{ THE GREAT MOVIES IV }

T H E

{GREAT MOVIES}

IV

ROGER EBERT

The University of Chicago Press

Chicago and London

Roger Ebert (1942–2013) was a Pulitzer Prize-winning film critic for the *Chicago Sun-Times*. In 1975, he teamed up with Gene Siskel of the *Chicago Tribune* to host the popular Sneak Peaks movie review program on PBS, which he continued for more than thirty-five years, including at Tribune Entertainment and Disney/Buena Vista Television. He is the author of numerous books, including *Awake in the Dark: The Best of Roger Ebert*; the Great Movies collections; and a memoir, *Life Itself*.

The University of Chicago Press, Chicago 60637
The University of Chicago Press, Ltd., London
© 2016 by The Ebert Company, Ltd.
Foreword © 2016 by The University of Chicago
All rights reserved. Published 2016.
Printed in the United States of America

25 24 23 22 21 20 19 18 17 16   1 2 3 4 5

ISBN-13: 978-0-226-40398-4 (cloth)
ISBN-13: 978-0-226-40403-5 (e-book)
DOI: 10.7208/chicago/9780226404035.001.0001

Previous versions of these essays have appeared in the *Chicago Sun-Times*, 1997, 1999, 2006, and 2009–2013.

Library of Congress Cataloging-in-Publication Data

Names: Ebert, Roger, author.
Title: The great movies IV / Roger Ebert.
Other titles: Great movies four | Great movies 4
Description: Chicago : University of Chicago Press, 2016. | ©2016 | "Previous versions
   of these essays have appeared in the Chicago Sun-Times, 1997, 1999, 2006, and
   2009–2013."
Identifiers: LCCN 2016004179 | ISBN 9780226403984 (cloth : alkaline paper) |
   ISBN 9780226404035 (e-book)
Subjects: LCSH: Motion pictures. | Motion pictures—Reviews.
Classification: LCC PN1994 .E2324 2016 | DDC 791.43/75—dc23 LC record
   available at http://lccn.loc.gov/2016004179

♾ This paper meets the requirements of ANSI/NISO Z39.48-1992 (Permanence of Paper).

CONTENTS

CONTENTS

Contents

FOREWORD

Roger Ebert casts a long shadow. I was hired by his widow, Chaz Ebert, to edit the website they founded in 2002, RogerEbert.com, shortly after his death in 2013. Every day I get an e-mail message, Tweet, Facebook query, or blog comment wondering what Roger would have thought about a current film. Would he have loved it, liked it, been indifferent to it, or hated, hated, hated, hated, hated it? The comments sections on RogerEbert.com are filled with people insisting Roger would have loathed a film that the assigned reviewer adored, or adored a film she loathed. This spectacle becomes poignantly amusing when you see contradictory comments beneath a single review: "I am so glad you liked this! Roger would have given it four stars, though." "It's a disgrace that you gave this film a positive review, Roger would have seen right through it."

What everyone longs for is not just a body of opinion focused through Roger's keen eye, but something more basic: Roger the man. Roger the life force. Good old Roger.

It is Roger's personal touch that separates him from nearly all current film reviewers, even the good to great ones: the sense that there is a person behind the words, one who has interests beyond film, and opinions about the world at large, and wisdom gained through the experience of living 70 years, producing several dozen novels' worth of prose and thousands of hours of

TV with his onscreen partner Gene Siskel, visiting dozens of countries, and touching the lives of untold numbers of moviegoers.

Roger's best writing evokes the most useful advice an editor gave me. I was having trouble writing a breaking news story on deadline and my editor said, "Why don't you just come over here and sit in this chair and tell me what the story is about." So I sat in the chair beside him and started talking. Suddenly the gist of the story became clear. I found myself regaling him with colorful details that weren't in the current draft. The pressure was off. I was no longer writing a Big Important Piece for posterity, I was just talking to a friend who happened to be my editor. "See what you're doing?" he said. "It's like we're having a cup of coffee and you're telling me about a piece you already turned in. Just take all the stuff you just told me and put that in the story."

Most of Roger's best pieces feel like that—like he's just talking to you about things he finds interesting or funny or exciting, or riffing on a film he finds slipshod or dumb, or evangelizing on behalf of a work that moves him or that he believes is important or special. When you read Roger's work, you feel as if he's on the phone with you, or sitting across from you at a restaurant, or writing you a personal e-mail. Sometimes he's holding court, sometimes he's ruminating, sometimes he's on the warpath. But you always feel that there's a person there—a man with a consistent set of concerns and values, expressed in plain language whose lyricism reveals itself when you read it aloud or quote it to others.

That personal touch is what makes Roger a great critic. A great teacher, too: the Midwestern directness becomes a linguistic Trojan horse that lulls the casual moviegoer into a comfort zone where Roger can ruminate on a movie's place in film history, or explore why a particular scene works on the emotions, or dig into the sense of life expressed by the story, the characters, and the filmmaking.

All of this explains why I consider *The Great Movies* series to be Roger's masterpiece. The books are expansive but judicious in laying out which films Roger considers great and essential. In their terse, lyrical sentences you will find every quality I've praised here. And if you read between the lines you'll learn as much about Roger as you might watching the documentary *Life Itself* or poring over his archive of personal essays at RogerEbert.com.

In their concision and complexity, the essays contained in the *Great Movies* books are remarkable. Many of them are original; others take portions of earlier reviews and expand on them, intensify them, revise them, question them. (You often find old Roger refuting young Roger.) They all speak to the reader as one might to a friend. They seem to be written by a critic secure in the knowledge that his audience knows who he is. The sense of familiarity emboldens Roger to cut to the chase, avoid anything resembling pretense, and speak from the heart when the spirit moves him, without fear that he will be ridiculed for freely admitting sadness, anger, or joy. The *Great Movies* essays function equally well as primers aimed at budding cinephiles, as insightful celebrations of works that have been picked over by generations of academics, and as lucid and insightful personal essays that are simultaneously about films, the world that films reflect, and the emotional interior of Roger.

This new volume represents the concluding installment of the *Great Movies* series. It compiles sixty-two reviews of films stretching from the recent past back through the silent era. There are pieces on films that have been acclaimed as canonical for decades or more: *The Cabinet of Dr. Caligari, Diary of a Country Priest, In a Lonely Place, Ivan the Terrible, Parts I & II, Senso,* and *Viridiana.* And there are essays on films that have only recently begun to be considered masterpieces (*Mulholland Dr., Eternal Sunshine of the Spotless Mind, Spirited Away, A.I. Artificial Intelligence*) and movies that, while beloved by some, may not necessarily be works you'd instinctively call "great" (*Superman, The Pledge, Lost in Translation, The Big Lebowski, Pink Floyd: The Wall, The Grey Zone, Seven*).

Roger the teacher is well represented. Here he is writing about a Film History 101 touchstone, *The Cabinet of Dr. Caligari,* crystallizing its essence, tying form to function so gracefully that it takes a second to register that he's compressed what might have been several pages of a lesser text into a few sentences.

Here's a gem from Roger the teacher, about Luis Buñuel, writer and director of 1961's *Viridiana*: "Buñuel the satirist, Buñuel the anticlerical, Buñuel the fetishist. That's the usual litany, but we should not exclude Buñuel the grandmaster of black comedy. None of his films is lacking a cheerfully sardonic view of human nature. His object is always dry humor. Even when he was working for Hollywood studios, recycling the sets and costumes of English-language pictures into Spanish versions of the same screenplays, or later simply dubbing them into Spanish, he slyly slipped in a few touches that were lacking in the sources. He is one of the great originals, creator of satirical delight, sometimes hilariously funny, and if you love great movies you sooner or later get to him." This is Trojan horse observation, designed to lure viewers who have never seen a Buñuel film into watching this one: it emphasizes that Buñuel is funny, that you will laugh as you watch his movies, and that it's OK to laugh. Buñuel is much more than funny, but you can see why he led with funny, because who doesn't want to see a funny movie?

His piece on Alfred Hitchcock's *Shadow of a Doubt* explains why the director's films are still so effective at generating tension, but in terms that anyone can grasp: "Hitchcock was a master of the classical Hollywood compositional style. It is possible to recognize one of his films after a minute or so entirely because of the camera placement. He used well-known camera language just a little more elegantly. See here how he zooms slowly into faces to show dawning recognition or fear. Watch him use tilt shots to show us things that are not as they should be. He uses contrasting lighted and shadowed areas within the frame to make moral statements, sometimes in anticipation before they are indicated."

Nearly every page contains a nugget like that. The tone never suggests that Roger is seeking to overrule or displace anyone else's judgment, much less show off, only that he's trying to connect with us—with *you*; he always seems to be speaking to one reader, not masses. It's not easy to write about a film like *Viridiana* or *Caligari* in a way that invites newcomers into the fold while offering enough fresh insight and elegantly turned phrases to make cinephiles want to keep reading, rather than mutter, "I already *know* all this!" and close the book. But Roger is a master of that sort of writing. He never simply regurgitates facts or dates or film terms or bits of received wisdom. There's always a sense that we're seeing the film through a fresh set of eyes, from an angle that reveals aspects we might not have noticed, much less fixated on.

His review of Tim Blake Nelson's 2001 Holocaust drama *The Grey Zone*, about Jewish prisoners employed to do the menial daily work of extermination in a death camp, explores the imagery and sound and texture of the movie, and shows how it serves the story. The final paragraph jars readers out of any preconceived notion that a film set in the past is removed from present day concerns: "*The Grey Zone* ends with a narration observing that the bodies of the dead are turned into ashes of bones, gases and vapor, and a fine, invisible gray dust that settles everywhere and goes into lungs; they become so accustomed to it they lose the cough reflex. Thus do the living and the dead intermingle. I believe Tim Blake Nelson is suggesting that dust rises from many flames all over the world, and we breathe it today."

His piece on Robert Bresson's *Diary of a Country Priest* is startling because rather than fixating on the formal aspects of a drama beloved by formalists (good luck finding a consideration of Bresson that does not use the word "austere"), it instead zeroes in on the title character's predicament, describing it in physical as well as visual terms. In the middle of the essay is a paragraph that subtly reminds us that the writer is a recovering alcoholic from a city of punishing winters who has written with honesty about his journey, and therefore understands on a human level what it means to subsist on a liquid diet and grapple with depression when it's cold out: "It is a bleak winter. The landscape around his little church is barren. There is often no sign of life except for the distant, unfriendly barking of dogs. His church and the manor of the local count are closed off behind bars, as if gated against each other. Girls in catechism class play tricks on him. The locals gossip that he's a drunk, because of his diet, but we never see him drunk. Bresson often fills the frame with his face, passive, and the stare of his unfocused eyes."

Again and again, Roger's human touch enlivens pieces that might otherwise have been content to be observant, amusing, and faintly scholarly. Formal analysis, literary appreciation, observations about acting and lighting and music and sound effects are always woven throughout, but these are fused to observations about the characters, the world view of the filmmaker, and the feelings and associations that the work evokes in Roger.

His *Rio Bravo* essay contains a rare description of John Wayne's acting that speaks directly to his choices as an actor, rather than repeating grandiose summations of what he meant to cinema. "His Chance doesn't feel it necessary to impose himself, apart from the formidable fact of his presence," he writes, a sentence that could describe Roger's writing. "He never sweet-talks Feathers (Angie Dickinson), indeed tends to be gruff toward her, but his eyes and body language speak for him. There is a moment when he is angered that she didn't get on the stage out of town, stalks upstairs to her hotel room, barges through the door, and then—in the reverse shot—sees her and transforms his whole demeanor. Can you say a man 'softens' simply by the way he holds himself? With the most subtle of body movements, he unwinds into the faintest beginning of a courtly bow. You don't see it. You feel it."

This bit from his review of *Caché* does a better job of illuminating the film's puzzle-box quality than any of the so-called thinkpieces that were written about it when it came out: "A stationary camera is objective. A moving camera implies a subjective viewer, whether that viewer is a character, the director, or the audience. Haneke uses the technique of making the camera 'move' in time, not space. His locked-down shots are objective. When they're reversed on a VCR, they *become* subjective."

Of *Shoah*, a Holocaust documentary so monumental in both scope and length that many can't even face watching it, Roger searches the filmmaking itself, not merely the content of the film, and describes the director Claude Lanzmann's methods in ways that make the film accessible again, even intriguing, without ever seeming as though he's hyping it, selling it, or misrepresenting it: "*Shoah* is a torrent of words, and yet the overwhelming impression, when it is over, is one of silence. Lanzmann intercuts two kinds of images. He shows the faces of his witnesses. And then he uses quiet pastoral scenes of the places where the deaths took place. Steam engines move massively through the Polish countryside, down the same tracks where trains took countless Jews, gypsies, Poles, homosexuals, and other so-called undesirables to their deaths. Cameras pan silently across pastures, while we learn that underneath the tranquility are mass graves."

Roger the scholar, Roger the humanist, Roger the formalist, Roger the sneakily powerful prose stylist: all are Roger, and all are a pleasure to read. But none is more engaging than Roger the enthusiast, the guy who practically flings open the door of the coffee shop to tell you about a film that gobsmacked him and that you must *must* see, right now, come on, let's go!

You can picture Roger's eyes lighting up as he realizes why Jim Jarmusch's *Mystery Train*, despite all the images of deserted Memphis streets and trains passing people by, "isn't an embrace of misery. It's more an evocation of how the personal styles of the characters help them cope with life, or not."

His take on *A. I. Artificial Intelligence* comes to a devastating conclusion about the film's much-derided ending. It seems uncannily attuned to the alchemy of a film written by Stanley Kubrick, one of the most icy-cool filmmakers, and directed by Steven Spielberg, one of the warmest: "Why would one mecha care if another obtained satisfaction? What meaning is there in giving David 24 hours of bliss? If machines cannot feel, what does the closing sequence really mean? I believe it suggests the new mechas are trying to construct a mecha that they can love. They would play Mommy to their own Davids. And that mecha will love them. What does love mean in this context? No more, no less, than *check*, or *mate*, or π. That is the fate of Artificial Intelligence. No Mommy will ever, ever love them."

His piece on *The Hairdresser's Husband* contains a description of what it feels like to fall in love that could only have been written by a man who was still very much in love himself: "She smiles. She is radiant. She is kind, gentle, sexy. They are always in heat. While she is performing a shampoo, he kneels on the floor behind her and caresses her to ecstasy. They make love on the red leather bench. They're in full view, but nobody ever seems to see them."

A phrase from his review of Ingmar Bergman's *Smiles of a Summer Night* could double as a summary of this volume, a collection of criticism that is also a stealth memoir and a record of a mind that was always simultaneously scrutinizing cinema and life itself: "There is an abundance of passion here, but none of it reckless; the characters consider the moral weight of their actions, and while not reluctant to misbehave, feel a need to explain, if only to themselves."

MATT ZOLLER SEITZ

INTRODUCTION

I miss Roger's writing. I miss his wisdom, his clarity, his expansive world-view, his empathy, his enthusiasm, his humor, his goodness. I just miss him. Since his death on April 4, 2013, there hasn't been a Friday that I pored over the reviews for our website at RogerEbert.com without thinking, "What would Roger have thought of this film?" I guess that's normal, not only because I am Roger's wife and the publisher of the website but because Roger set a standard for excellence in film criticism that prevailed for 46 years. That's a long time. In retrospect it's clear to me that Roger's reviews transcended movies; he wrote about life itself. That, I believe, is one of the reasons his work continues to resonate so deeply.

Consistently since 2013 I have been asked hypothetically whether such-and-such a movie would have been considered for induction into Roger's list of The Great Movies. There are some that I can say with 100 percent certainty he would have included in his *Great Movies* essays. Others, I have to admit, I don't know.

Roger and I didn't always agree on what constituted "great," yet our disagreements often inspired some of our most revelatory conversations. He never warmed up to Stanley Kubrick's 1971 classic, *A Clockwork Orange*, a film that remains my favorite and that has turned up on the greatest lists of many other critics. He allowed that *Clockwork* was masterfully made, but it left him cold. He never connected with it, never felt the soul in what Kubrick was trying to convey. Roger even conceded that it could possibly belong in a canon of great movies, but not in his *Great Movies* series. As Roger noted, the selections contained in his series are not *the* "greatest films of all time, because all lists of great movies are a foolish attempt to codify works which must stand alone. But it's fair to say: If you want to make a tour of the landmarks of the first century of cinema, start here."

Over the years Roger chose films for the series for many reasons. Some he included because he thought they were important in the history of cinema, some because they made a point better than any other movie on the subject, some because of their social currency or topicality, some because he felt the filmmakers or actors deserved more praise, some because an anniversary of the film was looming, and some just because they delighted him. There was never a formula to his selection process.

Roger said that writing about a great movie was like an act of meditation for him. He didn't consider it work. It fed something deeper. And because he wrote these extra articles voluntarily, you would think they would appear erratically. But he was as dedicated to writing the *Great Movies* pieces as he was to all of his other work. It became a tradition, one that he said helped him later to deal with illness and, as we were to see with *The Ballad of Narayama*, even death.

When he first began writing the series there was no thought of publishing a book. But after he wrote the first 100 essays, his publisher suggested one, and before we knew it, there was a second set of 100 reviews, and then a third. Roger wanted to finish a fourth installment of *The Great Movies*, but he was able to complete only 62 essays before he passed away. It was suggested that perhaps we could get pieces written by others to round out the edition, but in my heart of hearts I wanted to keep his series pure. We may never know the other movies he would have chosen to write about, but we are fortunate enough to have these.

What makes this fourth and final edition of *The Great Movies* so meaningful for me is the fact that it contains some of Roger's final essays. His work had remarkable depth to it from the very beginning of his journalism career, even before he was hired as the *Chicago Sun-Times* film critic.

Roger could peel away the layers of an onion like few other writers, yet I truly believe that in his last years, Roger's writing achieved an even greater philosophical depth. He was dealing with much more than whether a film was great—he was grappling with the very nature of storytelling and the profound role that it plays in our lives. Illness may have robbed my husband of the ability to speak, but his voice resonated louder than ever before. As I used to tell him, his writing made me swoon.

There are so many wonderful reviews in this book, but I would like to draw your attention to one in particular. It was published on March 7, 2013, less than a month before Roger's death at age 70. The film was Keisuke Kinoshita's 1958 classic *The Ballad of Narayama*, and it was destined to be the last entry in Roger's *Great Movies* series. It is a haunting drama set in a Japanese village that follows a strict tradition: when village elders reach their 70th year, they are carried up the side of the Narayama mountain to meet their destiny. Some of the villagers envision merry, magical encounters. Do the elders meet their gods? Do they ascend divinely into the heavens?

Even among the select elders who suspect otherwise, some selflessly embrace the journey. Their death means more food and opportunity for the younger people in the village. Of course this is not discussed. It is even considered an honor for the family to carry the elders up Mount Narayama. And the unspoken agreement is that we all go up the mountain eventually. But at a certain point in the film we are disabused of the benign or magical aspect of the trip. Frozen skulls and bones spell out the real horror of what happens up there.

Roger defends the filmmaker's choice to juxtapose song and dance with this brutal imagery. "This harsh imagery contrasts with the way the film is structured around song and dance," wrote Roger. "Kinoshita is correct, I believe, in presenting his story in this stylized way; his form allows it to become more fable than narrative, and thus more bearable." Indeed the film's pronounced artifice makes its brutal subject matter easier to endure.

Roger, from his hospital bed, chose this film as a late addition to our film festival, Roger Ebert's Film Festival—Ebertfest. I thought he would be in attendance to see it, but Roger suspected that he would not. And so on that day in April 2013 when we screened *The Ballad of Narayama* at the Virginia

Theater in Champaign, Illinois, I was sitting next to Tilda Swinton, who had recently lost her mother, and we were both stunned by it. It left the audience in tears. It was clearly intended by Roger as a farewell to us. It was Roger's way of preparing us for his own trip up Mount Narayama.

Any clouds of sadness soon lifted, however, as they always did in the company of Roger and his words. Through his works, Roger's spirit is alive and well, reverberating within every word he ever wrote, and continuing to inspire movie lovers of all ages. In this fourth and final edition of *The Great Movies* you'll find Roger's vitality—a celebration of life and the legacy we leave. I thank Roger for these gifts. We are all privileged to experience them.

CHAZ EBERT

SELECTIONS FROM THE INTRODUCTIONS TO THE PREVIOUS VOLUMES

From *The Great Movies* (2002)

We live in a box of space and time. Movies are windows in its walls. They allow us to enter other minds—not simply in the sense of identifying with the characters, although that is an important part of it, but by seeing the world as another person sees it. François Truffaut said that for a director it was an inspiring sight to walk to the front of a movie theater, turn around, and look back at the faces of the audience, turned up to the light from the screen. If the film is any good, those faces reflect an out-of-the-body experience: The audience for a brief time is somewhere else, sometime else, concerned with lives that are not its own. Of all the arts, movies are the most powerful aid to empathy, and good ones make us into better people.

Not many of them are very good, however. Yes, there are the passable Friday night specials, measured by critics including myself in terms of their value in entertaining us for two hours. We buy our tickets and hope for diversion, and usually we get it, but we so rarely get anything more. Especially in these latter days of the marketing-driven Hollywood, and a world cinema dominated by the Hollywood machine, films aim coarsely at low tastes. "If you put three thoughts into a movie you've broken the law and none will come," Sean Penn told an audience at the Edinburgh Festival in 2001. The movies in this book have three thoughts, or more. They are not "the"

100 greatest films of all time, because all lists of great movies are a foolish attempt to codify works which must stand alone. But it's fair to say: If you want to make a tour of the landmarks of the first century of cinema, start here.

■■■■■■■■■■■■

I came to believe that the classics of earlier years were an unexplored country for many filmgoers, even the best ones. As a film critic for a daily newspaper, I didn't want to spend my life locked in the present. In 1996 I went to Nigel Wade, then the editor of the *Chicago Sun-Times*, and proposed a biweekly series of longer articles revisiting the great movies of the past. He gave his blessing. Not many editors would have; the emphasis in American film journalism is on "celebrity news," box office results, and other forms of bottom-feeding. Every other week since then, I have revisited a great movie, and the response has been encouraging. I received letters and e-mails from movie lovers; got into debates with other critics; heard from a university trustee and a teenager in Madison who both vowed to watch every movie on the list. The Library Media Project made discounted DVDs of the movies available to public libraries.

The relative invisibility of classic movies is directly related to the death of film societies. Until the rise of home video, every campus and many public libraries and community centers had film societies which held cheap and well-programmed 16mm screenings. My early film initiation took place at two such clubs at the University of Illinois, which also inspired me to see first-run films I might otherwise have avoided. I saw *Ikiru*, *The 400 Blows*, *The Maltese Falcon*, and *Swing Time* for the first time in those campus rooms—knowing little or nothing about them except that they cost only twenty-five cents, and that afterward people got together in the student union and drank coffee and talked about them.

From *The Great Movies II* (2005)

This is the second *Great Movies* book, but the titles in it are not the second team. I do not believe in rankings and lists and refuse all invitations to reveal my "ten all-time favorite musicals," etc., on the grounds that such lists are meaningless and might well change between Tuesday and Thursday. I make only two exceptions to this policy: I compile an annual list of the year's best films, because it is graven in stone that movie critics must do so, and I participate every ten years in the *Sight & Sound* poll of the world's directors and critics.

As I made clear in the introduction to the first *Great Movies* book, it was *not* a list of "the" 100 greatest movies but simply a collection of 100 great movies—unranked, selected because of my love for them and for their artistry, historical role, influence, and so on. I wrote the essays in no particular order, inspired sometimes by the availability of a newly restored print or DVD.

■■■■■■■■■■■■

I have cited before the British critic Derek Malcolm's definition of a great movie: any movie he could not bear the thought of never seeing again. During the course of a year I review about 250 films and see perhaps 200 more and could very easily bear the thought of not seeing many of them again, or even for the first time. What a pleasure it is to step aside from the production line and look closely and with love at films that vindicate the art form.

■■■■■■■■■■■■

One of my delights in these books . . . has been to include movies not often cited as "great"—some because they are dismissed as merely popular (*Jaws*, *Raiders of the Lost Ark*), some because they are frankly entertainments (*Planes, Trains, and Automobiles*, *Rififi*), some because they are too obscure (*The Fall of the House of Usher*, *Stroszek*). We go to different movies for different reasons, and greatness comes in many forms.

Of course there is no accounting for taste, and you may believe some of these titles don't belong in the book. The reviewer of the first volume for the *New York Times Book Review* ignored the introduction and the book jacket and persisted in the erroneous belief that it was a list of "*the*" 100 greatest movies. He felt such a listing was fatally compromised by my inclusion of Jacques Tati's *Mr. Hulot's Holiday*—which was not, he declared, a great film. Criticism is all opinion, so there is no such thing as right and wrong—except in the case of his opinion of *Mr. Hulot's Holiday*, which is wrong.

From *The Great Movies III* (2010)

You might be surprised by how many people have told me they're working their way through my book of Great Movies one film at a time. That's not to suggest that these books are in any way definitive. I loathe "best of" lists, which are not the best of anything except what someone was able to come up with that day. I look at a list of the "100 greatest horror films," or musicals, or whatever, and I want to ask the list maker, "But how do you *know*?" There are great films in my books, and films that are not great, but there is no film here to which I didn't respond strongly. That's the reassurance I can offer.

I believe good movies are a civilizing force. They allow us to empathize with those whose lives are different from our own. I like to say they open windows in our box of space and time. Here's a third book filled with windows.

▪▪▪▪▪▪▪▪▪▪▪▪▪

I ruffled some feathers after *Transformers: Revenge of the Fallen* was released in 2009. It was so stupid it was almost criminal. Noting that some of its fans considered it one of the greatest films ever made, I suggested perhaps they were not "sufficiently evolved." Oh, did that make people angry. What snobbery! Who did I think I was?

I was indeed a snob, if you agree with this definition: "A person who believes that their tastes in a particular area are superior to those of other people." I do. That is not ego. It is a faith that after writing and teaching about films for more than forty years, my tastes are more evolved than those of a fanboy. We are so terrified these days of showing disrespect for low taste. You can admire Miley Cyrus (God love her), but if I prefer Billie Holiday, why, I'm a snob. It is quite possible to devise a defense of *T2RF*, as its fans affectionately call it. One persuasive critic likened it to pop art. Well, okay.

He had an argument, he had his reasons, he considered it in a particular context. But to argue I am a snob for not *loving T2RF* as much as "everybody does" values less thought and experience over more.

What am I getting at here? The way to know more about anything is to deepen your experience of it. I have no way of proving it, but I would bet you a shiny new dime that it is impossible to start out loving *T2RF*, experience the films in this book, and end by loving it.

{ THE GREAT MOVIES IV }

{ 25TH HOUR }

Depend upon it, Sir, when a man knows he is to be hanged in a fortnight,
it concentrates his mind wonderfully.

DR. JOHNSON

Tomorrow morning, Monty Brogan is turning himself in to begin a prison term. His two best friends lean on a railing, look out over the river, and agree "it's over." They will never see Monty again. He may be alive in eight years, but he won't be the Monty they've known since they were kids. Monty Brogan also knows this. So do his girlfriend and his father. It will all end after tonight.

Monty's mind is very concentrated. There is a sense, in Spike Lee's *25th Hour* (2002), that he's experiencing his last day of freedom in a heightened state. Everything is more focused, more meaningful, sometimes dreamy. He has his ideas about how he got here and who may have been involved, but there is little he can do about that now. From the choices still open to him, he focuses now on the remaining important things: his woman, his father, his friends, and unsettled business.

Naturelle (Rosario Dawson) is on hold; supportive, loving, but feeling shut out. Jacob and Frank (Philip Seymour Hoffman and Barry Pepper) are very sympathetic, but after all they are still free to live their lives.

His father (Brian Cox) bitterly blames himself for drinking his way into such debt that he took "loans" from his son. Monty (Edward Norton) is intelligent. He sees his mistakes clearly. It was a mistake to get into drug dealing when he had the chance. It was a mistake to stay in it as long as he did. It was a mistake to think he could hide a lot of cash and cocaine, and a mistake to let *anyone* know where it was hidden.

This is another of Norton's exceptional performances. As usual, he doesn't act out a lot. He implodes. He keeps his own counsel. He is a realist, even in these drifting final hours. He thinks he knows who he can still trust, but what does he really know, and what can he really do?

Spike Lee, working with David Benioff's adaptation of his own novel, paints a portrait of a life in 24 hours. From a morning walk with his dog to a long drive the next morning with his father, Monty makes one last trip around the bases. He convinces Jacob to take care of the dog. He makes love with Naturelle but later seems distant to her. He goes to a nightclub with Jacob and Frank, and she joins them later. He does some final business and settles a last score.

The wonder of the rich screenplay is that it contains all of this material about Monty, and yet informs us so fully about the others. There could be a separate movie about Jacob, a pudgy and phlegmatic high school English teacher who is fascinated by a tattoo on the bare midriff of one of his students, and by the girl Mary (Anna Paquin) who wears it. But any move in that direction would be wrong, and he knows it.

Mary is charged with her own emerging sexuality and boldly flirts with him. Through chance they find themselves in the same club. He's had a martini and champagne and can't drink, and there's a moment when the two of them are alone that is one of the most perfect and complex that Lee has ever filmed. Frank, on the other hand, is a seasoned and careless ladies' man. His apartment literally overlooks the wreckage of 9/11, but he won't move because he can't get the right price. Thus 9/11 becomes an unspoken undercurrent in this 2002 film.

We know that all of these people may never be together again, no matter what their plans. But look at the strategies of style that Lee brings to their stories. The crucial moment between Jacob and Mary takes place up a flight of stairs. *After* it is over, after Jacob has returned to the booth, then Lee employs his trademark gliding shot, showing Jacob seemingly floating up the stairs without moving his feet. We understand Jacob is replaying the hypnotic compulsion that led him—drove him—up the stairs.

Consider too the extraordinary scene where Monty looks in the mirror of a sleazy restroom and loses his cool for the only time in the film, screaming f-yous at every ethnic, economic, sexual, and age group in the city and then arriving at the summation, directed at himself. When the movie was released, some said they didn't understand this scene. Haven't we all felt that way? When all of the f-yous are really about ourselves?

Lee uses a couple of subtle devices that can go unnoticed. He punches up a few moments by freeze-frames so brief they're like little stutters. We don't see them, but they work—like when someone is talking, and we particularly take note of an expression they use. He also plays with lighting. There's a shot when Norton and Hoffman are bathed in blue light, except for a little red in Norton's right eye. Think how hard Rodrigo Prieto, the cinematographer, worked to get that in there, and how hard he worked to keep us from "noticing" it.

Then there is the masterful conclusion of the film, as Monty's father, the old Irish saloon keeper, drives him upstate to the prison. They pass under the same freeway sign that opens the film. He suggests that they keep right on driving out west and find a small town and live under new names, and Monty can find the right girl and start a family and have the life his father's debts took from him. Lee pictures this life so convincingly that some viewers are seduced into wondering if it's really happening.

Who is the vision painted for? For Monty, or old James Brogan, to comfort himself that he did make the offer and it was sincere? Monty doesn't feel a "duty to pay his debt to society," but he's focused now on his destiny, and his trance of 24 hours will end only when he's in prison.

Everybody knows that Spike Lee is an important filmmaker, but do they realize how good he is with actors, and how innovative he is with style? We live in a period when many filmmakers use either a straightforward meat-and-potatoes style, or draw attention with meaningless over-editing, queasy cams, and showboat shots. With Lee, as with any classical director, the emphasis is on the story and the people. But he's always *there*, nudging us, being sure what we notice, moving his camera not merely with efficiency but with grace and innovation. Because he doesn't go out of his way to call attention, how many realize what a master stylist he is?

In this film he benefits from pitch-perfect performances from Norton and Hoffman of course; from Dawson, Cox, Pepper—and from Anna Paquin, that little girl from *The Piano*. How well she evokes her exact stage in life as she dances alone on the disco floor, or not alone, really, but with herself.

One more note about acting. I've seen a lot of people drinking in a lot of movies. I've seen them sobering up the morning after. But I don't remember anyone starting out sober, getting drunk, and then returning to sobriety quite like Hoffman does it here. We know exactly where he's at during these transitions, but we never see them happening.

A. I. ARTIFICIAL INTELLIGENCE

Stanley Kubrick always referred to the story as "Pinocchio." It mirrored the tale of a puppet who dreams of becoming a real boy. And what, after all, is an android but a puppet with a computer program pulling its strings? The project that eventually became Steven Spielberg's *A. I. Artificial Intelligence* (2001) was abandoned by Kubrick because he wasn't satisfied with his approaches to its central character, David, an android who appears to be a real little boy. Believing special effects wouldn't be adequate and a human actor would seem too human, he turned the project over to his friend Spielberg. Legend has it he made that decision after being impressed by Spielberg's special effects in *Jurassic Park*, but perhaps *E.T.* was also an influence: If Spielberg could create an alien who evoked human emotions, could he do the same with an android?

He could. As David, he cast Haley Joel Osment, who had scored a great success in *The Sixth Sense* (1999). Osment's presence is a crucial element in the film; other androids, including Gigolo Joe (Jude Law), are made to look artificial with makeup and unmoving hair, but not David. He is the most advanced "mecha" of the Cybertronics Corporation—so human that he can perhaps take the place of a couple's sick child. Spielberg and Osment work together to create David with unblinking eyes and deep naïveté; he seems a real little boy but lacking a certain *je ne sais quoi*. This reality works both for and against the film, at first by making David seem human and later by making him seem a very slow study.

David has been programmed to love. Once he is activated with a code, he fixes on the activator, in this case his Mommy (Frances O'Connor). He exists to love her and be loved by her. Because he is a very sophisticated android indeed, there's a natural tendency for us to believe him on that level. In fact he does not love and does not feel love; he simply reflects his coding. All of the love contained in the film is possessed by humans, and I didn't properly reflect this in my original review of the film.

"We are expert at projecting human emotions into non-human subjects, from animals to clouds to computer games," I wrote in 2001, "but the emotions reside only in our minds. *A. I.* evades its responsibility to deal rigorously with this trait and goes for an ending that wants us to cry, but had me asking questions just when I should have been finding answers."

That is true enough on the principal level of the film, which tells David's story. Watching it again recently, I became aware of something more: *A. I.* is not about humans at all. It is about the dilemma of artificial intelligence. A thinking machine cannot think. All it can do is run programs that may be sophisticated enough for it to fool us by seeming to think. A computer that passes the Turing Test is not thinking. All it is doing is passing the Turing Test.

The first act of the film involves Henry and Monica Swinton (Sam Robards and Frances O'Connor). Henry brings David home to fill the gap left by their own sick little boy, Martin (Jake Thomas). Monica resists him, and then accepts him. But after Martin is awakened from suspended animation and cured, there is a family of four; Martin is fully aware that David is a product, but David doesn't understand everything that implies. Possibly his programming didn't prepare him to deal one-on-one in real time with real boys. He can't spend all of his time loving Mommy and being loved by her.

He imitates life. He doesn't sleep, but he observes bedtime. He doesn't eat, but so strong is his desire to be like Martin that he damages his wiring by shoving spinach into his mouth. He's treated with cruelty by other kids; when he reveals he doesn't pee, a kid grabs his pants and says, "Let's see what you don't pee with." After faithfully following his instructions in such a way that he nearly drowns Martin, he loses the trust of the Swintons and they decide to get rid of him, just as parents might get rid of a dangerous dog.

Monica cannot bring herself to return David to Cybertronics. She pauses on the way and releases him into a forest, where he can join other free-range mechas. He will not die. He doesn't get cold, he doesn't get hungry, and apparently he has an indefinite supply of fuel. Monica's decision to release him instead of turning him in is based on her lingering identification with David; in activating him to love her, she activated herself to love him. His unconditional love must have been deeply appealing. We relate to pets in a similar way, especially to dogs, who seem to have been activated by evolution to love us.

The center act of the movie shows David wandering a world where mechas have no rights. He is accompanied by his mecha bear, Teddy, who is programmed to be a wise companion, and they are discovered by Gigolo Joe, a mecha programmed to be an expert lover. They visit two hallucinatory places designed by Spielberg on huge sound stages. One is a Flesh Fair, not unlike a WWF event, at which humans cheer as mechas are grotesquely destroyed. David, Joe, and Teddy escape, probably because of their survival programming, but is David dismayed by what he sees? How does he relate to the destruction of his kind?

Then there is Rouge City, sort of a psychedelic Universal City, where Joe takes him to consult a Wizard. Having been fascinated by the story of Pinocchio, who wanted to be a real boy, David has reasoned that a Blue Fairy might be able to transform him into a human and allow Monica to love him and be loved. The Wizard gives him a clue. After Joe and David capture a flying machine, they visit New York, which like many coastal cities has been drowned by global warming. But on an upper floor of Rockefeller Center, he finds that Cybertronics still operates, and he meets the scientist who created him, Dr. Hobby (William Hurt). Hobby is Geppetto to David's Pinocchio.

Now again there are events which contradict David's conception of himself. In an eerie scene, he comes across a storeroom containing dozens of Davids who look just like him. Is he devastated? Does he thrash out at them? No, he remains possessed. He is still focused on his quest for the Blue Fairy, who can make him a real little boy. But why, we may ask, does he want to be real so very much? Is it because of envy, hurt, or jealousy? No, he doesn't seem to possess such emotions—or any emotions, save those he is programmed to counterfeit. I assume he wants to be a real boy for abstract reasons of computer logic. To fulfill his mission to love and be loved by Mommy, he concludes he should be like Martin, whom Mommy prefers. This involves no more emotion than Big Blue determining its next move in chess.

In the final act, events take David and Teddy in a submersible to the drowned Coney Island, where they find not only Geppetto's workshop but a Blue Fairy. A collapsing Ferris wheel pins the submarine, and there they remain, trapped and immobile, for 2,000 years, as above them an ice age descends and humans become extinct. David is finally rescued by a group of impossibly slender beings that might be aliens, but are apparently very advanced androids. For them, David is an incalculable treasure: "He is the last who knew humans." From his mind they download all of his memories, and they move him into an exact replica of his childhood home. This reminded me of the bedroom beyond Jupiter constructed for Dave by aliens in Kubrick's *2001*. It has the same purpose, to provide a familiar environment in an incomprehensible world. It allows these beings, like the unseen beings in *2001*, to observe and learn from behavior.

Watching the film again, I asked myself why I wrote that the final scenes are "problematical," go over the top, and raise questions they aren't prepared to answer. This time they worked for me and had a greater impact. I began with the assumption that the skeletal silver figures are indeed androids, of a much advanced generation from David's. They too must be programmed to know, love, and serve Man. Let's assume such instructions would be embedded in their programming DNA. They now find themselves in a position analogous to David in his search for his Mommy. They are missing an element crucial to their function.

After some pseudoscientific legerdemain involving a lock of Monica's hair, they are able to bring her back after 2,000 years of death—but only for 24 hours, which is all the space-time continuum permits. Do they do this to make David happy? No, because would they care? And is a computer happier when it performs its program than when it does not? No. It is either functioning or not functioning. It doesn't know how it feels.

Here is how I now read the film: These new generation mechas are advanced enough to perceive that they cannot function with humans in the absence of humans, and I didn't properly reflect this in my original review of the film. David is their only link to the human past. Whatever can be known about them, he is an invaluable source. In watching his 24 hours with Mommy, they observe him functioning at the top of his ability.

Of course we must ask in what sense Monica is really there. The filmmaker Jamie Stuart informs me she is not there at all—that an illusion has merely been implanted in David's mind, and that the concluding scenes take place entirely within David's point of view. Having downloaded all of David's memories and knowledge, the new mechas have no further use for him, but provide him a final day of satisfaction before terminating him. At the end, when we are told he is dreaming, that is only David's impression. Earlier in the film, it was established that he could not sleep or therefore dream.

Why would one mecha care if another obtained satisfaction? What meaning is there in giving David 24 hours of bliss? If machines cannot feel, what does the closing sequence really mean? I believe it suggests the new mechas are trying to construct a mecha that they can love. They would play Mommy to their own Davids. And that mecha will love them. What does love mean in this context? No more, no less, than *check*, or *mate*, or π. That is the fate of Artificial Intelligence. No Mommy will ever, ever love them.

{ AN AUTUMN AFTERNOON }

Two middle-aged students take their old teacher out to dinner, and he gets thoroughly drunk and is overtaken by sadness. We are alone in life, he tells them. Always alone. He lives with his daughter, who takes care of him, who has never married, who will be left all alone when he dies. He tells Hirayama, the hero of *An Autumn Afternoon*, to avoid the same mistake: marry his daughter now, before she is too old.

"Ummm," responds Hirayama. He reveals no apparent emotion. He lives at home with a son and daughter, and she waits on both of them. Another son is married. He considers his teacher's sorrowful advice. At his office, a young woman his daughter's age is getting married. Perhaps the old man is correct. The night of the dinner, the students take their teacher home. They find he and his daughter now run a noodle shop, and she is fed up with him for getting drunk again. She cares for her father, but is trapped and unhappy.

The more you learn about Yasujiro Ozu, the director of *An Autumn Afternoon* (1962), the more you realize how very deep the waters reach beneath his serene surfaces. Ozu is one of the greatest artists to ever make a film. This was his last one. He never married. He lived for 60 years with his mother, and when she died, he was dead a few months later. Over and over again, in almost all of his films, he turned to the same central themes, of loneliness, of family, of dependence, of marriage, of parents and children. He holds these themes to the light and their prisms cast variations on each screenplay. His films are all made within the emotional space of his life, in which he finds not melodramatic joy or tragedy, but *mono no aware*, which is how the Japanese refer to the bittersweet transience of all things.

From time to time I return to Ozu feeling a need to be calmed and restored. He is a man with a profound understanding of human nature, about which he makes no dramatic statements. We are here, we hope to be happy, we want to do well, we are locked within our aloneness, life goes on. He embodies this vision in a cinematic style so distinctive that you can tell an Ozu film almost from a single shot. He films mostly indoors. His camera is at the eye level of a person seated on a tatami mat. The camera never moves. His shots often begin before anyone enters the frame, and end after the frame is empty again. There is foreground framing, from doors or walls or objects. There is meticulous attention to the things within the shot.

Ozu arranged the props in a shot with obsessive care, his collaborators recalled. In particular there is a little teapot that occurs in film after film, almost as the maker's mark. The objects themselves are not as important as their compositional function; he often composes on a lateral within the unmoving frame, leading our eyes forward and backward. *An Autumn Afternoon* is one of his six color films, made between 1958 and 1962, and in it he makes particular use of the color red to draw our eyes deeper into the frame. In almost every shot there is something red or orange in the foreground, middle distance, and back. These are not obvious. They may involve a stool, a sign on a wall, an item of clothing hanging from a hook, a vase, some books. They mean nothing in particular, but because red is a dominant color, they lead our eyes through his usually pastel compositions and prevent us from reading a shot only in a flat pane. They give his films a depth of space that mocks the pretension of 3D.

If you love Ozu you do not need to be told that *An Autumn Afternoon* stars Chishû Ryû, who appeared in almost every film Ozu ever made. He always plays, we feel, the Ozu character, reserved, neat, quiet, and, like Ozu himself, often a heavy drinker, more meditative than demonstrative. In *An Autumn Afternoon*, his Hirayama is a salaryman at an unspecified factory, who lives with his daughter Michiko (Shima Iwashita), 24, and son Kazuo (Shinichirô Mikami), a little younger. An older son, Koichi (Keiji Sada), is already married. Hirayama is tall, slender, always well-dressed. What he feels is left to us to infer; Ozu prefers the empathy of the audience to dialogue revealing inner feelings. That monosyllable "ummm" is used over and again as Chishû Ryû's character responds without committing himself. Two or three times in *An Autumn Afternoon*, I heard the older son also using it, and I smiled with recognition.

The film takes place in Hirayama's office and home, in a few bars and restaurants, and in his son's home. A great many scenes involve steady drinking. These have echoes in Ozu's work; a reunion with an old teacher can also be seen in the similar story of *There Was a Father* (1942), also starring the neither young nor old Chishû Ryû, this one living at home with his son.

There were a few things that happened to Ozu, apart from the military service he never displayed in his films: he went to school (where he smoked, drank, skipped class, and was expelled), he worked, he never married, he drank too much, he was lonely, he spent much time with colleagues who loved him. These are the elements of his stories. Whether he felt trapped by his mother, whether he wanted to marry, we cannot know for sure. There were rumors of some troubles over a geisha in the 1930s, but no engagements or great romances. He worked almost always for the same studio, Shochiku, which revered him. The Japanese considered him their greatest director, but unlike Kurosawa he was unknown in the West. Shochiku considered him "too Japanese" to travel well, until the critic Donald Richie arranged for some of his work to be shown at the Venice Film Festival in the early 1970s.

As an extra on the Criterion DVD of *An Autumn Afternoon*, we see the French critics Michel Ciment and Georges Perec from a TV show of that period discussing this great director who had come into their view a decade after his death. They try to describe the effect of his work. Ciment: "It is Zen, the rapture of the present lived moment." Perec: "It's what is happening when nothing is going on." *Mono no aware.*

Perec reveals he cried twice in what must be the film's emotional high point, on the daughter's wedding day. She turns, radiant in her traditional bridal costume, so her father can see her. What are they thinking? She had argued she should not marry because her father and brother could not manage without her. She agreed with her father's wishes. We haven't even met the man she will marry. It isn't who she is going to that's the point; it's who she is leaving. Hirayama looks at her. "Ummm," he says. Observing, recognizing, accepting. There is no laughter. This scene of separation is as close as Ozu comes to violence. There was no indication that father and daughter shared any great love or need. But they were settled into a fixed existence, and marriage has ruptured it.

The soundtrack music by Kojun Saitô sounds Western (Italian, indeed), as it often does in an Ozu film. This is not an anachronism; Western music was well known in Japan. It is winsome and nostalgic. Its cheer is muted. It states what no one says in words: We carry on. We do our best. We are contained within our fates. Things change. In the final shot, we see Hirayama alone at home, in the kitchen at the end of an empty corridor. He pours himself some tea, probably, from the common yet distinctive little teapot that accompanied Ozu on his journey through his life's work. The maker's mark.

$$\left\{\; \text{B ADLANDS} \;\right\}$$

Holly describes her life as if she's writing pulp fiction. "Little did I realize," she tells us, "that what began in the alleys and back ways of this quiet town would end in the Badlands of Montana." It is the wondering narrative voice that lingers beneath all of Terrence Malick's films, sometimes unspoken: human lives diminish beneath the overarching majesty of the world.

Holly is practicing her baton-twirling on the front lawn when she meets Kit. She is 15. He is 25, and has just walked off his job as a garbage man. We never learn anything about his earlier years. He walks out of nowhere, sees her, and sweeps her up in his whirlwind. Within a day or two he has shot her father dead, he has set her house afire, and they are on the run across South Dakota.

Terrence Malick's *Badlands* (1973) tells a story that has been told many times, of two lovers who are criminals and are pursued across the vastness of America. *Bonnie and Clyde* (1967) comes first to mind. Malick's direct inspiration was the story of Charles Starkweather, the "Mad Dog Killer," who in 1957–58 with his girlfriend Caril Ann Fugate went on a killing spree that left 11 dead, including her parents and younger sister. She was 13, he was 18.

Malick finds no meaning in their crimes, no psychological explanation. Kit is a handsome psychopath who, Holly tells him, looks like James

Dean. Holly is an unformed child who seems simple and remote. She describes their odyssey in the third person, as predestined fate. Neither seems to react emotionally to death. Listen here to how she slides over the death of her dog: "Then sure enough Dad found out I been running around behind his back. He was madder than I ever seen him. His punishment for deceiving him: he went and shot my dog. He made me take extra music lessons every day after school, and wait there 'till he came to pick me up. He said that if the piano didn't keep me off the streets, maybe the clarinet would."

Malick opens on the leafy streets of a small town, where Holly's house on the corner resembles the house Malick used in *The Tree of Life* (2011). We sense his own memories at work. Then he moves into hiding with them in a series of breathtaking scenes, as they live in a forest and roam mindlessly across the empty Great Plains, the quarry of a national manhunt. In the last of their stolen cars, a big Cadillac, they leave the roads and cut cross-country over unfenced prairies, summoning associations with pioneer settlers. "At the very edge of the horizon," Holly said, "we could make out the gas fires of the refineries at Missoula, while to the south we could see the lights of Cheyenne, a city bigger and grander than I'd ever seen."

Badlands was one of the great films of the flowering of American auteurs in the 1970s, a debut film chosen to close the New York Film Festival. It starred Martin Sheen and Sissy Spacek. He was 33 and had done much television acting, but this was his first important feature. She was 24, and it was her second movie. Both looked younger than their years. Sheen, with carefully combed hair, blue jeans, checked shirts, and Lucky Strikes, had the Dean look; after Charles Starkweather saw *Rebel Without a Cause*, he deliberately patterned himself on the movie star. Spacek, red-haired, freckled, slight, seemed a girl, not a woman. Sex has little to do with Kit and Holly's relationship, although we see some kissing; they seem to be children who are role-playing.

Their shallowness is in conflict with their deadliness. A friend of Kit's, who seems to help them but then runs for a phone, is shot in the stomach and left to sit, dazed, dying, and contemplative. He'd attempted to lure them into a field with a tale of treasure. That Kit believed him took childlike credulity. A family is killed for no other reason than that Kit and

Holly come across their farmhouse. A rich man is spared for no reason at all, and Kit later observes how lucky he was. He uses the man's Dictaphone to record a fatuous final statement: "Listen to your parents and teachers. They got a line on most things, so don't treat 'em like enemies. There's always an outside chance you can learn something. Try to keep an open mind." He thinks that because he's famous, his words have meaning.

Nature is always deeply embedded in Malick's films. It occupies the stage and then humans edge tentatively onto it, uncertain of their roles. There is always much detail, of birds and small animals, of trees and skies, of empty fields or dense forests, of leaves and grain, and always of too much space for the characters to fill. They are nudged here and there by events which they confuse with their destinies. In his *Days of Heaven* (1978), his characters ride the rails into a Texas prairie. In his *The Thin Red Line* (1998), a war movie, his characters are embedded in the jungles of Guadalcanal. His *The New World* (2005) shows Native Americans at home in primeval forests while British explorers build forts to hide in. There is a strong sense of humans uneasily accommodated by the land.

Badlands is technically a road movie. That is a form which breaks filmmakers free of tight plotting and opens them to whatever happens along the way. They can introduce and dispose of characters and subplots at will. The travelers are all that is constant. In *Badlands* Kit and Holly are fleeing toward nowhere, although Kit talks vaguely of "heading north" and becoming a Mountie. Holly follows along not so much because she must, but because she had a crush on Kit and her father (Warren Oates) angered her by forbidding her to see him. She seems to regard her father's death only as a convenience.

There is an idyll in a dense forest, where Kit constructs an improbable tree house possibly intended to evoke Tarzan. He rigs alarms and sets booby traps. They lead a natural life, an idle one, aimless. Lacking personal resources, they occupy a default state of boredom. One early shot of Kit shows him walking down an alley, stamping on a tin can to flatten it, then kicking it away. That gives him something to do.

The film has a mystical scene in which Malick has Holly looking at slides of faraway places through her father's 3D Stereopticon: "It hit me that I was just this little girl, born in Texas, whose father was a sign painter, who only had just so many years to live. It sent a chill down my spine and I thought, where would I be this very moment if Kit had never met me?" She realizes perhaps that she had no meaningful existence before Kit. Toward the end of their long flight over the land, Kit's appeal runs out: "I'd stopped even paying attention to him. Instead I sat in the car and read a map and spelled out entire sentences with my tongue on the roof of mouth where nobody could read them."

Terrence Malick, born in 1943, is a legendary figure in American film, often described as reclusive. In fact, he is simply private, absorbed in his own work, happy with a circle of friends, and declining to join in even token efforts at publicity. I am unaware of a single interview he has given; the many secondhand reports from those who know him paint a cheerful man, friendly, obsessed with details, enraptured by nature. There is a hint of Kubrick. "He can talk to anyone about anything," Jessica Chastain, the star of *The Tree of Life*, told Steven Zeitchik of the *Los Angeles Times*. He declined to appear at the premiere or press conference for *Tree of Life* at Cannes 2011 (where it won the Palme d'Or), but was seen all over town at dinners and screenings. In five movies in four decades, he has, in his own way, fashioned one of the most distinctive bodies of work of his time. Very much in his own way.

THE BALLAD
OF NARAYAMA

The Ballad of Narayama is a Japanese film of great beauty and elegant artifice, telling a story of startling cruelty. What a space it opens up between its origins in the kabuki style and its subject of starvation in a mountain village! The village enforces a tradition of carrying those who have reached the age of 70 up the side of a mountain and abandoning them there to die of exposure.

Keisuke Kinoshita's 1958 film tells its story with deliberate artifice, using an elaborate set with a path beside a bubbling brook, matte paintings for the backgrounds, mist on dewy evenings, and lighting that drops the backgrounds to black at dramatic moments and then brings up realistic lighting again. Some of its exteriors use black foregrounds and bloody red skies; others use grays and blues. As in kabuki theater, there is a black-clad narrator to tell us what's happening.

This artifice supports a story that contains great emotional charge. Kinuyo Tanaka plays Orin, a 70-year-old widow whose resignation in the face of her traditional fate is in stark contrast with the behavior of her neighbor Mata (Seiji Miyaguchi), who protests violently against his destiny. Their family attitudes are similarly opposed; while Orin's son Tatsuhei (Teiji Takahashi) loves his mother and doesn't have any desire to carry her up the mountainside, Mata's family has already cut off his food, and he wanders the village as a desperate scavenger; Orin invites him in and offers him a bowl of rice, which be gobbles hungrily.

In contrast with her resignation and her son's reluctance to carry out her sentence, Orin's vile grandson Kesakichi (Danshi Ichikawa) can't wait to be done with the old woman and begins singing a song mocking the fact that she retains, at 70, all 33 of her original teeth. This is taken up by the villagers, who materialize as a vindictive chorus, their song implying she kept her teeth because of a deal with demons. Eager to qualify for her doom, Orin bites down hard on a stone and when they see her again her mouth reveals bloody stumps.

This harsh imagery contrasts with the way the film is structured around song and dance. Although presented in the kabuki style, it isn't based on an actual kabuki play but on a novel. Kinoshita is correct, I believe, in presenting his story in this stylized way; his form allows it to become more fable than narrative, and thus more bearable.

His sets and backdrops reflect the changing seasons with lush beauty: spring, summer, the red leaves of autumn, then the wintry snows on the slopes of Narayama. On the mountaintop, blackbirds perch on snowy crags as the camera uses lateral moves to sweep across the desolate landscape. Finally depositing his mother in an empty place on the mountain, Tatsuhei greets the snow with relief: She will freeze more quickly. This he can sing only to himself, because the journey up the mountain has three strict rules: (1) you must not talk after starting up Narayama; (2) be sure no one sees you leave in the morning; (3) never look back. His adherence is in contrast with the adventures of the fearful neighbor Mata, who appears soon after bound head and foot, dragged protesting by his son ("Don't do this!").

Orin's goodness and resignation are at the center of the story. In particular, notice her kind welcome for Tama (Yuko Mochizuki), a 40-year-old widow she has decided will be the ideal new wife for her widower son. Known for her ability to catch trout when no one else can, she leads Tama through the forest on a foggy night and reveals a secret place beneath a rock in the brook where a trout is always to be found. This secret was never revealed to her first daughter-in-law. She even wants to die before her first grandchild arrives. She wants to rid the village from a hungry mouth.

Some will find Orin's behavior strange. So it is. Perhaps, in the years soon after World War II, she is intended in praise of the Japanese ability to present acceptance in the face of the appalling. You can attach any set of parallels to Kinoshita's parable and make them work, but that seems to fit.

Keisuke Kinoshita (1912–98) is of the same generation as Akira Kurosawa. Saying that ideas sprang quickly into his mind, he moved between periods and genres and made 42 films in the first 23 years of his career. He was immediately attracted to motion pictures; a film was shot in his hometown when he was in high school and he ran away to a studio in Kyoto. His family made him return home, but later dropped its opposition to his career plans. Without a college education, he started humbly as a set photographer and worked his way up, sending in one screenplay after another to the studio chief.

He made dramas, musicals, thrillers, anything, but he never made another film like *The Ballad of Narayama*. In its matter-of-fact juxtaposition of fate and art, it leaves an indelible impression. Tatsuhei's second bride Tama tells him: "When we turn 70, we'll go together up Narayama."

{ BARRY LYNDON }

Stanley Kubrick's *Barry Lyndon*, received indifferently in 1975, has grown in stature in the years since and is now widely regarded as one of the master's best. It is certainly in every frame a Kubrick film: technically awesome, emotionally distant, remorseless in its doubt of human goodness. Based on a novel published in 1844, it takes a form common in the nineteenth-century novel, following the life of the hero from birth to death. The novel by Thackeray, called the first novel without a hero, observes a man without morals, character, or judgment, unrepentant, unredeemed. Born in Ireland in modest circumstances, he rises through two armies and the British aristocracy with cold calculation.

Barry Lyndon is aggressive in its cool detachment. It defies us to care, it asks us to remain only observers of its stately elegance. Many of its developments take place offscreen, the narrator informing us what's about to happen, and we learn long before the film ends that its hero is doomed. This news doesn't much depress us, because Kubrick has directed Ryan O'Neal in the title role as if he were a still life. It's difficult to imagine such tumultuous events whirling around such a passive character. He loses a fortune, a wife, or a leg with as little emotion as he might in losing a dog. Only the death of his son devastates him, and that perhaps because he sees himself in the boy.

The casting choice of O'Neal is bold. Not a particularly charismatic actor, he is ideal for the role. Consider Albert Finney in *Tom Jones*, for example, bursting with vitality. Finney could not possibly have played Lyndon. O'Neal easily seems self-pitying, narcissistic, on the verge of tears. As one terrible event after another occurs to him, he projects an eerie calm. Nor do his triumphs—in gambling, con games, a fortunate marriage, and even acquiring a title—seem to bring him much joy. He is a man to whom things happen.

The other characters seem cast primarily for their faces and their presence, certainly not for their personalities. Look at the curling sneer of the lips of Leonard Rossiter, as Captain Quin, who ends Barry's youthful affair with a cousin by an advantageous offer of marriage. Study the face of Marisa Berenson, as Lady Lyndon. Is there any passion in her marriage? She loves their son as Barry does, but that seems to be their only feeling in common. When the time comes for her to sign an annuity check for the man who nearly destroyed her family, her pen pauses momentarily, then smoothly advances.

The film has the arrogance of genius. Never mind its budget or the perfectionism in its 300-day shooting schedule. How many directors would have had Kubrick's confidence in taking this ultimately inconsequential story of a man's rise and fall, and realizing it in a style that dictates our attitude toward it? We don't simply see Kubrick's movie, we see it in the frame of mind he insists on—unless we're so closed to the notion of directorial styles that the whole thing just seems like a beautiful extravagance (which it is). There is no other way to see Barry than the way Kubrick sees him.

Kubrick's work has a sense of detachment and bloodlessness. The most "human" character in *2001: A Space Odyssey* (1968) is the computer, and *A Clockwork Orange* (1971) is disturbing specifically in its objectivity about violence. The title of *Clockwork*, from Anthony Burgess's novel, illustrates Kubrick's attitude to his material. He likes to take organic subjects and disassemble them as if they were mechanical. It's not just that he wants to know what makes us tick; he wants to demonstrate that we do all tick. After *Spartacus* (1960), he never again created a major character driven by idealism or emotion.

The events in *Barry Lyndon* could furnish a swashbuckling romance. He falls into a foolish adolescent love, has to leave his home suddenly after a duel, enlists almost accidentally in the British army, fights in Europe, deserts from not one but two armies, falls in with unscrupulous companions, marries a woman of wealth and beauty, and then destroys himself because he lacks the character to survive.

But Kubrick examines Barry's life with microscopic clarity. He has the confidence of the great nineteenth-century novelists, authors who stood above their material and accepted without question their right to manipulate and interpret it with omniscience. Kubrick has appropriated Thackeray's attitude—or Trollope's or George Eliot's. There isn't Dickens's humor or relish of human character. Barry Lyndon, falling in and out of love and success, may see no pattern in his own affairs, but the artist sees one for him, one of consistent selfish opportunism.

Perhaps Kubrick's buried theme in *Barry Lyndon* is even similar to his outlook in *2001: A Space Odyssey*. Both films are about organisms striving to endure and prevail—and never mind the reason. The earlier film was about the human race itself; this one is about a depraved minor example of it. Barry journeys without plan, sees what he desires, tries to acquire it, and perhaps succeeds because he plays roles so well without being remotely dedicated to them. He looks the part of a lover, a soldier, a husband. But there is no *there* there.

There's a sense in both this film and *2001* that a superior force hovers above these struggles and controls them. In *2001*, it was a never-clarified form of higher intelligence. In *Barry Lyndon*, it's Kubrick himself, standing aloof from the action by two distancing devices: the narrator (Michael Hordern), who deliberately destroys suspense and tension by informing us of all key developments in advance, and the photography, which is a succession of meticulously, almost coldly, composed set images. It's notable that three of the film's four Oscars were awarded for cinematography (John Alcott), art direction (Ken Adam), and costumes (Ulla-Britt Soderlund and Milena Canonero). The many landscapes are often filmed in long shots; the fields, hills, and clouds could be from a landscape by Gainsborough. The interior compositions could be by Joshua Reynolds.

This must be one of the most beautiful films ever made, and yet the beauty isn't in the service of emotion. Against magnificent settings, the characters play at intrigues and scandals. They cheat at cards and marriage, they fight ridiculous duels. This is a film with a backdrop of the Seven Years' War that engulfed Europe, and it hardly seems to think the war worth noticing, except as a series of challenges posed for Barry Lyndon. By placing such small characters on such a big stage, by forcing our detachment from them, Kubrick supplies a philosophical position just as clearly as if he'd put speeches in his characters' mouths.

The images proceed in elegant stages through the events, often accompanied by the inexorable funereal progression of Handel's "Sarabande." For such an eventful life, there is no attempt to speed the events along. Kubrick told the critic Michel Ciment he used the narrator because the novel had too much incident even for a three-hour film, but there isn't the slightest sense he's condensing.

Some people find *Barry Lyndon* a fascinating, if cold, exercise in masterful filmmaking; others find it a terrific bore. I have little sympathy for the second opinion; how can anyone be bored by such an audacious film? *Barry Lyndon* isn't a great entertainment in the usual way, but it's a great example of directorial vision: Kubrick saying he's going to make this material function as an illustration of the way he sees the world.

{ THE BIG LEBOWSKI }

The Big Lebowski (1998) is about an attitude, not a story. It's easy to miss that, because the story is so urgently pursued. It involves kidnapping, ransom money, a porno king, a reclusive millionaire, a runaway girl, the Malibu police, a woman who paints while nude and strapped to an overhead harness, and the last act of the disagreement between Vietnam veterans and Flower Power. It has more scenes about bowling than anything else.

This is a plot and dialogue that perhaps only the Coen brothers could have devised. I'm thinking less of their clarity in *Fargo* and *No Country for Old Men* than of the almost hallucinatory logic of *Raising Arizona* and *The Hudsucker Proxy*. Only a steady hand in the midst of madness allows them to hold it all together—that, and the delirious richness of their visual approach.

Anyone who cares about movies must surely have heard something about the plot. This is a movie that has inspired an annual convention and the Church of the Latter-Day Dude. Its star, Jeff Bridges, has become so identified with the starring role that when he won the 2010 Oscar for Best Actor, Twitterland mourned that his acceptance speech didn't begin with, "The Dude Abides." These words are so emblematic that they inspired a book title, *The Dude Abides: The Gospel According to the Coen Brothers*, by Cathleen Falsani. This is a serious book, though far from a dreary theological work.

The Dude is Jeff Lebowski, an unemployed layabout whose days are spent sipping White Russians and nights are spent at the bowling alley. There is always a little pot available. He has a leonine mane of chestnut hair, a shaggy goatee, and a wardrobe of Bermuda shorts, rummage sale shirts, bathrobes, and flip-flops. He went to Woodstock and never left. He lives in what may be the last crummy run-down low-rent structure in Malibu. Trust the Dude to find it.

It is widely known that the Dude was inspired by a real man named Jeff Dowd, a freelance publicist who was instrumental in launching *Blood Simple* (1984), the first film in the Coen canon. I have long known Jeff Dowd. I can easily see how he might have inspired the Dude. He is as tall, as shaggy, and sometimes as mood-altered as Jeff Lebowski, although much more motivated. He remembers names better than a politician, is crafty in his strategies, and burns with a fiery zeal on behalf of those films he consents to represent.

In the film, Jeff Lebowski tells the millionaire's daughter (Julianne Moore) that in his youth he helped draft the Port Huron Statement that founded Students for a Democratic Society, and was a member of the Seattle Seven. In real life Jeff Dowd was indeed one of the Seattle Seven, and remains so militant that at Sundance 2009 he took a punch to the jaw for insisting too fervently that a critic see *Dirt*, an ecological documentary Dowd believed was essential to the survival of the planet. True to his credo of nonviolence, the Dude did not punch back.

In *The Big Lebowski* our hero has left politics far behind, and exists primarily to keep a buzz on, and bowl. He is never actually drunk in the movie, and always far from sober. His bowling partners are Walter Sobchak (John Goodman) and Donny Kerabatsos (Steve Buscemi). Walter, even taller than the Dude, is a proud Vietnam veteran and the strategist of the three. He and the Dude never mention politics. Donny is their meek sidekick, always a step behind the big guys. He says perhaps three complete sentences in the film, all brief, and is often interrupted by Walter telling him to shut the f--- up. He is happy to exist on the fringes of their glory.

Details of the plot need not concern us. It involves a mean-tempered millionaire in a wheelchair who is the Big Lebowski (the Dude becomes, by logic, the Little Lebowski). He broods before the fire in a vast pan-eled library, reminding me of no one so much as Major Amberson in *The Magnificent Ambersons*. His trophy wife Bunny (Tara Reid) appears to have been kidnapped. This leads indirectly to the Dude being savagely beaten by hit men who mistake him for the Big Lebowski. Well, how many Jeff Lebowskis can there be in Malibu? One of them urinates on the Dude's rug, which he valued highly ("it pulled the room together"), and the whole movie can be loosely described as being about the Dude's attempts to get payback for his rug.

The inspiration for the supporting characters can perhaps be found in the novels of Raymond Chandler. The Southern California setting, the millionaire, the kidnapped wife, the bohemian daughter, the enforcers, the cops who know the hero by name, can all be found in Chandler. The Dude is in a sense Philip Marlowe—not in his energy or focus, but in the code he lives by. Down these mean streets walks a man who won't allow his rug to be pissed on. "That will not stand," he says, perhaps unconsciously quoting George H. W. Bush about Saddam's invasion of Kuwait. The Dude does not lie, steal, or cheat. He does swear. He wants what is right. With the earliest flags of the republic, he insists, "Don't tread on me."

The Coens have always had a remarkable visual style, tending toward overwhelming architectural detail—long corridors, odd interior decoration, forced perspectives, lonely vistas, lurid cityscapes. Even in ostensibly realis-tic settings, such as the suburbs of *A Serious Man* (2009), they like to insist beyond the point of realism. Their suburb is the distillation of Suburbhood. In *The Big Lebowski*, their anchor location is the bowling alley, their domi-nant colors what might be described as Brunswick Orange and turquoise. The alley is strangely underpopulated, its lanes vertiginous in length. There is one POV shot from within a rolling bowling ball. When Jeff hallucinates or is unconscious, he inhabits bizarre fantasy worlds.

One of their fellow bowlers is Jesus Quintana (John Turturro), a man who has converted himself into an artwork in his own honor. An-other trio of supporting characters, the Nihilists, is led by Peter Stormare (who played the man feeding the body of Buscemi into the wood chipper in *Fargo*). A considerable role is played by Philip Seymour Hoffman, as Brandt, the worshipful assistant to the Big Lebowski. Some of its fans have seen this movie dozens of times. I suppose they've already observed that Hoffman and David Huddleston, who plays the Big Lebowski, bear a strong family resemblance. Someone knowing nothing about the film could be excused for suspecting that Philip Seymour Hoffman plays both characters, the older man with skillful makeup effects. A coincidence? I would not for one moment put it beyond the Coens, Ethan and Joel, to encourage this misapprehension. I suspect they cast Huddleston for the physical resemblance.

The film is all about Jeff Lebowski's equanimity in the face of vicissitudes. He is pounded, water-boarded, lied to, and insulted. His rug is pissed on and his car set aflame. He is seduced by a woman who wants only his seed. He has a fortune dangled before his eyes, only to have it replaced by telephone books and used boxer shorts. To heal and keep himself whole he stirs himself another White Russian, has a toke, sits in a warm bath. Like the Buddha, he focuses on the big picture.

The film is narrated by the Stranger (Sam Elliott, never more gloriously mustached). It is he who observes at the end that the Dude Abides, and says he hears there is a little Lebowski on the way. The Dude however is denied matrimony, and indeed seems to have no women at all in his life, except by lucky chance. Does this depress him? Is he concerned about being chronically unemployed? No. If a man has a roof over his head, fresh half-and-half for his White Russians, a little weed, and his bowling buddies, what more, really, does he need?

THE CABINET OF DR. CALIGARI

The first thing everyone notices and best remembers about *The Cabinet of Dr. Caligari* (1920) is the film's bizarre look. The actors inhabit a jagged landscape of sharp angles and tilted walls and windows, staircases climbing crazy diagonals, trees with spiky leaves, grass that looks like knives. These radical distortions immediately set the film apart from all earlier ones, which were based on the camera's innate tendency to record reality.

The stylized sets, obviously two-dimensional, must have been a lot less expensive than realistic sets and locations, but I doubt that's why the director, Robert Wiene, wanted them. He is making a film of delusions and deceptive appearances, about madmen and murder, and his characters exist at right angles to reality. None of them can quite be believed, nor can they believe one another.

The film opens in the German town of Holstenwall, seen in a drawing as houses like shrieks climbing a steep hill. After a prologue, a story is told: A sideshow operator named Caligari (Werner Krauss) arrives at the fair to exhibit the Somnambulist, a man he claims has been sleeping since his birth 23 years ago. This figure, named Cesare (Conrad Veidt), sleeps in a coffin and is hand-fed by the crazed-looking doctor, who claims he can answer any question.

The hero, Francis (Frederich Feher), visits the show with his friend

Alan (Hans Heinz von Twardowski), who boldly asks, "When will I die?" The reply is chilling: "At first dawn!" At dawn Alan is dead. Suspicion falls on Cesare. Francis keeps watch all night through a window as Caligari sleeps next to the closed coffin. But the next morning, his fiancée, Jane (Lil Dagover), has been abducted. Does that clear the doctor and the Somnambulist from suspicion?

In itself, this is not a startling plot. The film's design transforms it into something very weird, especially as Cesare is seen carrying the unconscious Jane and is pursued by a mob. The chase carries them through streets of stark lights and shadows and up a zigzagging mountain trail. Caligari, meanwhile, is followed by Francis as he returns to where he apparently lives—the insane asylum, where he is the . . . director! Evidence is discovered by Francis and the local police that Caligari, influenced by an occult medieval manuscript, yearned to find a somnambulist and place him under a hypnotic spell, subjecting him to his will.

A case can be made that *Caligari* was the first true horror film. There had been earlier ghost stories and the eerie serial *Fantomas* made in 1913–14, but their characters were inhabiting a recognizable world. *Caligari* creates a mindscape, a subjective psychological fantasy. In this world, unspeakable horror becomes possible.

Caligari is said to be the first example in cinema of German expressionism, a visual style in which not only the characters but the world itself is out of joint. I don't know of another film that used its extreme distortions and discordant angles, but its over-all attitude certainly cleared the way for *The Golem, Nosferatu, Metropolis,* and *M.* In one of the best-known books ever written about film, *From Caligari to Hitler,* the art historian Siegfried Kracauer argued that the rise of Nazism was foretold by the preceding years of German films, which reflected a world at wrong angles and lost values. In this reading, Caligari was Hitler and the German people were sleepwalkers under his spell.

I don't believe the films caused Nazism in Germany, and whether they predicted it depends a great deal on hindsight. What is certain is that the expressionist horror films created the most durable and bulletproof of genres. No other genre has box-office appeal all by itself, although film noir, also deeply influenced by expressionism, comes close. All a horror film need promise is horror—the unspeakable, the terrifying, the merciless, the lurching monstrous figure of destruction. It needs no stars, only basic production values, just the ability to promise horror.

The 1920s were the decade that saw the rise of the Dada and surrealist movements. The first rejected all pretense, all standards, all sincerity. It was a profound expression of hopelessness and alienation. It led to the rise of the related art movement surrealism, which cut loose from order and propriety, rejected common values, scorned tradition, and sought to overthrow society with anarchy. It's said such movements were a reaction to the horror of World War I, which upset decades of relative tranquility and order, threw the European nations into unstable new relationships, and presented the inhuman spectacle of modern mechanized battle. After the brutality of trench warfare, it would be difficult to return to landscapes and still life.

The Cabinet of Dr. Caligari as a viewing experience must have been unsettling to the audiences of 1920. The original *Variety* review, which cheerfully reveals the ending, tries in its stilted wording to express enthusiasm: "This has resulted in a series of actions so perfectly dovetailed as to carry the story through at a perfect tempo. Robert Wiene has made perfect use of settings designed by Hermann Warm, Walter Reimann and Walter Roehrig, settings that squeeze and turn and adjust the eye and through the eye the mentality."

Although the prose suggests chiropractic, I imagine some viewers indeed felt squeezed, turned, and adjusted by the images. The film today still casts its spell. I viewed the version on a DVD from Kino, which (unusual with silent films of its vintage) includes all the original footage. The film has not been digitally restored to remove all flaws, but in a way those that remain—spots, blemishes—add to the effect. You feel as if you're watching an old record of an old story, which includes within itself an even older one. The original film was tinted, so there are no purely black-and-white scenes, only those mostly in shades of reddish-brown and slate blue.

Wiene is fond of the iris shot, which opens or closes upon a scene like an eye. This makes the point that we are *looking* and are privileged to witness events closed to other people. He also sparingly uses a device of superimposing words on the image to show Alan feeling surrounded by voices. Wiene's close-ups lean heavily on Caligari's fierce and sinister scowl, the dewy innocence of Jane, and the wide-eyed determination of Alan. The somnambulist is not very expressive—he certainly lacks the charisma of Frankenstein's monster, who in a way he inspired—and is most often seen in long shot, as if the camera considers him an object, not a person.

The sets are presented, as they must be, in mostly longer shots, establishing their spiky and ragged points and edges. The visual environment plays like a wilderness of blades; the effect is to deny the characters any place of safety or rest. It isn't surprising that the *Caligari* set design inspired so few other films, although its camera angles, lighting, and drama can clearly be seen throughout film noir, for example in the visual style of *The Third Man* (1949).

Robert Wiene (1873–1938) began his career in 1913 and directed 47 films, including *Raskolnikow* based on *Crime and Punishment*, and the famous *The Hands of Orlac* (1924). He fled the rise of Hitler and at the time of his death was working on *Ultimatum* (1938), with another refugee, Erich von Stroheim. Conrad Veidt (1893–1943), another refugee, made 119 films and was a major star of the time, whose credits included the great *The Man Who Laughs* (1928) and of course *Casablanca* (1942), where he played Major Strasser, who met an unexpected end at the airport.

{ CACHÉ }

How is it possible to watch a thriller intently two times and completely miss a smoking gun that's in full view? Yet I did. Only on my third trip through Michael Haneke's *Caché* (2006) did I consciously observe a shot which forced me to redefine the film. I was not alone. I haven't read all of the reviews of the film, but after seeing that shot I looked up a lot of them, and the shot is never referred to. For that matter, no one seems to point to a conclusion that it might suggest.

I described the film as "a thriller." So it is, but a thriller that implodes, not releasing its tension in action but coiling it deeper inside. *Caché* on its fundamental level is about a family that becomes aware it is being watched. And not merely watched, but *seen*. The family's bourgeois home, in a side street in an ordinary district of Paris, is observed in an opening shot that lasts about five minutes.

The camera is locked down. We see the house. Its facade is almost entirely hidden from the street by shrubbery. Nothing happens. After perhaps three minutes, a bicyclist passes: that reveals it's footage, and not a photograph. Later, people emerge from the front door and head out for the day. And *then* we see the stripes a videotape displays when it's being rewound, and hear voices discussing it. The shot was watching, and now it is being watched.

It was on a tape left at the door of Anne and Georges Laurent (Juliette Binoche and Daniel Auteuil). They have a 15-year-old son, Pierrot (Lester Makedonsky). Georges hosts a public television talk show about books. She has a job in publishing. The walls in their home are lined with books, and the rooms filled with computers, editing equipment, all the tools of virtual labor.

The mysterious video is maddening. Others arrive, some are accompanied by childish drawings: a black-and-white cartoon head, with a slash of red blood at its mouth or neck. Who sends them? What message do they contain? Georges and Anne have lived comfortably behind their shrubbery for years, in what seems a stable marriage. Friends often come for dinner and good conversation. Their lives proceed on shared assumptions. Now this.

It introduces a wedge between them—the small point at first, then forcing a wider separation. Georges says he knows nothing about the tapes. We believe him. But Anne knows him so well that she senses they make him uncomfortable about *something*. He has secrets, perhaps even from himself. He grows unreasonably irritated by her questions. She discovers him withholding information.

Juliette Binoche, that actress of perfect tone, modulates Anne's feelings realistically. She doesn't become hysterical, simply offended. She regards Georges, and we see she knows him well. He may be hiding nothing, but in that case, he is nevertheless hiding it. Daniel Auteuil seems almost like a child found out at something.

I'll be brief. Other tapes arrive, suggesting Georges drive to a particular address and knock on a particular door. There he meets Majid (Maurice Benichou), a man about his age. They haven't seen one another since both were five or six. This was the man sending the tapes? Majid says he knows nothing about it. We believe him. We really do. Georges conceals details of his visit from Anne. Why? He asserts that Majid *must* be the source of the tapes. Then he must know Majid has a reason.

One subdued night in their bedroom, Anne regards him and asks simply, "What did you do to him?" Does Georges know? I will let you discover how the two men knew each other as children. Whatever happened, it is still there in the air between them.

Haneke surrounds this mystery with the details of everyday life. Dinner parties, meetings at the office, meal preparation, tapings of the TV show, a lunch between Anne and a mutual friend, a visit by Georges to his elderly mother. Problems with Pierrot, a teenager who is sulky and distant in the way that teenagers are when they have little to complain about except their discontent. Pierrot frightens them by being missing all night. The police are called in. Pierrot's disappearance is explained. The police leave. Georges doesn't want to press the matter of the tapes with the police. His wife believes he protests too much.

We ask ourselves: Is the real mystery not who is sending the tapes, but how they cause Georges to feel? The focus shifts from an outside threat to one hidden in his character. Haneke's attention is on the couple forced apart, not on the source of the tapes and drawings. Indeed, when we discover the origin of the bloody mouth and neck images, it does nothing, really, to suggest Majid sent them. That's largely because Maurice Benichou, the actor playing Majid, does such a convincing job of playing innocence. To repeat: we believe him.

Haneke, a masterful Austrian whose *The White Ribbon* won Cannes 2009, is a meticulous filmmaker. His camera is precisely placed, and he firmly controls what we see and how we see it. Point of view is all-important. Background images of TV news may be relevant. We learn from Georges of a long-suppressed incident in 1961, during Algerian demonstrations in Paris, when the bodies of 200 demonstrators were found floating in the Seine. How could this be forgotten? Has France hidden it in its memory?

A stationary camera is objective. A moving camera implies a subjective viewer, whether that viewer is a character, the director, or the audience. Haneke uses the technique of making the camera "move" in time, not space. His locked-down shots are objective. When they're reversed on a VCR, they *become* subjective. Likewise shots within the Laurent house sometimes seem to be objective. This is underlined by the fact that some of the tapes seem to have been shot from positions that must have been in full view. A tape taken *within* Majid's apartment, for example. If Majid didn't make it, who did? There's a reverse shot in Majid's apartment, showing the shelves where a camera must have been hidden to film the video. If you advance through it a frame at a time, on the bottom shelf you'll see in plain view what could be a camera lens, or maybe not. It seems too large.

Someone knows something. Georges may suspect what it is. It refers to his fifth year: How much do we recall or understand from then? Majid knows what it is. His grown son (Walid Afkir) may know, but says not, and he is also convincing. Given the Law of Economy of Characters, there is only one remaining player: Pierrot, the son. What could he possibly know, and how could he have learned a secret probably not clear even to his father, who has certainly never discussed it with him?

Yet the son, too, seems ruled out. Everyone seems ruled out. In an interview on the DVD Haneke is pleased by confounding our expectations. Those raised on the mainstream cinema, he says, are accustomed to an ending that resolves things, "so they can leave the film and forget it." He discusses many explanations for Caché, and points out none are necessary.

Yet there is the film's final shot, which has been so much discussed, showing two characters meeting who shouldn't know one another. What does that mean? Does it solve anything? Haneke is delighted that he constructed the shot so about half of all viewers fail to even notice them on a large canvas filled with extras. That works for him, too. Now I call your attention to the shot I missed the first time through. You will find it on the DVD, centering around 20:39. You tell me what it means. It's the smoking gun, but did it shoot anybody?

{La Ceremonie}

The French have a name for the events leading up to a death by guillotine. They call it "the ceremony." Although Claude Chabrol's *La Ceremonie* (1995) contains no guillotines, there is a relentless feeling to it, as if the characters are engaged in a performance that can have only one outcome. It comes as a surprise to all of them, and to us. But given these people in this situation, can we really say in hindsight that we're surprised?

Chabrol, a founding member of the French New Wave who died in September 2010 having made 54 features, is sometimes said to be influenced by Hitchcock, perhaps because many of his characters become involved in murder but few of them make it a profession. It often comes into their lives as the result of a psychological compulsion set in action by particular circumstances.

"Of course, murder always heightens the interest in a film," he told me in 1971, at the New York Film Festival. "Even a banal situation takes on importance when there's a murder involved. I suppose that's why I choose to work with murder so often. That's the area of human activity where the choices are most crucial and have the greatest consequences. On the other hand, I'm not at all interested in who-done-its. If you conceal a character's guilt, you imply that his guilt is the most important thing about him. I want the audience to know who the murderer is, so that we can consider his personality."

That leads to the question: Does he let us know who will commit murder(s) in *La Ceremonie*? I think he does, although there will be some in the audience who are surprised that anyone in the film is killed. Assuming that some must die (this is a film by Chabrol, after all), it is obvious who they must be. That's why I won't issue a spoiler warning; this isn't a who-done-it. It's more about how the two murderers do something together that neither would be capable of doing by themselves.

So *La Ceremonie* is about murder. It is also about faces, two in particular. They belong to Isabelle Huppert, as Jeanne, the rude postmistress in a small French town, and Sandrine Bonnaire, as Sophie, a young woman who comes to the town seeking work as a maid. In these roles they share a facial quality both often display: they have an almost maddening secrecy. There is also a difference: Jeanne seems all-knowing, cocky, dominant. Sophie, submissive, grateful for attention, doesn't seem very bright. When she's told something, she has a way of turning her head slowly and letting it sink in before reacting. The film consistently plants hints of a secret Sophie conceals—a handicap I will not reveal—that indicates that her ability to hold a job indicates she has a gift for deception.

Huppert, the busiest major actress of her generation, wears so well in so many different roles because she only reluctantly reveals a character's feelings. She leaves it up to us to figure them out; there may be some play-acting involved, but we sense that most is hidden. Above all she's ideal for characters with an enormous stubborn determination that she holds very much inside. Chabrol has used her seven times, most inevitably in the title role of *Madame Bovary*.

Bonnaire's face can be equally concealing, but she is better at seeming vulnerable. Her great early role was in Agnes Varda's *Vagabond* (1985), the story of a young office worker who walks away from her job and sets off optimistically to backpack around France. When she's found dead in a ditch some months later, we wonder why she continued to fall, and fall, when she had many opportunities to save herself. She will never tell us.

The film opens with a job interview. She meets with a wealthy bourgeois wife named Catherine Lelievre (the bilingual Jacqueline Bisset) in a cafe. They have tea. Catherine explains that she lives in an isolated house in the country, with her husband Georges (Jean-Pierre Cassel) and their son Gilles (Valentin Merlet). Melinda (Virginie Ledoyen), his daughter by an earlier marriage, sometimes comes to visit. They require a live-in maid and cook. All very well with Sophie, who takes command of the interview with almost imperious self-confidence. She has her papers, her letter of reference, her salary requirement. An isolated house is no problem. At the end of their conversation, it's almost as if Sophie dismisses Catherine.

We see the large, luxurious country estate. Its stone walls contain a service wing, so that family and servants live privately. Everyone gets along at first. In contrast to her manner in the cafe, Sophie seems quiet and submissive here, performing her tasks and then going to her room. There she seems a different person, a naive adolescent, sitting on the floor, leaning against the bed, hypnotized by whatever happens to be on TV.

One day she accompanies Georges into the village, where she meets the postmistress, Jeanne. As portrayed by Huppert, Jeanne seems instinctively to sniff out some quality in Sophie that puts her on alert. She contrives opportunities for them to meet. She is hungry for gossip about the Lelievre family. She has class-conscious scorn for their comfortable lifestyle. She especially believes Madame Lelievre is stuck up and insufferable.

We are watching a seduction. Despite our expectations that lesbianism is possible, it isn't sexual, but has to do with power. Jeanne senses a weakness in Sophie, a secret, and perhaps believes she can make the other young woman her instrument—to do what, remains to be seen. With nothing in particular in mind, Jeanne knows she will be able to control Sophie in a mutual action. Jeanne drives out to the house frequently, and they meet in Sophie's room, sneaking up the back stairs, devouring TV programs; when the Lelievres discover her in the house, Georges explodes. Earlier, he accused her of opening his mail. Now he forbids them to see one another. Jeanne's eyes narrow. Georges has taken a fatal step.

Earlier in the film, Georges discovered alarming background details about both women. Earlier, in other towns, they were touched by two deaths—Sophie's father, and Jeanne's young daughter. There is no particular reason to believe either woman was responsible for these deaths, but Georges's research into provincial newspapers indicates there was a certain amount of suspicion. Well, are they murderers? Chabrol never declares himself, and that sets up one of the most disturbing scenes in the movie. Giggling like schoolgirls with a crush, the two tease each other that they know the other's secret, and the secret is murder. Neither denies it. We suspect one, maybe both, are innocent. By passively allowing such things to be said about them, they create a titillating tension in the relationship. We begin to understand that regardless of whether either has committed murder, together they are certainly capable of it.

Chabrol is at home in the world of the wealthy and does an effortless job of showing the Lelievre family, confident, affectionate, dining in style, appreciating fine wines, lining themselves up all four on a sofa to watch an opera by Mozart on TV. This is a contrast to the two young working-class women upstairs, whose relationship and the TV they watch is attuned to Sophie's simplistic mind. Assuming Jeanne is much smarter than Sophie, what we see taking shape is an act of resentful violence, in which the childlike maid is the murder weapon. The film implacably moves toward a horrifying conclusion.

{ THE CIRCUS }

Charlie Chaplin was a perfectionist in his films and a calamity in his private life. These two traits clashed as he was making *The Circus*, one of his funniest films and certainly the most troubled. When he sat down to write his autobiography, he simply never mentioned it, perhaps because he wanted to sidestep that entire period. Yet a delightful movie emerged from the turmoil.

When he released it in 1928, Charlie was long since established as the greatest star in Hollywood. He must have feared the advent of the talkies, which by bringing sound to the movies would rob him of his silence. But more than sound was on his mind during the two years it took him to finally finish his production.

Always attracted to young girls, he married the 16-year-old Mildred Harris in 1918, when he was 29. After affairs with Pola Negri and Marion Davies, in 1924 he married Lita Grey, who said she was 16 but may have been 15. He learned she was pregnant while preparing *The Circus*, and after she sued for divorce and threatened scandal, her family scented a big settlement. They agreed on $600,000, while the IRS simultaneously determined he owed $1 million in back taxes.

Meanwhile, Chaplin had hired Lita's friend Merna Kennedy as his lead in *The Circus*; Lita charged that they had an affair, and he also had an affair during the same period with the great silent star Louise Brooks.

There were also rumors of wild parties, apparently true; his genitals led an undisciplined existence.

I mention these matters to underline his accomplishment with *The Circus*. Calamities struck the production. The circus tent set burned down. A reel of finished film was lost. His perfectionism demanded 200 takes for a difficult scene on a tightrope. He was divorcing Grey, he was romancing at least two other women, his funds were in disarray, the talkies were coming, and yet his Little Tramp carried on unperturbed.

It's interesting to ponder how smart the Tramp really is, and how much he understands the situations he finds himself in. He's sort of a Holy Fool. In *The Circus*, he gets hired as a clown by accident after he proves so incompetent as a property man that he steals the laughter from the real clowns. He's the star of the circus, but has to have this explained to him by Merna, who plays the ringmaster's mistreated stepdaughter. He has no idea what made him funny, no clear idea of why he stops being funny, and usually seems the unwitting pawn of events outside his comprehension.

This makes him, for me, a little less inspired than Buster Keaton, whose characters are smart and calculating, if also beset by life's disappointments. But both get many of their laughs by their sheer physical grace and acrobatic skills. The physical world conspires against them, and they prevail. They are often yearning romantics, with this difference: Buster seems a plausible mate, and the Tramp hardly seems to possess a libido, only idealized notions. If their comedies had been made in a more liberated time, it is possible to imagine Keaton in bed with a woman, but disquieting to think of the Tramp as a sexual being.

Yet here he contrives a giant crush on Merna (the character takes the actress's name). They are brought together in the first place by one of the constant motifs in Chaplin, hunger. In *The Gold Rush*, he had eaten a shoe, and now his only piece of bread is stolen by the girl, who has been forbidden to eat as the ringmaster's punishment for a bad performance. At one point, he slyly filches a baby's bun. Later, in a lovely bit of pantomime, he rehearses for a comic bit as William Tell's son, but grabs stolen bites of the apple. Merna and the Tramp are brought together in the first place as comrades in hunger and travail, and in the Tramp's mind, they're lovers.

The film is rich in sight gags. It opens with a complex pickpocket scenario, continues with a famous chase around the fairgrounds, includes a house of mirrors scene in which multiple Tramps, cops, and strangers chase one another's reflections. One scene has him locked in a lion's cage; measures must have been taken to assure his safety, but CGI was unknown and the lion seems real enough. The editing here, coordinating the lion and the Tramp, must have been daunting. There are also bits showing Chaplin's flawless timing, as when he wreaks havoc with the magician's elaborate tricks.

The piece de resistance is the extended tightrope scene. The Tramp watches morosely as Rex, King of the Air (Harry Crocker), performs on the high wire, and Merna sighs and bats her eyes. Later Rex misses a performance, and the Tramp seizes the chance to go on the wire himself to win back her admiration. With the device of a secret safety wire supposedly manned by a prop man, he performs stunts that are extraordinary because of their difficulty; he uses the wire as a means of making the performance much harder than ordinary tightrope walking would be.

Yes, camera angles no doubt disguise his distance from the ground. Yes, there must have been a net. Yes, the "wire" must have only been the half of it. But still, what remarkable agility, a reminder of a time when Chaplin and other great stars (Fairbanks, Keaton, Lloyd) did their own stunts and could be seen doing them. And the addition of the pestering monkeys is a masterstroke.

The ending is rather a letdown, involving the Tramp's oddly motivated reasons for reuniting Merna and Rex. There is a comeuppance for the ringmaster, and then, of course, the familiar closing iris shot of the Tramp, alone and forlorn but with a defiant little hop, going back on the road.

Chaplin was a considerable artist, brave and gifted, but I am in a minority in placing him second to Keaton among the silent clowns. My reasons for that are admittedly impulsive: I sense Keaton was the better man. Chaplin was so famous, so rich, so powerful when so young that there is a kind of conceit in the Tramp, a reverse noblesse oblige. Yes, he had a miserable childhood, and in his films, he often plays the friend of waifs, but there's an air of back-patting about it. The Buster Keaton character has his feet on the ground. He would be embarrassed to parade his goodness. He uses ingenuity rather than divinity. Chaplin's untidy love life suggests he felt he deserved whomever he wanted; Keaton in private life seems to have been melancholic because of alcoholism, but a decent enough sort with women.

But is this merely arbitrary judgment on my part? No doubt. A lesser man can make a better film, and a great man can make a bad one. I feel Keaton's work has aged better than Chaplin's. His films are drier, less lachrymose, less in love with their hero. Audiences still snuffle on cue at the end of *City Lights*, when the little blind flower girl discovers the identity of her benefactor. I'm touched, too. But it's a set-up, isn't it? You write a movie in which you are the benefactor of a blind flower girl, you're gonna come out looking great. Buster is engaged in immediate practical problems.

I realize these are cavils. The wonderment is that we still have the silent clowns, many now available in restored versions. Almost all of Keaton, of Lloyd, of Chaplin. They were artists who depended on silence, and sound was powerless to add a thing. They live in their time, and we must be willing to visit it. An inability to admire silent films, like a dislike of black and white, is a sad inadequacy. Those who dismiss such pleasures must have deficient imaginations.

LA COLLECTIONNEUSE

During lazy summer days and nights, the subjects of *La Collectionneuse* (1967) practice idleness and slow-motion mind games in a villa in the hills above St. Tropez on the French Riviera. Sensuality is always in the air, where it drifts aimlessly. This is the third of Eric Rohmer's Moral Tales, the first at feature length, the first filmed in color. It functions as a jumping-off point for the rest of his long career.

Rohmer (1920–2010) was older than his fellow directors in the French New Wave, and it's remarkable that he was already 47 when he made the film that enfolds so much of the indolence and narcissism of youth. Much of his prolific output fell into three groupings: six Moral Tales, Comedies and Proverbs, and Tales of the Four Seasons. The Moral Tales studied tricky questions of romance, and there was little or no sex in them but much discussion about it. He found actors of undeniable physical appeal, and his camera caressed them as they spoke, and spoke, about the possibility of caressing each other.

La Collectionneuse, which refers to a female collector (of men, in this case) centers on a young woman named Haydée who finds herself living at the villa with Adrien and Daniel, two friends about ten years older than she is. They watch her being picked up by a series of young guys who drive up to the villa and then speed off to the fashionable beachfront city, bringing her back after dawn. Both men claim they have no desire to sleep with her, and talk themselves into an undeclared contest to see which will be the first to succumb.

This assumes that Haydée can be had for the taking, which is by no means the case. The film is narrated by Adrien, and information is filtered through his unreliable opinions of Haydée and Daniel and his high opinion of himself. There is no scene at which he isn't present, but since he can't control what is said, we are invited to arrive at our own conclusions. Rohmer had a deliberate narrative style that postponed or sidestepped events that a conventional director would have supplied right on schedule. The Moral Tales demonstrated that his characters were not fated to do obvious things, and reserved the option of thinking about the meaning of their actions. They were not invariably moral, nor was their alleged morality necessarily one we would agree with.

But step back a moment and look at these three. Daniel (Daniel Pommereulle) is the least interesting, a lanky layabout who fancies wearing kaftans to the beach, who smokes and drinks a lot, who boasts of his indolence, and who expects to sleep with Haydée sooner or later. Haydée (Haydée Politoff), about 20 when the film was made, is a slender woman with a pretty, round face, full lips, and a saucy haircut. She has a lot of self-confidence and knows how to keep her secrets. Adrien is played by Patrick Bauchau, a strikingly handsome youth who is described in the dialogue (which he cowrote) as "six feet six with the profile of an eagle." He is actually only 6´3″, but when I saw him for the first time at Telluride I wanted to stop and stare: he would have been in his 40s then, and age had only added character and intrigue to his face. In 1967 he was already a New Wave actor, writer, and producer, and appeared in Rohmer's *Suzanne's Career* (1963), a 55-minute short that counts as the second Moral Tale.

They live at a languorous pace. The men decide she is a "slut," because they assume she sleeps with the revolving roster of guys who take her into town. When a rich art collector visits the villa to look at a vase Adrien is selling, Adrien essentially offers her to the older man. The way she handles that speaks well for her insight into the situation.

Although it must be near St. Tropez, the villa is on an unspoiled hillside, and the characters can walk directly down to the sea. It has been loaned to them by a friend. It's sparsely furnished, and as the three sit on a veranda or under trees, nature is well-represented with the bird songs Rohmer is fond of.

Adrien, who hopes to raise money to open a gallery, has confided in his narration that he plans, for a month, to do as little as possible. He doesn't even want Daniel around, and is annoyed when Haydée turns out to have been invited by the absentee owner. Determined not to get involved with a silly younger girl, he begins a private game to maneuver Haydée and Daniel into bed together. Sensing his plan, Daniel tries to turn the tables on them. Haydée keeps her own hopes completely to herself.

To watch a film like this, or any Rohmer film, creates a sense of peaceful regard in me. He isn't afraid of losing my attention with too much dialogue, or too little action. He invites me to arrive at my own moral judgments. Immediately after this film came the celebrated *My Night at Maud's* (1968), the first Rohmer most Americans had seen, and then came the seductive and wickedly funny *Claire's Knee*, an entire movie about the lengths the hero Jerome will go to find an excuse to touch the delectable knee of Claire.

Rarely has a knee seemed more touchable. *La Collectionneuse* opens with a series of three brief prologues showing the characters before they meet at the villa, and the camera watches as Haydée, wearing a bikini, wades in the waves at the edge of the sea. The camera's gaze is bold and objective, regarding her body part by part: her legs, her thighs, her stomach, her chest, her ears, hands, throat. It's diabolical how well Rohmer sets her up as an object of desire in a film that will indefinitely postpone the realization of any desire we may feel. I wonder if this prologue in some way inspired the idea for *Claire's Knee*.

Rohmer was late to join the New Wave, although as the editor of the influential *Cahiers du Cinema* he published the film reviews of such future directors as Godard, Truffaut, and Chabrol. He made a film named *The Sign of the Lion* in 1959, to little effect. Finally, partnering with Barbet Schroeder as his producer and sometime actor, he made the two shorts in 1963. When *La Collectionneuse* appeared in 1967, he was late to the table; Godard, Resnais, Chabrol, Varda, and Truffaut were already well-established.

La Collectionneuse was the first feature photographed by Nestor Almendros, the Spanish cinematographer who won an Oscar for *Days of Heaven* and was nominated three more times. He earlier worked with Rohmer on *A Student of Today*, the short that was the first Moral Tale, and they went on to collaborate on nine features in all. His lush, contemplative approach fit perfectly with Rohmer's desire to look at characters and think about them, instead of forcing them through their paces.

I saw my first Rohmer, *My Night at Maud's*, at the 1969 New York Film Festival, and wrote: "It is so good to see a movie where the characters have beliefs, and articulate them, and talk to each other (instead of at each other). It is so good, in fact, that you realize how hungry you've been for this sort of thing." I've been in love with Rohmer ever since.

{ COME AND SEE }

It's said that you can't make an effective antiwar film because war by its nature is exciting, and the end of the film belongs to the survivors. No one would ever make the mistake of saying that about Elem Klimov's *Come and See*. This 1985 film from Russia is one of the most devastating films ever about anything, and in it, the survivors must envy the dead.

The film begins with an ambiguous scene, as a man calls out commands to invisible others on a beach. Who is he? Who is he calling to? Why is he fed up with them? It's revealed that he's calling out to children who have concealed themselves among the reeds. They are playing games of war, and digging in the sand for weapons concealed or lost during some earlier conflict.

We meet them. Florya, perhaps 14, lives nearby with his family. It is 1943, Hitler's troops are invading the Soviet republic of Byelorussia, and Florya (Aleksey Kravchenko) dreams of becoming a heroic partisan and defending his homeland. He wants to leave home and volunteer. His family forbids him. But as events unfold, he leaves, is accepted in a fighting unit, is forced to change his newer shoes with a veteran's worn-out ones, and is taken under the wing of these battle-weary foot soldiers.

He is still young. He seems younger than his years in early scenes, and much, much older in later ones. At first he is eager to do a good job;

posted as a sentry, told to fire on anyone who doesn't know the password, he challenges a girl scarcely older than he is. He does not shoot her; indeed, he never shoots anybody. They grow friendly. Glasha (Olga Mironova), innocent and warm, dreams of her future. Florya is not articulate and may be mentally slow, but he is touched.

The film follows him for its entire length, sometimes pausing to look aside at details of horror. He doesn't see everything. In particular, there's a scene where he and the girl, separated from the army unit, return to his family farm, where he expects a warm welcome. There is nobody there, furniture is upturned, but it seems they've just left. A pot of soup is still warm. He suddenly becomes convinced he knows where they're gone, and pulls her to run with him to an island in a marshland. Then she sees a sight that he doesn't.

Such a departure from his point of view doesn't let us off easy. All he sees is horror, and all he doesn't see is horror, too. Later Florya finds himself in a village as Nazi occupiers arrive. There is a sustained sequence as they methodically round up all the villagers and lock them into a barn. The images evoke the Holocaust. As he's shoved in as part of the seething crowd, Florya's eyes never leave the windows high above the floor. By now his only instinct in life has become to escape death. Parents and children, old people and infants, are all packed in. The Nazis call for any able-bodied men to come out. The fathers stay with their families. Florya scrambles out a window and watches as the Nazis burn down the barn, its locked double doors heaving from the desperation inside. This is a horrifying scene, avoiding facile cutaways and simply standing back and regarding.

This incident, and the story of the boy himself, are based on fact. Many Russian films have depicted the horror of Nazism, because Hitler was a safe target and a convenient stand-in for political allegory closer to home. This film is much more than an allegory. I have rarely seen a film more ruthless in its depiction of human evil.

The principal Nazi monster in the film, S. S. Major Sturmbannfuhrer, is a suave, heartless beast not a million miles distant from Tarantino's Col. Hans Landa. He toys with an unpleasant little simian pet that clings to his neck. He is almost studious in his murderous commands. His detachment embodies power, which is the thing Florya never for a moment possesses throughout the movie. It is possible that Florya survives because he is so manifestly powerless. To look at him is to see a mind reeling from shock. One would like to think the depiction of the Nazis is exaggerated, but no. The final title card says, "The Nazis burned down 628 Byelorussian villages together with all the people in them."

It strains credulity to imagine Florya surviving all the horrors that he witnesses, but there was a real Florya, and Klimov's script was written with Ales Adamovich; Klimov told Ron Holloway in a 1986 interview, "Adamovich was the same age as the hero in the film. He and his family fought with the partisans and witnessed the genocide perpetrated by the Nazis on Belarussian soil." Klimov added that his film was shot in Byelorussia (now known as Belarus) near where the events took place, and that he used no professional actors.

The film depicts brutality and is occasionally very realistic, but there's an overlay of muted nightmarish exaggeration. The swamp that Florya and Glasha wade through, for example, has a thick gelatinous top layer that seems like a living, malevolent skin. There's a sequence in which Florya becomes involved with some cows who will become food for starving troops. He and the cow are in a field obscured by a thick fog when machine-gun fire breaks out—from where, he cannot tell. The eventual death of the beast is told in a series of images that mirror the inexorable shutting down of life. The cow's life was doomed one way or another, but these suggest how utterly incomprehensible death is to the cow. The nightmare intensifies after Florya is too near an artillery bombardment and is deafened. The sound becomes muted, and there is a faint ringing, which makes the reality of sound frustratingly out of reach for him.

Is it true that audiences demand some kind of release or catharsis? That we cannot accept a film that leaves us with no hope? That we struggle to find uplift in the mire of malevolence? There's a curious scene here in a wood, the sun falling down through the leaves, when the soundtrack, which has been grim and mournful, suddenly breaks free into Mozart. And what does this signify? A fantasy, I believe, and not Florya's, who has probably never heard such music. The Mozart descends into the film like a deus ex machina, to lift us from its despair. We can accept it if we want, but it changes nothing. It is like an ironic taunt.

I must not describe the famous sequence at the end. It must unfold as a surprise for you. It pretends to roll back history. You will see how. It is unutterably depressing, because history can never undo itself, and is with us forever.

I learn from IMDb.com that the film's title, seemingly so straight-forward, has a bleak context. It comes from the Book of Revelation: "And when he had opened the fourth seal, I heard the voice of the fourth beast say, 'Come and see.' And I looked, and behold a pale horse: and his name that sat on him was Death, and Hell followed with him. And power was given unto them over the fourth part of the earth, to kill with sword, and with hunger, and with death, and with the beasts of the earth."

{ CONTACT }

Contact (1997) is a film that takes place at the intersection of science, politics, and faith. Those are three subjects that don't always fit easily together. In the film, an alien intelligence transmits an image of three pages of encrypted symbols. It is clear where the corners of each page are. It is also clear that the three corners are intended to come together in some way to make a single image. Scientists are baffled in their attempts to bring the pages together. The solution, when we see it, provides a Eureka Moment. It is so simple, and yet so difficult to conceive of. It may be intended as a sort of intelligence test.

Watching the film again after 14 years, I was startled by how bold it is. Its heroine is a radio astronomer named Dr. Eleanor Arroway (Jodie Foster), who is an atheist. In the film she forms a cautious relationship with Palmer Joss (Matthew McConaughey), a believer in God who writes about science. Key roles are played by science advisors to the president, who see aliens, God, and messages from space all in cynical political terms. They justify their politics with the catch-all motive of "national defense."

When the movie was released in July 1997 I had more or less the same beliefs I have now about the existence of God and the possibility of life elsewhere in the universe. Yet reading my review I find the movie didn't seem as brave to me then as it does now. Perhaps that's because I've since become involved in so much discussion about Creationism, another topic that stands at the intersection of science, politics, and faith. Hollywood treats movies like a polite dinner party: don't bring up religion or politics.

The encrypted signal, when opened, contains plans for the manufacture of an enormous machine, apparently a spacecraft of some sort, which will presumably take a single human to a meeting with the alien intelligence on a planet circling Vega, the fifth brightest star in the night sky, about 25 light years away from Earth.

A key element of the film involves congressional hearings to determine who should be the astronaut aboard the ship. Although an international team of candidates has been selected, the cost of the ship has mostly been paid by the United States, and for political reasons the astronaut will be American. Ellie, whose team received the message, is one of the candidates. At a late point in the hearings, Palmer Joss blindsides Ellie by asking her if she believes in God. She answers honestly. This raises a question: Should the first human to meet an alien believe in God? Ellie loses the prize to her boss, David Drumlin (Tom Skerritt), an opportunist who has taken credit for her pioneering work in SETI (the Search for Extraterrestrial Intelligence). That she eventually ends up making the trip owes something to the actions of another true believer.

The movie is based on a novel by Carl Sagan, who told us with such joy that there are "billions and billions of stars up there." As a child fascinated by the stars, Ellie asks her father (David Morse) if there are humans on other planets, and he tells her: "If we are alone in the Universe, it sure seems like an awful waste of space." The quote is often attributed to Sagan. Despite her disbelief in an afterlife, Ellie has always yearned to meet her mother, who died in childbirth, and perhaps that was what drew her eyes to the sky as a small girl. Later, as an honored academic, she turns down a teaching post at Harvard to work on a SETI project in Puerto Rico. Funding for that search is withdrawn by the hypocritical David Drumlin, who doesn't approve of pure research and believes science should provide "practical results."

Contact was directed by Robert Zemeckis, whose work often employs daring technical methods. Remember his mixture of animation and live action in the pre-CGI days of *Who Framed Roger Rabbit* (1988). Look at the way he embedded Forrest Gump (1994) amid real people. Look at the way he used motion capture in *The Polar Express* (2004), *Beowulf* (2007), and *Disney's A Christmas Carol* (2009). In *Contact* he startled his audiences by using real CNN anchors to cover the story in the movie, and embedding an obviously real President Bill Clinton.

Clinton didn't actually act in the movie (his scenes sound appropriate but could be about anything). But those were real CNN people. Was it proper for reporters to play themselves in fiction? Network president Tom Johnson said at the time that the experiment was a bad idea, and would not be repeated; that memo apparently didn't get read. What worked in *Gump* as a joke struck a false note in the greater realism of *Contact*.

In *Contact*, I was particularly absorbed by the conversations between Ellie and Palmer, the atheist and the believer. They like one another; indeed, they even go to bed once, but love is cut short because Ellie can do the math and realizes if she gets to travel on the alien machine the logic of moving at light speed means no one she knows will be alive when she returns—including Palmer and their children, if any. Still, he loves her, and much is made of a little plastic toy he finds in a Cracker Jack box—a compass. But if the woman he loves doesn't believe in God, she shouldn't make the trip. (The various astronaut candidates presumably believe in different gods, but that's only a detail.)

I will not describe what happens to Ellie after she takes the trip. There was much debate at the time about whether she, in fact, ever left earth, although a line of dialogue about 18 hours of static seems to be significant. The more you think about the logic involved, the more fascinating the movie becomes. The original signal received from space is the first television signal ever broadcast on earth, and since we know when that was, we know how many years it would have needed to make the round trip.

That suggests at the least an alien program to search for such signals and bounce them back along with code for a series of prime numbers, a universal indication of intelligence. What else does it suggest? That the aliens are still alive, or only their program? What would be the purpose of their machine? Actual physical space travel, or an experience not unlike the one had by the hero of *2001*, who finds himself in an environment that has apparently been created by information in his own mind? What does she learn from the aliens of any use? What could be taught?

Jodie Foster is an ideal candidate for the role of Ellie Arroway. Smart, to the point, she explains that the purpose of Science is to discover Truth, wherever it is. That's where scientists disagree with Creationists, who believe they already know the Truth and it's the purpose of Science to find the Truth they know. You can see how that could engender some uneasiness about pure research; the danger is that you could find out something you don't want to know.

Matthew McConaughey's character is a good and sincere man, but I was confused by his ability to turn up everywhere. Just because he's written books on science and religion, why is he mysteriously invited to every high-level meeting and given so much influence? Another problematical character is Joseph (Jake Busey), who is way over the top as an evangelist, and curiously immune to routine security procedures.

The strength of *Contact* is in the way it engages in issues that are relevant today and still only rarely discussed in the movies. Consider the opposition to stem cell research, which in a sense is "pure research." Consider the politicians who disparage separation of church and state. When Ellie was asked by Congress if she believed in God, the correct reply would have been, "that is none of your business." That would have been the correct reply of any American, no matter whether they believed in God or not.

{ Day for Night }

Producer: "Aren't we one big happy family?" Actor: "So are the people in Greek tragedies."

The actor in this exchange, which comes midway through François Truffaut's *Day for Night*, is overstating his case. He should have said, "So are the people in French farces." He's talking about the sort of family that forms every time a movie shoots and breaks up when it wraps. For several weeks there's a kind of forced community where privacy is rare, everyone is exhausted, and emotional desperation is epidemic.

Truffaut's film, made in 1973 and being revived this week with a newly-struck 35-mm. print, is a poem in praise of making movies. Not good movies, not bad movies—movies. It takes place at the Victorine Studio in Nice, in the south of France, which has produced movies since the silent days. Truffaut himself plays Ferrand, the director of a movie named *Meet Pamela*, which is pretty clearly going to be a stinker. Ferrand exhibits not the slightest sign that he knows this, or would care if he did; he isn't intended to be a director of ambitious movies (like Truffaut), but a technician, in love with the process—with the stunts and special effects, the chemistry between the actors, the daily shooting schedule.

Strange, seeing this movie again in 1997, how much it reminded me of the recent films *Ed Wood* and *Boogie Nights*. Those are both films about people for whom the end product—the film itself—is only the necessary byproduct of their real reason to be in the movie business, which is to be on the set. To be making a movie. For a certain kind of emotionally footloose, artistic personality, a movie production is like a homeless shelter: their basic animal needs are satisfied, they are too tired to see beyond the morning call, and sex, when it comes, is between people who are careful to agree it doesn't mean too much.

When visitors from the real world arrive (husbands, lovers, bankers, journalists), they are provided with a director's chair to sit in, and they watch the action and nod and smile like proud grandparents. They'll never understand. "I'd drop a guy for a film," a character says in *Day for Night*. "I'd never drop a film for a guy."

Truffaut's film is like a little anthology of anecdotes from movie sets. We recognize all the familiar types: the callow young love-mad star (Jean-Pierre Leaud); the alcoholic diva past her prime (Valentina Cortese); the sexy romantic lead (Jacqueline Bisset), whose breakdowns are hopefully behind her now that she's married her doctor; and the aging leading man (Jean-Pierre Aumont) who is finally coming to terms with his homosexuality. There are also the functionaries with supporting roles: the script girl, the stunt man, the producer, the woman who runs the hotel.

During the course of the movie romances end and begin, marriages are threatened and repaired, people lock themselves in their rooms, and a cat refuses to lap up the milk on cue. We learn in an offhand way some of the trade secrets of moviemaking, such as how they make it snow in the summertime, how a third-floor balcony can have no building beneath it, and how scenes are shot "day for night" (a filter is used to give the effect of night while shooting in daylight).

The movie is narrated by the Truffaut character. "Shooting a movie is like a stagecoach trip," he says. "At first you hope for a nice ride. Then you just hope to reach your destination." At night he has a dream, in black and white of course, in which he's a small boy going downtown after dark. He reaches through the grating in front of the local theater, and steals the 8-by-10 glossy publicity stills for *Citizen Kane*. Earlier there's a scene where Ferrand and his producer (Jean Champion) shuffle through glossy photos of their actress (Bisset). The parallel is clear. As a youth, Ferrand dreamed of being another Welles, but now he's pleased to simply work in the same industry.

In her review of the film, Pauline Kael wrote that it was "a movie for the movie-struck, the essentially naive—those who would rather see a movie, any movie (a bad one, a stupid one, or an evanescent, sweet-but-dry little wafer of a movie like this one), than do anything else." It may not be for them, but it's certainly about them. When Leaud's girlfriend says she's glad to be in Nice with all of its restaurants, he's shocked: "Little restaurants? You must be joking! Don't you know Nice has 37 movies? We can grab a sandwich."

Kael's review is indignant: "I don't share Truffaut's fond regard for the kind of moviemaking that *Meet Pamela* represents." No, but it's possible to share Truffaut's affection for the people who make them. I asked Jeanne Moreau once about one of her famous scenes. She told me she hadn't seen any of her movies, except for a handful at film festivals, where her presence was required. "I get paid to make them," she said. "You get paid to see them."

François Truffaut (1932–84) was one of the most beloved of filmmakers, a man whose own love of film was obvious in such details as the old-fashioned iris shots he borrowed from silent films. (That's a shot where the screen seems to screw down to circle one detail, before going to black). "The most beautiful thing I have seen in a movie theater," he once said, "is to go down to the front, and turn around, and look at all the uplifted faces, the light from the screen reflected upon them."

Truffaut was a founder of the New Wave generation—French film critics who celebrated Hollywood's veterans in the 1950s and then made their own films. He was there at the start, with *The 400 Blows* (1959), *Shoot the Piano Player* (1960), and *Jules and Jim* (1961, starring Moreau—I hope she saw it). In 25 years he directed 23 films. Why did he make so many? I think because he loved to be on the set. The young actor in *Day for Night* is heartbroken after his girl runs off with the stuntman. Truffaut's character consoles him: "People like us are only happy in our work."

{ DEPARTURES }

It is a bad time for the young couple. He plays the cello in a small provincial orchestra. Their audiences have been sparse. The owner of the orchestra sadly tells them it must shut down. He comes home and informs his wife. There is more bad news. He recently purchased a new cello, paying far more than they could afford. He didn't tell her because he knew she would say it was a bad idea. Now she knows.

The opening scenes of *Departures* (2009) give no hint of what direction the film will take. It begins as a narrative about a couple in financial crisis. We have no way of knowing, and indeed neither do they, that this is the beginning of a journey of profound growth and discovery, brought about through the instrument of death.

I showed Yojiro Takita's film at Ebertfest 2010, and it had as great an impact as any film in the festival's history. At the end the audience rose as one person. Many standing ovations are perfunctory. This one was long, loud, and passionate. That alone doesn't have anything to do with making a film great, and 2011 may seem too soon to include a 2009 film in this collection of Great Movies. I'm including it because having seen it three times I am convinced that *Departures* will hold its power and appeal.

The Japanese cinema reserves a special place for death. In films like Kurosawa's *Ikiru*, Ozu's *Tokyo Story*, Itami's *Ososhiki* (*The Funeral*), and Kore

62

Eda's *Maborosi* and *After Life*, it is handled in terms of ongoing life. There is mourning, but not hopeless grief. The mourning is channeled into ritual which provides comfort. There is no great focus on an afterlife. Attention centers on the survivors and on the meaning of the life that has just ended. Watching *Departures* again most recently, I was reminded of these words spoken in Errol Morris's *Gates of Heaven*: *Life is for the living and not for the dead so much.*

The hero of *Departures* is Daigo (Masahiro Motoki), an impulsive young man, likable, easy to read. His wife Mika (Ryoko Hirosue) loves him and believes in him. When disaster strikes, she's quick to agree they must return to the small town where he was born and move into his childhood home, which was left to him after his mother's death not long ago. He sells the expensive cello and they make the trip. This is defeat for him: unemployed, owning not even an instrument, back where he began.

Looking into the employment ads, he finds a promising offer at what sounds like a travel agency. Daigo applies at a quiet little office managed by an assistant (Yo Kimiko), and soon the owner, Mr. Sasaki (Tsutomu Yamazaki), appears. The interview is brief. He gets the job and a cash advance. He discovers the agency handles travel, all right—to the next world. It is an "encoffinment," or undertaking, business.

Before he has time to absorb this idea, Daigo is taken along by his new boss to observe the process. It strikes me as more humane than the Western practice of out of sight embalming and so on. The body of the departed is displayed on a mat in front of the mourners, who kneel together and watch the process of preparation. It is a ceremony of precise ritual and grace. Carefully arranged sheets preserve the dead person's privacy as the corpse is washed and dressed. Then the face is made up with exquisite attention to detail. Finally the body is placed in a simple wooden coffin. Most family members remain silent, but sometimes there are outbursts of emotion—or truth—and young Daigo starts learning lessons of life.

He delays telling his wife what the job entails because it would shock her. Undertaking is an important occupation in Japan, I gather, but not a respectable one. In his childhood house they grow closer than ever before, and play old LP records his father left behind. He reveals his bitterness toward the man, who disappeared and never contacted the family again. Mika is content until the day she discovers what her husband is doing for a living. As much as she loves him, she tells him she must leave him; she doesn't even want to be touched by a man who prepares the dead.

The construction of Takita's screenplay is rock-solid in its fundamentals, and yet such is the film's flow that we don't sense the machinery creaking. Subplots are introduced and we hardly notice. Mr. Sasaki misses his late wife. The office assistant has a sad story of her own. We learn something of the several families that employ the Departures firm. We meet the old lady who runs a public bath, and her oldest customer, and later the attendant at a crematorium. We watch the quiet, sweet way in which the assistant informs Daigo he was born for this work. We understand why, when his wife leaves, Daigo knows he must stay. He provides a service that has become meaningful to him.

Takita's music and cinematography are part of the film's success. Cello music, some performed in a beautiful fantasy outdoor scene by Daigo, more at home with the little cello he owned as a child, is right for this material. (A discreet shot shows the marks still on the floorboards from where it rested while he practiced.) The cinematography by Takeshi Hamada can perhaps be called polite. No shots for effect. It has the decorum of a mourner at a funeral. Beauty shots, such as the outdoor cello performance, feel as if the camera has been granted sudden freedom. Close-ups don't punch up points, but allow us to peer into these faces we have come to value.

Casting is vital in this movie, in no role more than Mr. Sasaki. The actor Tsutomu Yamazaki has a wise and serene face. He makes the character not demonstrative but understated, as he plays the young man's personality gently. We understand why his assistant reveres him. He never makes speeches about the importance of his work. All is implied or demonstrated. At the end, when several plot threads come together, it happens so naturally and is so deeply satisfying.

This film is not a stylistic breakthrough or a bold artistic statement. But it is rare because it is so well-made. The universal reason people attend movies is in the hopes of being told an absorbing story that will move them. They would rather be touched emotionally, I believe, than thrilled, frightened, or made to laugh. Yet there are few things more deadening than manipulative sentimental melodramas—what *Variety* likes to call "weepers."

Departures plays fair. It brings four main characters onstage (and the sweet old couple from a bath house). We know and understand them. We care about them. They are involved in an enterprise we probably knew nothing about. It touches on death, a subject of general fascination. There is nothing contrived about its problems; they belong naturally to the narrative. It doesn't drag its feet and bewail fate, but even permits itself some laughter, which is never out of tone. It functions flawlessly.

Because the audience at Ebertfest doesn't choose the films and often knows nothing about them, some of the members must have been uneasy to discover they were watching a Japanese film about undertaking. They seemed to become quickly involved. I heard the sounds of emotion in the dark. They cheered at the end because they had seen a film that was excellent at achieving the universal ends of narrative. How often does that happen?

Departures won the 2009 Academy Award for best foreign language film.

DIARY OF A COUNTRY PRIEST

The young priest only smiles once. It is on the day he leaves the cruel country town to catch a train and see a doctor. A passing motorcyclist gives him a lift to the station, and as he climbs on behind him we see a flash of the boy inside the sad man. It is a nice day, it's fun to race though the breeze, and he is leaving behind the village of Ambricourt.

For the rest of the time in Robert Bresson's *Diary of a Country Priest* (1951), the young man's face scarcely betrays an emotion. He looks solemn, withdrawn, stunned by the enormity of his job. His faith and vocation are real to him, but the parishioners in Ambricourt scorn and insult him and tell lies about him. He is unwilling or unable to defend himself. He cannot understand the hostility. He keeps a daily journal in which he records his actions, which seem futile to him.

This film is the story of a man who seems in the process of offering himself to God as a sacrifice. He lives only on bread, wine, and a little potato soup. He gives up meat and vegetables. Whether this is because his stomach won't hold down anything else or whether his diet is destroying his health is unclear until later. He is thin and weak, he coughs up blood, he grows faint in the houses of parishioners, one late night he falls in the mud and cannot get up.

It is a bleak winter. The landscape around his little church is barren.

There is often no sign of life except for the distant, unfriendly barking of dogs. His church and the manor of the local count are closed off behind bars, as if gated against each other. Girls in catechism class play tricks on him. The locals gossip that he's a drunk, because of his diet, but we never see him drunk. Bresson often fills the frame with his face, passive, and the stare of his unfocused eyes.

Diary of a Country Priest has been called one of the two greatest Catholic films, along with Dreyer's *The Passion of Joan of Arc*. I see them both as tragedies about true believers in the face of cruel societies. Both lives end in death, as Christ's did. The priest goes about his duties. He says a daily Mass, often attended by only one person—and her motive is not spiritual. He calls on the people in his parish, so weak he can hardly speak with them, crossing their names from a list and stumbling back into the cold. A local man quarrels with him about the cost of his wife's funeral. People sneer at him as "the little priest."

He tries to counsel the governess of the count's daughter, who the count is having an affair with. The count insults him. The daughter is angry with her father and everyone else. The countess knows of the affair but doesn't care; she lost her son at a young age and is still in mourning. In the great scene that supplies the center of the film, the priest urges the countess to have faith and accept Christ's love, and she undergoes a remarkable spiritual rebirth. Even this conversation is lied about and held against him.

Robert Bresson does nothing in a superficial way to please his audiences. The rewards of his films unfold slowly from their stories and pierce deeply. He is very serious about human nature and the indifference of the world. He is not a Catholic but an agnostic who values any consolation his characters can find, in or out of faith.

His visual strategy doesn't break scenes down into easy storytelling elements but regards them as unyielding facts. In this film he opens and closes many passages with old-fashioned iris shots, reproducing the act of opening our eyes to the world, seeing its reality, and closing them again. There is a lot of background music, some of it vaguely spiritual, some of it saccharine, all of it more ironic than consoling. The look seems dark and depressing at first, but his films live not in the moment but in their complete length, and for the last hour I was more spellbound than during a thriller. Bresson does nothing to make me "like" the priest, but my empathy was urgently involved.

Bresson (1901–99) was one of the great figures in the French cinema. In 50 years he made only 13 features. I saw the final one, *L'Argent*, at the 1983 Cannes Film Festival, and recall that the press screening was unlike those of most directors; you would have thought the critics were in church. It is ironic that his films are more deeply spiritual than, in my opinion, anyone else's. He did not believe, but he respected belief, and hope.

Not for his characters the consolations of tidy plots and snappy conversations. They are faced with the existential dilemma: What is the point of life when its destination is death? In *Diary of a Country Priest*, the young hero welcomes the advice he receives from the local doctor and the old priest of a nearby parish. The doctor examines him, observes all the local people have been weakened by the alcoholism of their parents, warns him that he is undernourished, admonishes him, "face up to it!" The priest (as only a French priest might) attributes some of his problems to the fact that he doesn't drink better wine. The priest's advice is kind, practical, involved with the management of a parish. He treats the young man like a son. We sense he is a good old man and a good priest, but wary of devotion carried to dangerous extremes.

The star of this film, Claude Laydu, can hardly be seen to act at all. In life he was quite lively, and indeed hosted a TV show for children. Bresson had a famous theory that actors were "models." He didn't require them to act, and indeed would repeat a shot time and time again to remove visible signs of "acting." The scenario, the visual strategy, and the editing would encompass his story. The actor must not seem too proactive because his character is after all only a figure pushed here and there by life and fate. This sounds like a severe artistic discipline, but the result can be purifying. After emerging from one of his films, you may sometimes see conventional movie acting as foolish: the characters actually believe they can influence the outcome!

A film like *Diary of a Country Priest* gathers its strength as it continues. There's always the sense that Bresson knows exactly where he's going and the simplest way to get there. Consider the devastating effect of the priest's journey to visit a specialist in Lisle. We never even hear the second doctor's opinion. We learn it through the journal, read aloud, as all through the film key moments are narrated. After leaving the doctor's office the priest goes to visit a friend of his from the seminary, now living a secular life in poverty because of illness, and seeks this man (who is living in sin) because he is still, after all, a priest, and can offer consolation and absolution.

One thing we are sure of is that the "little country priest" takes his vocation and faith very seriously. Nor does the film question them. It is about precisely the dilemma we must all face: How far can our ideas support us in the approach to death? The young priest's ideas prove to sustain him in the final moments, but they did little earlier to console him. He leaves behind a world of cruelty and petty ignorance. He did nothing deserving blame.

Note: The hand and handwriting in the film belong to Bresson.

DIARY OF A LOST GIRL

When they were leaving the world premiere of G. W. Pabst's film *Pandora's Box* (1928), Louise Brooks could hear her name in the crowd around her, but she didn't like the tone they were using. She asked Pabst what they were saying. He translated: "She doesn't act. She does nothing." This perhaps delighted the great German director, who also chose Brooks to star in his next film, *Diary of a Lost Girl* (1929).

In her autobiography, *Lulu in Hollywood*, one of the most charming and honest books about the movies ever written, Brooks says Pabst refused to discuss the details of a performance with her and never held group discussions with his actors: "He wanted the shocks of life to release unpredictable emotions." Nor did he encourage his actors to associate with one another. "Every actor has a natural animosity toward every other actor, present or absent, living or dead," she writes, and Pabst used that tension to enhance the emotions in a scene. She tells another story. In the scenes in their films where Brooks wears thin dresses or nightgowns while dancing with an actor, he forbid her to wear anything under them. "No one will know," she told him. "The actor will know," he said.

In not acting, in "doing nothing," Louise Brooks became one of the most modern and effective of actors, projecting a presence that could be startling. Among those who know the movies, it might be true to say that

Brooks is one actor who still, to this day, inspires deep affection. She is so simple, so direct, so *there*. Watching her fourth-billed in *The Show-Off* (1926), I watched her effortlessly steal every scene she was in. The others were there in front of the camera. She seemed actually in the scenes.

I don't mean to suggest that in "not acting" Brooks was wooden or robotic. There was no doubt when she was expressing sadness, happiness, enthusiasm, fear. But she suggested an unusual degree of self-possession; in the middle of a happy scene, the others might act out mirth, but her reaction would be more one of regarding it, recognizing it. Her job as an actress wasn't to lead us in the proper reaction. It was to observe its reality.

Fancy hair styles were not for her. She had that crisp pageboy bob that Vidal Sassoon pilfered 25 years later. She had those strong, straight eyebrows, unlike the coy arches of her contemporaries. She was so slender and fit that she seemed poised for flight. The most extraordinary things happened to her in her best films, and instead of visibly reacting and telegraphing emotions, she acted as the instrument to transmit them to us. She encourages identification to an unusual degree.

By 1928 she was one of the best-known movie stars in the world, but she was fed up with Hollywood and too smart for the way the industry treated actresses. She was brought to Berlin by Pabst, who was tired of overeager actresses; he had worked in 1925 with Greta Garbo, another restrained performer. Together they made two of the greatest of silent films. They were both scandalous for their portrayals of lesbianism and prostitution, and after returning to Hollywood she offended the sensibilities of a company town by turning down the lead in *Public Enemy* opposite James Cagney. She made several unsuccessful films in the 1930s, and then, she writes in her book, "I found that the only well-paying career open to me, as an unsuccessful actress of thirty-six, was that of a call girl." One of her clients was William S. Paley, the founder of CBS, who sent her a check every month for the rest of her life.

The French film critics rediscovered her; as often, they were ten years early in telling Americans what was best about our movies. In its article Wikipedia quotes Henri Langois, founder of the Cinematheque François and the great influence of the auteur school: "There is no Garbo, there is no

Dietrich, there is only Louise Brooks!" It is well known that James Card, film curator for George Eastman House, found her in New York in the late 1950s, bonded with her, brought her to live in Rochester, encouraged the writing of *Lulu in Hollywood*, and launched the second life of her career. He found her "living as a recluse," Wikipedia says, but because of Paley's loyalty she was not precisely on Skid Row. A veteran film publicist named John Springer told me: "At a dinner party at my house one night, Card said he would give anything to find Louise Brooks. I told him he might not have to look too hard: she had the apartment across the hall."

Diary of a Lost Girl was the close of her glory days. It's not the equal of *Pandora's Box*, but her performance is on the same high level. It has a frankness that would largely disappear from mainstream films after the rise of censorship in the early 1930s. She plays Thymian, an innocent young girl we meet on the day of her First Communion. Her family lives upstairs over her father's drug store, which is managed by a man named Meinert (the actor Fritz Rasp has a lupine face and cruel smile). It is revealed that her father has made the family's young maid pregnant, and she is thrown from the house. The next maid, Meta, observes that the father can be seduced, and efficiently does so.

Thymian feels shut out at home as her father and Meta start a new family. She becomes pregnant by Meinert, and the scandal is too great for the bourgeois family; after her child's birth Thymian is sent to a cruel "reformatory" run by a sadistic lesbian taskmaster of a woman and her towering, shaven-headed husband. Running away with another girl, she finds her way to a whorehouse, where the grandmotherly madam makes it clear what Thymian's duties will now consist of.

One of the clients is Count Osdorff, an old friend of her family and a wastrel whose half-hearted attempts to help the girl come to nothing. In an ending of unrestrained irony, Osdorff's wealthy uncle marries Thymian, who now becomes a member of Society for the Rescue of Endangered Female Youth. The Society pays a visit on the whorehouse, where Thymian attempts to play the reformer role expected of her, but finally rises up in wrath.

One notable element of the film is that it's entirely the story of

Thymian, just as *Pandora's Box* was entirely the story of Lulu. Louise Brooks didn't have a personality or screen presence that lent itself to supporting roles. If both young women are victims, neither is helpless, and the men who would exploit her find their evil turned against them. In a world of cruelty, the Brooks characters stand as enduring figures. How she accomplishes this is the mystery of her acting. "The great art of films," she wrote, "does not consist of descriptive movement of face and body but in the movements of thought and soul transmitted in a kind of intense isolation."

ETERNAL SUNSHINE
OF THE SPOTLESS MIND

Visiting an old people's home, I walked down a corridor on the floor given over to advanced Alzheimer's patients. Some seemed anxious. Some were angry. Some simply sat there. Knowing nothing of what was happening in their minds, I wondered if the anxious and angry ones had some notion of who they were and that something was wrong. I was reminded of the passive ones while watching *Eternal Sunshine of the Spotless Mind* (2004). Wiped free of memory, they exist always in the moment, which they accept because it is everything.

In his screenplay for the film, Charlie Kaufman has a character quote some lines by Alexander Pope:

> *How happy is the blameless vestal's lot!*
> *The world forgetting, by the world forgot.*
> *Eternal sunshine of the spotless mind!*
> *Each pray'r accepted, and each wish resigned...*

This passage comes well into a very long poem which I doubt the character Mary would have memorized. The audience needn't know that; many may know no more than she does when she calls the author Pope Alexander. She quotes as she's trying to impress a boss she loves. Kaufman has that knack of painlessly explaining his subject right there on the screen. Consider how much information about evolution he embeds in his screenplay for *Adaptation*.

Kaufman, the most gifted screenwriter of the 2000s, is concerned above all about the processes of thought and memory. His screenplay for Spike Jonze's *Being John Malkovich* (1999) involved a way to spend 15 minutes inside the mind of another person. Michel Gondry's *Human Nature* (2001) is concerned about the Nature vs. Nurture theories of our behavior: Do we start this way, or do we learn it? Jonze's *Adaptation* (2002) contrasts the physical evolution of orchids (which assume fantastic forms to earn a living) with identical twins, one who writes from his nature and the other from his nurture. In George Clooney's *Confessions of a Dangerous Mind* (2002), he shows the game show creator Chuck Barris leading a double life as a deadly CIA assassin (Barris believes this story is factual). Kaufman's first film as a director, *Synecdoche, New York* (2008), is his most challenging. He attempts no less than to dramatize the ways in which our minds cope with our various personas and try to organize aspects of our experience into separate compartments we can control.

These sound like topics for a class in evolution or neuroscience, but Kaufman and his directors structure them like films that proceed quite clearly along paths we seem to be following, until we arrive at the limits of identity. *Eternal Sunshine of the Spotless Mind*, like *Malkovich*, invents a fantastic device for its peculiarities, and wisely declines to explain it. All we know is that an obscure company in Boston offers to erase your memories of a particular person or anything else. Period.

The film opens like a meet cute. Indeed, it's a film built around meet cutes, some not so cute. A solemn, worried man named Joel (Jim Carrey) takes a train for no reason and at a station encounters Clementine (Kate Winslet), who thinks they've met before. He doesn't think so. She persists. He goes home with her and they sleep together. In fact they have met before and were in love, but it ended badly and they both had the memory erased.

That much is quite clear. It also becomes clear, later, that when the wounded Joel discovered what Clementine did, in revenge he sought to wipe her from his memories. His head is encased in a sort of aluminum football helmet attached to an alarmingly small laptop controlled by a technician named Stan (Mark Ruffalo), who drinks beer with his coworker Mary (Kirsten Dunst). They're jumping on his bed in their underwear when Joel's mind goes "off the map."

Terrified, Stan calls in the boss, Dr. Mierzwiak (Tom Wilkinson), who is alarmed, as well he might be. Inside the helmet, Joel struggles desperately to resist the loss of his memories of Clementine. He has literally changed his mind about changing his mind. Kaufman by now has jumped the rails and tumbled us into a labyrinth of time and reality. We see Joel and Clementine at various times before both erasures, after hers, and during his—when he even tries to hide his memories by disguising them both as childhood playmates.

Some viewers have been confused by the film's movement through chronology and locations, but I think the paradoxes are explained if we realize that everything is happening in only one place, Joel's mind. The disconnects are explained by his fragmented memories of when they were together before, during, and after the erasure. The train station sequence at the beginning is closer to the end of the movie's timeline.

Not that we're required to piece it all together. Gondry and Kaufman use qualities of the cinema itself to allow it to make emotional sense when it's baffling any other way. We know our minds easily comprehend and accept flashbacks, hallucinations, and conflicting realities. Even small children seeing a flashback for the first time understand what's being conveyed. As impossible events occur, we understand they're subjective—generated in the minds of the beholders. That explains the crumbling beach house in *Eternal Sunshine* and the constantly burning home in *Synecdoche*. We know at the time they aren't "real," and afterwards we're missing the point if we ask for an "explanation." These films are made with insight into how the mind translates information.

Kaufman isn't merely an ingenious screenwriter but a shrewd one. Notice how he uses the comic subplot involving Stan, Mary, and Patrick (Elijah Wood), the clueless office assistant, as counterpoint to his fraught central story. And how Dr. Mierzwiak functions as the Prospero figure, lending gravitas to an absurd premise. If we complain about these "extra characters," we may as well complain about their parallels in Shakespeare. It's difficult to focus on two people in an impossible situation for three acts, and even harder to make that entertaining, as a film like this must. Kaufman uses comic relief as an important device in his construction.

His screenplays require actors who can keep a straight face in the center of farce. Nothing is more fatal than an actor signaling that material is funny. That's for us to decide. To the character, it's his life, and there's nothing funny about it. Keaton never allowed himself a smile or a wink; Chaplin a few smiles, but too many. Jim Carrey in *Eternal Sunshine* is a sad sack throughout; John Cusack in *Malkovich* earnestly desires to do good, and Malkovich himself has made a career of probity; Philip Seymour Hoffman in *Synecdoche* desperately seeks to hold together his mental machinery (and the film itself is far from funny).

Why I respond so intensely to this material must involve my obsession with who we are and who we think we are. The secret of communicating with another person, I suspect, may be in communicating with who he thinks he is. Do that, and you can kid a great man and treat an insignificant one with deep respect. They'll credit you with insight.

The wisdom in *Eternal Sunshine* is how it illuminates the way memory interacts with love. We more readily recall pleasure than pain. From the hospital I remember laughing nurses and not sleepless nights. A drunk remembers the good times better than the hangovers. A failed political candidate remembers the applause. An unsuccessful romantic lover remembers the times when it worked.

What Joel and Clementine cling to are those perfect moments when lives seem blessed by heaven, and sunshine will fall upon it forever. I hope those are the moments some of those patients are frozen in. They seem at peace.

{ FRENCH CANCAN }

It is universally agreed that Jean Renoir was one of the greatest of all directors, and he was also one of the warmest and most entertaining. *Grand Illusion* and *Rules of the Game* are routinely included on lists of the greatest films, and deserve to be. But although *Rules* contains scenes of delightful humor, neither suggest the Renoir who made *Boulu Saved from Drowning* (1932) or *French Cancan* (1954), a delicious musical comedy that deserves comparison with the golden age Hollywood musicals of the same period.

In them one can sense the cherub that his father, Auguste Renoir, painted more than once. That same twinkle is captured in the photographs taken later in his life. Some people are essentially happy, and it shows in their faces. Renoir lived to be 84, his last years at home in Beverly Hills, where he was interviewed by a parade of worshipful young critics. He won an honorary Academy Award in 1975. He had moved to America after the Nazi invasion of France in 1940. Although most of his great films were made in the 1930s, in the 1950s he returned to France to make a remarkable trilogy which were all in Technicolor and all musical comedies: *The Golden Coach* (1955), named by Andrew Sarris as the greatest film ever made, *French Cancan*, and *Elena and Her Men* (1956).

French Cancan uses one of the most familiar of musical formulas, loosely summarized as, "Hey, gang! Let's rent the old barn and put on a show!" In this case he was inspired by the origins of the Moulin Rouge, the Montmartre cabaret theater which to this day still has success with the kinds of shows it opened with. It is a backstage story centering in the life of the (fictional) impresario Henri Danglard, a womanizer whose career was a series of narrow escapes from bankruptcy.

For his Danglard, Renoir cast Jean Gabin, the greatest of all French leading men, whose genius, like that of so many stars, involved never seeming to try very hard, and simply reflecting his own inner nature. It was their fourth film together, and after the weighty characters Gabin played in *The Lower Depths* (1936), *Grand Illusion* (1937), and *Le Bête Humaine* (1938), a complete change of tone. Danglard is the always insolvent owner of the Chinese Screen, which headlines the infamous courtesan La Belle Abbesse (Maria Felix) as a sultry belly dancer, known to all as Lola, his mistress.

One night he goes out slumming with Lola and some friends, and in a Montmartre dive sees the patrons doing a jolly cancan. This scene, early in the film, has a freshness that delights; it feels almost plausible, not staged, although it surely is. And it establishes two key characters, the pretty bakery girl Nini (Françoise Arnoul) and her possessive lover Paolo (Franco Pastorino). When Lola haughtily declines to dance, Danglard asks Nini to be his partner, inflaming the jealousy of both Lola and Paolo and giving him an inspiration. The Chinese Screen is failing and falling into the hands of his creditors. He will open a new theater, and revive the cancan, an oldfashioned dance from the 1870s, renaming the "French Cancan" as a strategy to make it sound more exotic—not to the French, but, as we see on opening night, to American tourists and Russian sailors.

Danglard is a man who faces emergencies with serenity. His face never betrays concern. He occupies a series of unpaid hotel suites, always alert to find a financial backer, and not above offering Lola herself as the prize to one rich prospect. He makes no pretense of faithfulness, to her or anyone else, and makes it clear that his only loyalty is to the stage. The three 1950s musical comedies are often described as Renoir's "art trilogy," and this one is most single-mindedly dedicated to the bond between performer and audience.

French Cancan was shot entirely on sound stages, including one big set of a Montmartre street scene, with stone steps leading up to a little square above where we find the bakery that employs Nini. (This square providentially opens onto a charming little grassy area for a romantic scene, although such a space is unimaginable in such a crowded part of the city.) A cafe on the street provides the setting for a chummy older couple who observe and comment on all the activity, and are covered with dust when Danglard's workmen detonate explosives to bring down the White Queen, a failing club which is destined to provide the land for the Moulin Rouge.

The stairs up to Nini's bakery are well-traveled by three hopeful lovers: not only Danglard and of course Paolo, but Prince Alexandre (Giani Esposito), the unimaginably rich heir to a kingdom obscurely located somewhere in the Middle East. Fidelity is much valued by Paolo and Alexandre, but in the cases of Danglard and Nini, if they can't have the one they love, they love the one they're with. These revolving romantic subplots provide Renoir with love scenes verging on farce, especially as Danglard, always with an eye out for the main chance, realizes that Nini might be useful in coaxing funds out of the prince.

In the meantime, construction advances on the Moulin Rouge, despite troubles. A government official arrives for the dedication of the new foundations, and Lola, enraged to find Nini there, attacks her. What results is one of those movie scenes, much beloved in the taverns of Westerns, in which everybody in the room inexplicably joins in and starts pummeling each other. Danglard ends up being pushed into a pit.

His complete attention is now devoted to holding auditions and putting together a show. Great charm enters in the person of an elderly dance coach (Lydia Jeanson), who danced the cancan as a girl and now teaches the hopefuls that Danglard has recruited. Although I once attended the Moulin Rouge, as a sin-seeking college student, I thought of the cancan more as spectacle than effort, and those rehearsal sessions establish what very hard work it is.

Two of the film's best sequences take place backstage on opening night. One involves Nini realizing that the heartless Danglard, having exploited her prince, still has a roving eye. The other involves the drama when she locks herself in her dressing room and threatens the evening's big cancan number. No entreaties will budge her—not even those of her mother. Then Danglard winds up and delivers an extraordinary speech, unlike anything he has said before, in which he explains to Nini that trifles like love and money mean nothing to a true performer. For such a person, nothing matters but winning the will of the audience by putting on a show. I can imagine Ethel Merman delivering such a speech, but from the lips of Jean Gabin, who probably played more murderers than anything else, they are astonishing. You have the feeling that Gabin, and through him Renoir, are speaking from the heart.

That compulsion to go on with the show is the driving engine in *French Cancan*, and helps explain why it's more fictive than a more routine musical (such as, oh, say *There's No Business Like Show Business*). This is a musical and a comedy, but it's something more, a portrait of an impresario for whom opening a theater and producing a show are the highest goals in life.

Gabin has a late scene when he's alone backstage, sprawled exhausted in a big prop chair, hearing the orchestra and the applause from behind the curtain. He lifts his hands as if to conduct, and we realize this is as happy as he'll ever be in his life, or ever hope to be. It reminded me curiously of a scene he has in Jacques Backer's *Touchez pas au Grisbi*, a film he also made in 1954. In that one, as a failing gang leader, he's alone in a room and has a monologue about an ungrateful pal who has let him down: "There's not a tooth in his head that hasn't cost me a bundle." One sign of a great actor is when he can be alone by himself on the screen, doing almost nothing, and produce one of a film's defining moments.

{ THE GREY ZONE }

Rare among films about the Holocaust, Tim Blake Nelson's *The Grey Zone* (2001) lacks an upbeat ending. Even a great film like Steven Spielberg's *Schindler's List* works largely because in a universe of horror, the director found a narrative of courage and hope. One Holocaust film after another does the same thing: finds a story that doesn't end with everyone dead, so that we can somehow be reassured that life carries on. But such stories deny the central fact that the overwhelming mass of Holocaust victims disappeared into the maw of evil.

I sometimes ask myself what I would do if I were faced with an inescapable death. I know I will die someday; that is in the nature of things. But to be plucked from life and exterminated by a malevolent human machine is not natural. In a death camp, would I passively await the end? Would I seek accommodation for myself? Would I work to resist, however hopelessly?

The Grey Zone begins with the fact that the Nazis employed groups of Jewish prisoners to do much of the hard physical work of extermination. They led victims into gas chambers, fed their bodies into incinerators, shoveled up their ashes, and disposed of them. For this work, they were paid with privileges: food, tobacco, wine, and medicines plundered from the dead, and above all, perhaps a few more months of life.

It was rumored that Russian soldiers were a few months from reaching the camps and liberating them. If I could save my life by bargaining for those months, would that be wrong? It would be the wrong choice from a standpoint of objective morality; I should not collaborate in murder. Yet as I await a certain fate in despair, can I be blamed for attempting a bargain with destiny?

The central characters in *The Grey Zone* have accepted the Nazi deal at Auschwitz and labor as exterminators. They usher their fellow Jews into the gas chambers, tell them to place their clothing on numbered pegs, lie to them to remember the numbers for after their "shower." One Jew has a better job. This is Dr. Miklos Nyiszli (Allan Corduner), a surgeon highly prized by the monstrous Josef Mengele for carrying out medical "experiments." His guard is an SS officer named Muhsfeldt (Harvey Keitel). Nyiszli values his position, which includes an indefinite stay of execution and even the lives of his wife and daughter. Muhsfeldt values his, which brings him prestige in the service of Mengele. The two men have something in common.

The others are involved in a plot to steal gunpowder from a nearby munitions factory. They have weapons smuggled in to them by members of the Polish resistance movement. They hope to blow up one or more of the crematoriums at Auschwitz, limiting the efficiency and speed of the death process. They're collaborating with women at the factory. Contraband is smuggled in with dead bodies. They hope to act soon.

This much is based on fact, as recorded in a postwar memoir by Nyiszli. The crucial element in the plot, however, was created by Nelson's screenplay. One day, hauling out the dead bodies from a gas chamber, Hoffman (David Arquette) discovers a young girl who has survived huddled beneath a pile of bodies. He carries her out as if she were dead, hides her, and summons Nyiszli, who returns her to consciousness. Now the leader of the group, Schlermer (Daniel Benzali), is faced with a dilemma. Hiding the girl could jeopardize the entire sabotage operation.

But what else can they do? If they betray her, they kill her as personally as if they had pulled a trigger. They could no longer rationalize that they are only carrying out secondary tasks for the actual murderers.

Muhsfeldt, who discovers the girl, agrees not to betray the secret—in return for information, and perhaps in small part because he, too, cannot resolve the dilemma of one individual girl whom chance has set aside from a collective fate.

Tim Blake Nelson's film presents this story with straightforward realism. He constructed a nearly scale-model duplicate of Auschwitz in Poland and brings to the crematorium scenes a sense of the forges of hell. His cast, mostly American apart from Corduner, includes not only Keitel and Arquette but Michael Stuhlbarg, Steve Buscemi, Mira Sorvino, and Natasha Lyonne. Apart from Keitel, they use non-German accents. Probably just as well.

Nelson's dialogue deserves attention. It's not unadorned realism, but a flat back-and-forth stylized directness that at times rather reminded me of Mamet. As often in Mamet, the undertone is a sort of patient explaining of the obvious. This approach is useful in scenes where the characters are discussing the moral implications of their situation. These discussions aren't theoretical but bear immediate practical results. They aren't discussing what "one" should do in "such" a situation, but what they must do in the case of this particular sad-eyed young girl standing before them. Then there's a striking exchange between Nyiszli and Muhsfeldt, in which they discuss the doctor's situation and Muhsfeldt's position of some power in the camp. This conversation is almost in code, each clearly implying what neither is willing to state aloud.

The physical production, always convincing, never shows off its extent. There are repeated shots of the crematorium smokestacks, the plumes of black smoke by day joined by visible flames at night. These shots reopen the persistent question: What did the nearby Poles *think* was happening in those camps? Trainloads of humans went in, and smoke emerged. Well, some Poles risked their lives in the resistance. Others sheltered Jews in their homes. Most knew and did nothing. All over the Earth, no population is outstanding for its moral courage. That's one reason the moral math of *The Grey Zone* is so sobering.

To accompany the plumes of smoke, there is a persistent very low-level roar on the soundtrack during many scenes. In the ovens, the work continues 24 hours a day, its results hauled away in truckloads of ashes, some of the Jewish laborers sitting on them. In the incineration process, there is no conveyor belt to distance the workers from the flames. Sometimes they shove in someone they know. Soon it will be their turn.

Tim Blake Nelson is primarily known as an actor (*O Brother, Where Art Thou?, Minority Report, Syriana*). This was his fourth feature as a director. If he only directed, he would be more recognizable as a leading contemporary filmmaker, because his credits are so notable. *Eye of God* (1997) stars Martha Plimpton as a bored woman who enters into correspondence with a prisoner (Kevin Anderson). They marry, and her misery increases. *O* (2001) transposes the story of Shakespeare's *Othello* to a high school in the South. *Leaves of Grass* (2009), my favorite film at Toronto 2009, stars Edward Norton in a dual role as twins, one an Oklahoma marijuana grower, the other a professor of philosophy at Brown. All of the scripts, except for *O*, were originals by Nelson. They are united by the close observation of situations where one character comes from outside the conventional world of the film.

The Grey Zone ends with a narration observing that the bodies of the dead are turned into ashes of bones, gases and vapor, and a fine, invisible gray dust that settles everywhere and goes into lungs; they become so accustomed to it they lose the cough reflex. Thus do the living and the dead intermingle. I believe Tim Blake Nelson is suggesting that dust rises from many flames all over the world, and we breathe it today.

THE
{ HAIRDRESSER'S }
HUSBAND

The hairdressing shop is their ocean liner, their lives are a cruise around the world. They will sail the Nile, kiss in the shadows of the Great Pyramids, see the sun set on every earthly paradise, and it will always be exactly like this. Perfect. *The Hairdresser's Husband* (1990) tells the story of two romantics besotted with love, living in a French hairdressing salon, she reading magazines on her perch by the widow, he working crosswords on the red leather bench, the sunlight flooding in. The yellows, blues, tropical colors. The exotic music he dances to. Occasionally at some unheard signal their eyes meet and they smile in shared bliss.

Isn't it pretty to think so. What is remarkable is that they both fully agree on this vision. From his early adolescence, Antoine (Jean Rochefort) has desired only one thing in life: to be a hairdresser's husband. Many men have been attracted by the beauty of Mathilde (Anna Galiena), but until now, in her early 30s, none has been perfect. Perfection. That's what they're looking for. He has known the barbershop for years. When old Monsieur Ambroise (Maurice Chevit) retired, he gave it to her, for she would carry on in his tradition. One day, she gives Antoine a shampoo and a trim, and he says, "Will you marry me?" She doesn't answer. Two weeks later he comes in for his next visit. She tells him yes. Her answer is yes.

The Hairdresser's Husband carries their shared perfection as far as it can—further, in fact, than we might desire. Perfection admits no compromise. It is not possible in a world made of time and men and women. But how wonderful it can be. This 1990 film by Patrice Leconte is funny, as warm as a hug, as fanciful as a dream. It is a fairy tale set in a real shop on a real street with real people. Of course, the shop and the street exist only in a movie studio, and the people are characters, but that's a movie for you. Film is an art form that permits perfection.

The film is awesome in how it begins, how it continues, and how it ends. It is profound. It is about our foolish dreams. I doubt it has ever found a single viewer who yearns to be a hairdresser's husband, but it allows us all to understand such a thing is quite possible. He isn't a hair fetishist. He is a hairdresser fetishist. Leconte shows us the very moment when he was seized by his desire. His young eyes are wide and solemn as he glimpses in a gap in another hairdresser's blouse that form we all learn, as our first lesson, is the source of all goodness, love and comfort: a woman's breast. He is lost.

Not only lost, but mad. There is no sanity in his intense focus. Is she mad? She must be. But they're both so happy. Real life hardly seems to be a factor. We never see them eat. We never see them sleep. We know they live in a room above the shop, but we don't see it.

Their days pass in a serene parade, sometimes enlivened by his fondness for dancing to recordings of the music of *The Arabian Nights*. He can't dance, as he is the first to admit. But what he does is wonderful, and Rochefort's gyrations, always with a solemn face, are very funny. Why this music? Why this dance? Why do we need to ask?

She smiles. She is radiant. She is kind, gentle, sexy. They are always in heat. While she is performing a shampoo, he kneels on the floor behind her and caresses her to ecstasy. They make love on the red leather bench. They're in full view, but nobody ever seems to see them. They make each other very happy.

Leconte, working from his own screenplay, interrupts their solitude with customers. Two inseparable friends, always deep in a dispute. A little boy who does *not* want to have his hair cut. A husband who dashes in to hide from his fearsome wife, who follows him. There aren't a lot of customers, which is all right with them. She is patient, attentive, expert. He is tactful and always helpful. The sun shines in. Their wedding day takes place in the shop, with old Monsieur Ambroise in attendance.

In a rare visit outside the shop one Sunday afternoon, they visit Ambroise in the retirement home where he lives. He observes that the home's gardens, so well-tended, have a sort of film over them, an aura: "These are the last trees and flowers these old people will ever see." He is not consoled by retirement. He was happy, now he is lonely. His relatives visit, but are impatient to leave. In such small dark clouds as these, Leconte allows his lovers to observe that nothing is forever.

Patrice Leconte is a director who should be better known. Like Ang Lee, he never repeats himself. Each film seems a fresh start from a new idea. His flawless *Monsieur Hire* (1989) is also about a fetishist—a voyeur. That is its *only* similarity with *The Hairdresser's Husband*. His *Ridicule* (1996), set at the court of Louis XVI, involved a provincial farmer, much agitated about the need for irrigation. Told that the king listens to no one who doesn't amuse him, he learns to be funny. He was never funny before. *The Widow of Saint-Pierre* (2000), based on a true story, involves a man condemned to the guillotine on a remote French island off Canada. The colony lacks a guillotine. The courts are sticklers for the letter of the law. The condemned man and the warden's wife undergo a transformation during the wait for the guillotine to arrive from France. It is very deep and moving.

My Best Friend (2007) is about a man who learns he truly has no friends, only acquaintances and associates. He hires a sunny taxi driver to instruct him in the act of making friends. *Man on the Train* (2003) stars French rock star Johnny Hallyday and Jean Rochefort again, as a bank robber and a retired literature teacher. Circumstances lead the teacher to admit the robber as an overnight guest. Each old man envies the other, who represents a road not traveled. *The Girl on the Bridge* (1999) is about a professional knife-thrower who hangs around bridges looking for young women about to leap off them. He offers them a job as his target. There is always the possibility he might miss. If he doesn't, they get an interesting job with lots of travel. If he does hit them, well, what do they have to lose?

I have never seen a bad film by Patrice Leconte. As you can see, they share no genre. They share no style, either, except his clear, sure strokes at the service of his story. I have been thinking for years of including him in the Great Movies collection, but delayed, unable to choose among them. I could make an excellent case for every film I mentioned.

What they have in common is his gift for inventing unforgettable characters. Some are remarkable only in their ordinariness. They have this in common: they're fascinating. Admit that in my brief remarks about those titles you were intrigued by every character I mentioned. The French have affection for Leconte, because he doesn't disappoint them. But in the world market, he offers no hook or "high concept." For the global mass audience, if it requires an entire sentence to describe a film, that's too much complexity to deal with. Yet Leconte's kind of film is why I go to the movies with hope.

You will have noted I revealed nothing of the destiny of his couple who are so very happy. Surely their happiness cannot last forever? No? Are you sure? Surely we believe we are immune to the sad outcomes experienced by others. I want to say this much about the ending: it is a happy ending. Happy for her, happy for him, and their love remains inviolate and undiminished. Can you deny that?

{ H A R A K I R I }

Samurai films, like Westerns, need not be familiar genre stories. They can expand to contain stories of ethical challenges and human tragedy. *Harakiri* (1962), one of the best of them, is about an older wandering samurai who takes his time to create an unanswerable dilemma for the elder of a powerful clan. By playing strictly within the rules of Bushido Code which governs the conduct of all samurai, he lures the powerful leader into a situation where sheer naked logic leaves him humiliated before his retainers.

The time is 1630. Unemployed samurai, called ronin, wander the land. There is peace in Japan, and that leads to their unemployment. Their hearts, minds, and swords have been pledged to their masters, and now they are cast adrift, unable to feed and shelter their families. It would be much the same with a corporation today, when a loyal employee with long tenure is "downsized." Loyalty runs only from the bottom up.

At the gate of the official mansion of Lord Iyi, a shabby ronin named Tsugumo Hanshiro applies for an audience with the clan elder, Saito Kayegu (Rentaro Mikuni). He has been set loose by Lord Geishu and has no job. He requests permission to kill himself in the clan's forecourt. The ritual act is known as harakiri, or seppuku (which is the film's title in Japanese). It involves using a short blade for self-disembowelment. After the blade plunges in and slices from left to right, a designated master swordsman stands by to decapitate the samurai with one powerful stroke.

Tsugumo desires to kill himself because of the disgrace of being a jobless samurai. Saito tells him a story designed to discourage this. In the district there have been many appeals like this, and in some cases the desperate samurais had their lives spared and were given work by the clan they appealed to. They didn't really want to commit harakiri at all. However, Saito says, many clans have wised up to this tactic. He tells a story of Chijiwa Motome (Akira Ishihama), another cast-off from Lord Geishu. He turned up not long ago here in this very forecourt, he says, asking the same permission. Saito granted it—but only if he performed the ritual immediately. Motome gave his word as a samurai that he would indeed kill himself, but asked permission to first pay a short personal visit. Saito saw this as a delaying tactic, and commanded Motome to disembowel himself then and there. This was not easy, because Motome had pawned his short sword and had a cheap bamboo replacement. As a man of honor, he fell on this blunt blade and caused great damage and pain before being decapitated.

So you see, Saito tells Tsugumo, you had better be sincere. "I assure you I'm quite sincere," Tsugumo says, "but first I request your permission to tell a story"—one that will be heard by Saito and the retainers of the household, who are seated solemnly around the edges of the courtyard.

Harakiri was released in 1962, the work of Masaki Kobayashi (1916–96), best known for *Kwaidan* (1965), an assembly of ghost stories that is among the most beautiful films I've seen. He also made the nine-hour epic *The Human Condition* (1959–61), which was critical of the way the Bushido Code permeated Japanese life and helped create the state of mind which led to World War II. And he made *Samurai Rebellion* (1967), about a man who refuses to offer his wife to a superior.

His recurring theme, seen clearly in *Harakiri*, is that fanatic adherence to codes of honor, by granting them a value greater than life itself, sets up a situation where humanist values are forbidden. The samurai class eventually created the Japanese militarist class, whose members were so indoctrinated with worship of their superiors that the deaths of kamikaze pilots and the slaughter of soldiers in hopeless charges under fire were seen not as military acts, but as a seeking for honorable death. The modern Japanese novelist Yukio Mishima was famously so devoted to the code that he saw its decay as the shame of Japan, and himself committed seppuku in 1970 after leading his small private army in an ill-advised uprising to restore the honor of the Emperor. The American writer-director Paul Schrader told his story in *Mishima: A Life in Four Chapters* (1985).

Opening in a way similar to *Rashomon*, in which a man arrives at a gate and begins telling one of four versions of the same story, Kobayashi makes a film where there is only one correct version of the story, but its meaning depends entirely on whose point of view you take. Who is right? Saito, who is determined not to have the charity of the Iyi clan exploited, or Tsugumo, who is determined that Saito and his household will hear the whole story of Motome which led up to his falling on his pathetic bamboo sword?

It would be wrong for me to reveal the details of the story Tsugumo tells. What I can say is that it is heartbreaking. He explains that Motome was not a man trying to avoid death by the excuse of asking for a delay. He was a man whose actual honor humbles Saito and other authoritarian bureaucrats. Sometimes it takes more courage to do the right thing than to do the traditional thing. Following the Bushido Code frees its adherents from the need to arrive at their own moral conclusions. *Harakiri* is a film reflecting situational ethics, in which the better you know a man the more deeply you understand his motives.

The telling of the story involves a feeling of ritual. Three times Tsugumo is given the privilege of choosing the master swordsman who will behead him. Three times a messenger is sent to fetch the man. Three times the messenger returns alone, with the news that the chosen man is feeling too ill today to survive. Tsugumo, who is obviously familiar with the retainers of the Iyi clan, doesn't seem very surprised. He will eventually explain the absence of the "sick" men by producing in the courtyard dramatic symbols of their lack of inner strength. This provides one of the great dramatic moments of all samurai films.

It's important how the director Kobayashi's own life reflects Tsugumo's ideals. He was a lifelong pacifist, but his way of acting on his beliefs was not to avoid military service but to refuse promotion to the officer class, so that he would take his chances along with other conscripts.

This black-and-white film is elegantly composed and photographed to reflect the values it contains. The camera often takes the POV of Saito, standing at the top of the stairs leading from the courtyard to the official residence, looking down from authority to Tsugumo the lowly petitioner. Then it will take a reverse POV of Tsugumo looking up to the man with the power. Angular shots incorporate the onlookers, who sit impassive and listen as their leader and the powerless ronin speak. Then, during a sword-play scene, a hand-held camera is used to suggest the breaking down of traditional patterns. It would take men with hearts of stone to resist being moved by Tsugumo's story, but these men have been born and bred to have such hearts.

The fist image in the film will raise questions in the minds of viewers. We are looking at the symbol of the Iyi clan, the repository of its traditions and ancestors—an empty suit of armor. Eventually this symbol will be disgraced and exposed as the hollow man it is. And when we listen to the heartless reasoning of Saito, it is easy to draw parallels with more recent political debates where rigid economic theories of both left and right are cited as good reason to disregard human suffering.

{ HEART OF GLASS }

Werner Herzog's *Heart of Glass* (1976) is a vision of man's future as desolation. In a film set entirely in a Bavarian village around 1800, it foresees the wars and calamities of the next two centuries and extends on into the twenty-first with humanity's nightfall. In the story of the failure of a small glassblowing factory, it sees the rise and collapse of the industrial revolution, the despair of communities depending on manufacture, the aimlessness of men and women without a sense of purpose.

None of these things is specifically stated. They come in the form of prophecies by a shepherd, who pronounces them in a trance to townspeople who think he must be mad. His words don't specify any of the events we know to have taken place, but they're uncanny in their ability to evoke what was coming. His words are the way a man might describe nuclear destruction, tyranny, ecological disaster, and the dominance of the crowd over the individual—if that man lacked words for the fearful images that appeared to him.

This is one of the least seen and most famous of Herzog's films, known as the one where most of the actors were hypnotized in most of the scenes. It hasn't been much seen, perhaps because it isn't to the taste of most people, seeming too slow, dark, and despairing. There's no proper story, no conclusion, and the final scene is a parable seemingly not connected to anything that has gone before. I think it should be approached like a piece of music, in which we comprehend everything in terms of mood and aura, and know how it makes us feel even if we can't say what it makes us think.

Herzog's canvas has two shots from the tops of peaks, looking down over the earth. For the rest, he sets his film entirely within the village, in a few houses, a beer hall, a glass factory, and the surrounding forest. The people depend for their existence on the manufacture of beautiful and valued rose-colored glassware. The master glassmaker Muhlbeck has died, taking to the grave the secret of the glass. Desperate experiments are undertaken to rediscover the recipe, but all fail. A reasonable person might say, "All right then, the factory can make other kinds of glass." There are no reasonable people in the village.

Herzog indeed hypnotized them for most of the scenes; that is not simply publicity. The dialogue which they repeat under hypnosis is pronounced with a dread certainty. It lacks life and individuality. Is this how hypnotized people speak? Not necessarily. Usually they speak more like— themselves. Eerily, it occurs to me that what we may actually be hearing are the intonations of Herzog's own voice as he hypnotized them and told them what to say. He is acting through them.

He removes all individuality from the performances. He removes all self-awareness. These are not "characters," although they have distinct characteristics. They are men who have had their souls taken from them by the failure of their work. With nothing to do and nothing to hope for, they no longer have the will to survive. I am reminded of the Chinese factory workers in the documentary Last Train Home, who leave the provinces and live in dormitories to work for meager wages that they send home to support their children. It is a dismal life, but it is a purpose, and if while absent 50 weeks a year they lose the love of their children, then the secret of the glass has been lost.

Certain citizens stand out from the small population. There is Hias (Joseph Bierbichler), the prophetic shepherd. The heir to the factory. The dwarfish sycophant. A brazen woman. A glass blower. Two friends, who quarrel and fall drunken from a hayloft, one living, one dying because his body cushions the other's fall. The survivor dances inconsolably with his friend's body. His macabre dance, and many other scenes, take place within a beer hall where the people drink and stare. In a well-known scene, one of the friends breaks a beer stein over the head of the other, who doesn't react. Then, slowly, he pours his own beer over the first one's head, again getting no reaction.

You can sense what Herzog is getting at. In the ordinary world one man doesn't break a mug over another's head without some ostensible reason, based on their personalities, the situation, and what they've said. All of that is redundant for Herzog's purpose. He shows the *essence* of the two men quarreling. They require no occasion. They are bereft of reason and a purpose for living, and reduced to automatons of hopelessness and hostility.

The interiors are darkly lit, with shadows gathered around them. The music of Popul Vul seems like melodies from Purgatory. Ordinary conversation is lacking, ordinary routines abandoned. These are people solemnly waiting for . . . nothing. Although some have found the film slow and one reported dozing off, I find it terrifying in its emptiness. It is like looking down into a vertiginous fall at the edge of time. Like many good "slow" films, it seems to move more quickly on additional viewings.

I mentioned two scenes on mountain peaks. They open and close the film. The first shows a man looking down into a vast valley, through which a river of clouds pours. In 1976 these clouds were not created by CGI; Herzog used special effects to combine the man and the image. I learn he worked 12 days to get the shot. The effect is haunting. What it evokes for me is the sense of Man standing above Time and glimpsing it on its flow toward Eternity. I learn from the critic Neil Young that Herzog's "debt to nineteenth-century German artists is evident, with Caspar David Friedrich prominent among the influences." He says this shot "recreates his famous *Wanderer above the Sea of Fog.*"

The final scene involves a man on a mountain peak who looks out to sea. Herzog intercuts sea birds on the mountain side, moving in nervous waves of flight. A narrator explains that the man concludes there must be something on the other side of the ocean. Transfixed by his conviction, men set out to cross the sea, rowing with fierce determination in a pitifully small boat after land disappears behind them and no land appears before them.

The narrator tells us they took it as a good omen that the birds followed them out to sea.

What does this mean? It is better to row into oblivion than to wait for it to come to you? I don't know. Some images are complete without translation into words. *Heart of Glass* strikes me as a film of such images. From it I get a feeling that evokes my gloom as I see a world sinking into self-destruction, and feel I am lucky to be old because there may not be another lifetime's length of happiness left for most people on this planet. For most of my time here there was still rose-colored glass.

Herzog fascinates me. I feel a film like *Heart of Glass* comes as close to any single one of his titles to expressing the inchoate feelings in his heart. He was once asked what he would do if he had one day to live. It's a meaningless question, but I appreciated his answer: "Martin Luther said that if he knew the world were ending tomorrow, he would plant a tree. I would start a new film."

{ IN A LONELY PLACE }

The courtyard of the Hollywood building occupied by Humphrey Bogart in *In a Lonely Place* (1950) is one of the most evocative spaces I've seen in a movie. Small apartments are lined up around a Spanish-style courtyard with a fountain. Each flat is occupied by a single person. If you look across from your window, you can see into the life of your neighbor.

One apartment is occupied by Dixon Steele, an alcoholic screenwriter who had some success but is now in the midst of a long, dry spell. Across from him is Laurel Gray (Gloria Grahame), a would-be actress and a smart cookie. Steele is a bitter, angry man. Drinking at noon in his usual hangout, he succeeds in insulting his agent, punching a man who is cruel to an aging has-been actor, and then getting in a fistfight with the son of a studio chief.

This concise opening scene, set in a bar inspired by Bogart's own hangout, Romanoff's, establishes Dixon Steele's character and summarizes some of the things we sense about Bogart, that enigmatic man. They both drink too much. They're both idealists who sympathize with underdogs. They both have a temper. Steele has, and Bogart was always able to evoke, self-pity; remember his Dobbs in *Treasure of the Sierra Madre*. Bogart was at his best in conflicted roles, at his weakest in straightforward macho parts. Steele's qualities make him an ideal partner for Laurel Gray, who has been around, knows the ropes, and is more likely to fall for a wounded pigeon than a regular guy.

In a Lonely Place has been described by the critic Kim Morgan as "one of the most heartbreaking love stories ever committed to film," and love is indeed what it's really about. It has the look, feel, and trappings of a film noir, and a murder takes place in it, but it is really about the dark places in a man's soul and a woman who thinks she can heal them.

As carefully constructed by Bogart, who produced it, and directed by Nicholas Ray, from a great noir novel by Dorothy Hughes, it's at pains to make its man and woman adults who know their way around. Neither is a victim, except of their own natures: Dixon Steele a drinker with rotten self-esteem, Laurel Gray a woman who should know better than to invest in him.

In the film, Steele is given the job of adapting a trashy best seller. He needs the work, but he can't even bear to read the novel. A friendly hat-check girl named Mildred (Martha Stewart) tells him she loved it, and he hires her to come home with him and tell him the story. On their way through his courtyard, they pass Laurel Gray, and Gloria Grahame is perfect in how she conveys to him that she notices him. The storytelling session drags on, Mildred becomes a bore, and Steele sends her away. The next morning she's found murdered. Steele, seen to leave the bar with her and with a long rap sheet involving assaults and fights, is the logical suspect.

Did anyone see Mildred leave his apartment? Yes, as it turns out, Laurel says she did, and provides an alibi when she's brought to the police station. Something happens between Laurel and Dixon in the captain's office that is unmistakable—and later that day they act upon it, no small talk, hungry with passion and hope.

Laurel gets Dixon off the sauce. He starts writing again. They're helplessly in love, a little giddy with happiness. But the possibility lingers that he did murder the girl, and that Laurel testified for him out of instinct more than certain knowledge. An idyllic interlude on the beach suddenly turns ugly and leads to worse. We, and Laurel, are presented with the possibility that her life is in danger, especially if he drinks again. Ambiguity about the true Dixon Steele provides the soul of the film. The fact that they truly love each other its poignancy.

This is a crisp black-and-white film with an almost ruthless efficiency of style. It taps into the psyches of the three principals: Bogart, who bought the story to produce with his company; Nicholas Ray, a lean iconoclast of films about wounded men (James Dean in *Rebel Without Cause*); and the legendary Gloria Grahame (1923–81), whose life story inspired Peter Turner's extraordinary book *Film Stars Don't Die in Liverpool*. Turner was the last of her many loves. She was married to Nicholas Ray but that ended during the making of this film, when Ray found her in bed with his 13-year-old son by an earlier marriage. (She and the boy, Tony, were married from 1960 to 1974.)

Life on the set was obviously fraught with emotional hazards. Ray had modeled the movie's apartment complex on an apartment he once occupied at Villa Primavera in West Hollywood. When he moved out on Grahame, I learn from critic J. Hoberman, Ray actually moved onto the set and started sleeping there. The relationship between Dixon and Laurel mirrored aspects of Bogart's own with the younger, strong-willed, nurturing Lauren Bacall. Yet perhaps they all sensed that they were doing the best work of their careers—a film could be based on those three people and that experience.

In a Lonely Place is a superb example of the mature Hollywood studio system at the top of its form. Photographed with masterful economy by Burnett Guffey (*Knock on Any Door*, *Bonnie and Clyde*), it understands space and uses the apartments across the courtyard to visualize the emotional relationship between Dixon and Laurel. Visible to each other, dependent on each other, they never officially move in together but remain enclosed, and no matter what they say, apart. Notice the way Guffey focuses light on Bogart's eyes during a frightening speech when he imagines how Mildred was murdered.

"You know, Miss Gray," he says, "you're one up on me. You can see into my apartment but I can't see into yours."

"I promise you, I won't take advantage of it."

"I would, if it were the other way around."

Bogart is so good at playing vulnerable men. It's strange he has an enduring image as a tough guy. It would be more accurate to say he was tempered by experience. A decade before this film, in *Casablanca*, he was already the man drinking alone late at night, afraid of hearing an old song.

About Grahame's characters there was often a doomed quality. She and Lee Marvin had an iconic scene in *The Big Heat* (1953) when he threw a pot of boiling coffee in her face. In *It's a Wonderful Life* (1946), she plays the grown-up Violet, who in the nightmare sequence becomes a prostitute. She won an Oscar for *The Bad and the Beautiful* (1952), playing an actress who hates the producer who betrayed her. And she gained the unfortunate nickname "the can't say no girl" after performing that song in *Oklahoma!* (1955).

If there is one key element of film noir, it is the flawed hero. That, usually joined with a distinctive visual style and tone, defines the genre. The hero is sympathetic but weak, often haunted by mistakes in the past or fatally tempted by greed or lust. He is likely to discover himself capable of evil he had never dreamed of, and is consumed by guilt and fear.

Bogart embodies this noir quality flawlessly in *In a Lonely Place*. He plays a good man with a hot temper who can fly into a rage when he drinks. This gives Dixon a Jekyll and Hyde quality that Laurel awakens to, leading to later scenes of terror. The monster inhabiting him is an acting-out of self-loathing, which infects his success and dooms his happiness. He foresees his fate when he quotes to her a line just written in his new screenplay: "I was born when you kissed me. I died when you left me. I lived a few weeks while you loved me."

{ IVAN THE TERRIBLE, PARTS I AND II }

The two parts of Eisenstein's *Ivan the Terrible* are epic in scope, awesome in visuals, and nonsensical in story. It is one of those works that has proceeded directly to the status of Great Movie without going through the intermediate stage of being a good movie. I hope earnest students of cinema will forgive me when I say every serious movie lover should see it—once.

The productions were backed by Stalin, who took Ivan as a personal hero. They were filmed during World War II, mostly at the Alma Ata studios in Kazakhstan, where major Soviet directors were relocated for greater safety. Even in wartime Eisenstein seems to have been under few limitations; in Part II, spectacular shots show a march of hundreds of costumed extras playing Ivan's army, and proletarians on a march to implore Ivan to return from exile. The first film, released in 1944, was met with great success (i.e., by Stalin who was the only one who counted). Part II was completed by 1946 but was suppressed because either state censors or Stalin himself found the Tsar uncomfortably close to the dictator (it was finally released in 1958). Eisenstein planned a third part of a trilogy and shot some scenes for it, but production was halted and the director died in 1948.

The film opens in a vast, towering throne room in Moscow, during the coronation of Ivan with the approval of the Boyars, the hereditary class of affluent bourgeois who exercised de facto control over the state. Their smiles turn to angry frowns as the tall, confident teenager immediately declares himself Tsar of all of Russia and vows to marry Princess Anastasia; he will to extend and protect Russian borders and hold sway over the Boyars.

This scene will set a tone for both films. The coronation ceremony is deliberate and stately. The costumes are particularly ornate and bejeweled, apparently so heavy they must be difficult to wear. The acting style is declamatory and bombastic. Eisenstein begins here, and will continue throughout the film, to use dramatic close-ups of faces. The actors he uses often look odd. Their features are sometimes exaggerated by lighting from below. His camera angles are oblique. Ivan's opponents are seen as a menagerie of grotesque human caricatures, seen separately with no attempt to establish their spatial location.

It is impossible to look at those faces and not think immediately of the Danish silent film *The Passion of Joan of Arc*, made by Carl Theodore Dreyer in 1928. Eisenstein had almost certainly seen it before he began filming in the early 1940s, if not in Russia then in Hollywood, where after the success of his early films *Potemkin* and *October* he was invited in 1930 to make a film by Paramount. His projects were rejected by the studio, he became the target of anticommunists, and he never made an American film. (He did however find himself greatly impressed by the early work of Walt Disney, and later declared *Snow White and the Seven Dwarfs* the greatest film ever made.)

During the trial of Joan of Arc, Dreyer placed his heroine in a subservient position below a bench of fearsome judges, who along with onlookers are seen in frowning or angry close-ups, at oblique angles, in stylized lighting. If that was an influence on Eisenstein, so also might have been Dreyer's set designs. Joan of Arc is seen placed in extreme architecture, its angled and exaggerated walls suggesting cold hostility.

Eisenstein's sets are incompatibly larger, but often evoke the same look. Some of them are unadorned walls, arches, nooks, stairs, and passageways. Others, the throne room for example, have walls covered with painted icons, decorations, and bas-relief. It's tempting here to assume we're looking at matte drawings or optical effects, but in some shots Eisenstein has characters walk into the background and behind pillars or posts, demonstrating the dimensionality. In many other dramatic shots he uses enormous and pre-sumably real shadows, for example to show a huge image of Ivan's head with its wickedly pointed beard, dwarfing the members of his court.

In Part I we meet those involved in the court intrigues surrounding the Tsar (Nikolai Cherkasov). His close friend Kolychev wants out of the situation altogether, and opts to join a distant monastery. Another friend, Kurbsky, is pressured by the Boyars to resist Ivan. Since the Boyars until now had a monopoly on power and Ivan's assumption of the Tsar's role came out of the blue, this is persuasive.

After Ivan marries the Princess Anastasia (who he accurately con-siders his only friend), they have a child. This inflames the already existing hatred of Ivan on the part of Euphrosinia, Ivan's aunt. She passionately fa-vors her own son, Prince Staritsky. Her choice introduces some humor into the film, because the baby-faced Staritsky, his blond hair in a choirboy cut, is a mamma's boy. At one point he flings himself into his mother's arms and protests that she is always trying to make him do things. He has no wish to ever be Tsar.

This Euphrosinia is an evil creature, often wearing a witch's hat. A peculiarity of the throne room is that many of its entrances are arches too low for anyone to pass through upright. The one apparently leading to her own apartment is so low she bends almost double, slithering into view like a snake. It is she who diabolically plots to have Ivan himself unknowingly bring a poisoned chalice to the sickbed of Anastasia. Later, Ivan has his re-venge after mockingly dressing Staritsky in the Tsar's clothes and placing his crown on the lad's head.

Part I features stagy historical pomp and circumstance. Part II un-dergoes a tonal shift and declares itself cheerfully over the top. Some critics have been so unkind as to say it works best as camp comedy. Nikolai Cher-kasov's performance as Tsar is generally impressive in Part I, but in Part II it occasionally seems to have wandered in from a Mel Brooks production of the same material. I personally felt little emotional involvement in either part of the film; it played for me like reluctant hagiography for a madman.

Why are *Ivan the Terrible, Parts I and II* so routinely included on lists of the great films? I imagine few viewers really love it (although watching

it inspires a visual fascination). In part it may be because Eisenstein has become one of the Sacred Monsters of the cinema. Film students are brought
up to revere him. In the 1940s and 1950s he was championed by Jay Leyda,
who studied under Eisenstein in Moscow in 1933 and later became an influential curator at the Museum of Modern Art. It was Leyda who brought
the only complete print of Eisenstein's *Battleship Potemkin*, certainly a great
film, to the West.

Still, to hail *Ivan the Terrible* is more a duty than a pleasure. While
those who consider it camp must enjoy it, is that what Eisenstein intended?
I invite comparison of this film with Josef von Sternberg's *The Scarlet Em-
press* (1934); camp is the least of the qualities that can be attributed to it.
Compared to the wicked, subversive eroticism von Sternberg brings to the
court of Marlene Dietrich's Catherine the Great, Eisenstein is a mechanic.

{ THE KILLING }

Stanley Kubrick considered *The Killing* (1956) to be his first mature feature, after a couple of short warm-ups. He was 28 when it was released, having already been an obsessed chess player, a photographer for *Look* magazine, and a director of *March of Time* newsreels. It's tempting to search here for themes and a style he would return to in his later masterpieces, but few directors seemed so determined to make every one of his films an individual, free-standing work. Seeing it without his credit, would you guess it was by Kubrick? Would you connect *Dr. Strangelove* with *Barry Lyndon?*

This is a heist movie. Like horror films, heists are a genre that make stars not so necessary. The durable form inspires directors to create plots that are baffling in their complexity or bold in their simplicity. In *Bonnie and Clyde*, the gang parks in front of a bank, walks in with guns, and walks out (in theory) with the loot. In David Mamet's *Heist*, the characters are involved in interlocking levels of cons being pulled on each other. In *Rififi*, a theft involves a plan of almost unnecessary acrobatic ingenuity. Kubrick's plan here for a race track robbery involves two of those plot aspects; not so much the acrobatics. His narrative approach seems blunt, but the narrative itself is so labyrinthine we abandon any hope of trying to piece it together and just abandon ourselves to letting it happen. We feel in safe hands.

Perhaps a motif can be found in the movie's storefront chess club which, I learn, Kubrick frequented as a kid. His gang leader Johnny Clay (Sterling Hayden) goes there to meet a professional wrestler named Maurice, played by a professional wrestler named Kola Kwariani. Maurice is big and strong and is needed to start a fight at the race track bar to divert attention during the heist. Like all the members of Johnny's team, he has no idea of the overall plot. He just knows his role and his payoff, and knows Johnny enough to trust him.

The game of chess involves holding in your mind several alternate possibilities. The shifting of one piece can result in a radically different game. Johnny Clay has devised a strategy seemingly as flawless as Bobby Fischer's *Perfect Games*, but it depends on all the players making the required moves on schedule. If a piece shifts, everything changes, a possibility Johnny should have given more thought to.

The movie is narrated in an exact, passionless voice by the uncredited Art Gilmore, a veteran radio announcer. He places great emphasis on precise dates and times of day, although really only one day and time are crucial—4 p.m., the starting time of a $100,000 high stakes horse race. The rest of his narration serves only to confirm what we can see for ourselves, that the events on screen are not happening in chronological order. The plot jumps around like a chess player's mind: "If he does this, and I do that, and then he . . ."

In the few days before the heist, Johnny makes the rounds of his team members. We meet them at the same time. There's a large cast, made easy to follow because of typecasting and the familiar faces of many supporting players. Let's see. In no particular order (which would please the narrator), there are Fay (Coleen Gray), Johnny's girl; Marvin Unger (Jay C. Flippen), an old friend who is putting up the cost of the operation; Randy Kennan (Ted de Corsia), a crooked cop; Sherry Peatty (Marie Windsor), a gold-digging floozy; her husband George Peatty (Elisha Cook), a weakling race track cashier who hopes to buy her affection; Val Cannon (Vince Edwards), Sherry's actual lover; Mike O'Reilly (Joe Sawyer), the racetrack bartender who needs money for his sick wife; Nikki Arcane (Timothy Carey), a rifle sharpshooter; Leo the loan shark (Jay Adler); and assorted others. Kubrick brings all these types onscreen, makes it clear who they are, and sees that we will remember them, while only gradually revealing their roles in the heist.

Filmed largely in San Mateo and Venice, California, and at the Bay Meadows Racetrack, the movie has the look and feel of glorious 1950s black-and-white film noir. On a budget of $230,000, Kubrick uses a lot of actual locations. We see a shabby motel with residential rooms by the week or month, the low-rent "luxury" of the Peatty's apartment, the sun-washed streets. Many heist movies feature a chalk talk in which the leader explains the scenario to his gang so that we can visualize it; Jean-Pierre Melville's version of this scene adds immeasurably to *Bob le Flambeur*. Kubrick puts his pieces in place, but only when the actual plan is underway do we understand them. We go in like a chess player who knows what the rook, knight, and queen do, but doesn't know what will happen in the game. Nor, it turns out, do they all know the rules.

I wouldn't think of giving away the game. The writing and editing are the keys to how this film never seems to be the deceptive assembly that it is, but appears to be proceeding on schedule, whatever that schedule is. We accept even action that makes absolutely no sense, as in a crucial moment involving Nikki the sharpshooter. Required to hit a moving target with a rifle with telescopic sights, he inexplicably parks his sports car, a convertible with the top down, in plain view in a parking lot so that anyone can see him take out the rifle, aim, and fire. In theory they're looking elsewhere. In practice his personality gets him in trouble.

Sterling Hayden was a considerable screen presence with his tough guy face and his pouting lower lip. His gravel voice lays out instructions and requirements in a flat, factual manner; his gang members take them at face value. He never displays much emotion, not even at the end, when a great deal might be justified. We don't see passion, fear, greed. He could be a chess player in the zone. He has a streak of nihilism. The most colorful players are Marie Windsor, famously known as Marie Windsor, and Elisha Cook, famous for playing milquetoasts and chumps in the movies of four decades. She wraps him around her little finger, and he comes back for more.

Considering that it cheerfully abandons any attempt at chronological suspense, *The Killing* is an unreasonable success. The prize will be

$2 million—the day's expected total receipts at the track. This heist is worth a lot of planning, and Johnny has gone the distance. In his mind his plan is superb. All it depends upon is everybody doing exactly what is required of them, exactly when and where. The word that occurs to me in describing Kubrick's approach to Johnny and the film is "control." That may suggest the link between this first mature feature and Kubrick's later films, so varied and brilliant.

In his films, he had the plan in his mind. He knew where everyone should be and what they should do. Such a perfectionist was Kubrick that he knew every theater his films were opening in, and the daily grosses. It's said that a projectionist in Kansas City received a phone call from Kubrick in England, informing him that the picture was out of focus. Is that story apocryphal? I've never thought so.

{ LEON MORIN, PRIEST }

In 1961, one year after he appeared in *Breathless* (1960) and two years after she appeared in *Hiroshima, Mon Amour*, Jean-Paul Belmondo and Emmanuelle Riva made *Leon Morin, Priest*. They were both in the white heat of their early careers; Belmondo would make five other films that year. The director was Jean-Pierre Melville, known for his films about gangsters and the Resistance. A crime film might have been ideal for them, but instead they filmed this story at the intersection of desire, religion, and politics.

When a film shows us a priest and a woman, both attractive and in their early 20s, alone together in a room with the door closed, we've been programmed to think about the possibility of sex. Certainly every priest and every young woman knows this. Fifty years ago, many young women in France would have been reluctant to accept such an invitation from a man they scarcely knew—but a priest, of course, has taken the vow of celibacy, and so . . .

And so, what? She counts on him not making a move and is intrigued by the situation? He counts on her thinking that way and takes advantage? Possibly. Then again, they may both sincerely intend to discuss religion. Their discussion has in fact started earlier in the confessional, which Barny (Riva) entered looking for a fight. Her opening words weren't "Bless me, father, for I have sinned," but "Religion is the opiate of the masses!"

She chose her confessor sight unseen on the basis of his name, thinking working-class parents might well name a boy "Leon."

She is a communist. Such an affiliation was common enough in France during the German occupation, when the centrist parties were playing along with the collaborationist Vichy government. She's also a widow with a half-Jewish daughter, and a worker for a correspondence school that relocated from Paris to a town in the French Alps after the Germans marched in. The town has been occupied by genial Italians wearing feathers in their hats, who seem largely concerned with going on hikes and eating pastries. Then the German tanks rumble in, and the Nazis round up their Italian allies, shoot them, and get down to the business of rounding up Jews.

Barny and two other mothers with half-Jewish children have them baptized as Catholics in an attempt to protect them. Perhaps it was during this ceremony that she began to brood about the arbitrary line separating Christians and Jews. As an atheist, she finds religion a paltry reason for murder. Seeking out a priest to argue with, she is startled to find one whose tactic is to agree with her as far as he can. Yes, many members of the masses use religion as an opiate. Yes, the expensive furnishings in a church appall him. He points out that the church no longer makes distinctions between social classes: "Why should it take three priests to bury a rich man? We're not undertakers."

After her "confession," he offers to lend her a book and asks her to meet him in his room. She thinks of little else for four days. We know from the earlier scenes that this young widow is awake to sexual desire; she's obsessed with the woman who runs her office and thinks of her as beautiful, perfect, an amazon. When this woman stands behind her to point out something in a document and allows her breasts to cradle Barny's neck, the effect is electric.

We perhaps anticipate *Leon Morin, Priest* will lead to sex. Melville is too good a filmmaker to settle for such a simple solution. To our astonishment, it leads to instruction in the Catholic faith, Barny visiting the room once or twice a week to debate Leon and read his books. For both of them, I believe, these visits have a strong sexual undercurrent, and indeed he discovers that Barny sees other young women from the parish, but apparently no men, for religious instruction. Does he enjoy being close but not touching?

A sexy office mate of Barny's with easy morals vows she'll seduce him, "because I never fail." Is that what the film's about? Seduction interruptus? Only in small part. The German occupation draws a tighter net. Barny hides her daughter with two old maids living on a farm. An old Jewish scholar at work gets a new passport and a new name. The amazon at work learns her brother has been killed by Nazis, visibly ages, and loses her spirit. Barny gets in fierce arguments against collaborating with the Vichy government, although it must be said she makes no move to join the Resistance.

There's a striking scene when the children are baptized; some of their fathers, Resistance fighters, appear for the ceremony, and then melt back into the nearby forest. "It's as if you were watching fathers leaving for that day's work," writes critic Manohla Dargis. Melville, usually a classic stylist, uses a style unusual for him. He breaks the action into brief scenes punctuated by fades to black. It's as if a window opens and closes on the series of events—as if one need not necessarily lead to the next.

We rarely see the priest when he isn't in the same room with Barny. Once, during mass, he seems to go out of his way to allow the sleeve of his cassock to brush against her breast. She is sure this is not coincidence. So am I. Dissolve. In general, he has a curious way of touching her. She approaches him in church one day after confession while he's talking with an old lady, and he pushes her roughly aside: "Meet me in my room."

Once as she's entering his room he pushes, not gently, to hurry her from behind. When the office temptress sits provocatively on the edge of his desk with her legs crossed, he rudely pulls down her skirt to cover her knee. A polite man would not lightly treat women in this way. The priest has a license. In a way, the film is about his license. When Barny flirts with him ("Would you marry me if I were a Protestant?"), he reacts with anger. She's calling his bluff. She no longer feels free to visit him.

Leon Morin, Priest is a consistently intriguing film, because Melville so cleverly plays with our expectations. There is an undercurrent of sincere religiosity at work. Morin is a sincere priest who is prepared to accept a posting in a remote district where no one will be interested in his books. "I will convert the nations," he says, "starting with this village."

He has persuasive answers to all of Barny's questions about the faith, and you will discover what effect they have. He's a worldly realist. Asking "Are your hands pure?" and learning that she masturbates using a piece of wood, he asks, "Does it hurt?"

Jean-Pierre Melville (1917–73), born Grumbach, changed his name in admiration of Herman Melville; he was a major 1950s French director who had an important influence on the New Wave. Unable to break into the French studio system after the war, Melville was a pioneering independent who shot on location, had to suspend productions to raise more money to buy film stock, paid poorly, and yet under these conditions made his two great first films, *Les Enfants Terribles* (1950) and *Bob le Flambeur* (1956). Yet as Truffaut, Godard, and their fellow Wavers swept American art houses, his films were late to be discovered. Since his work has been restored on DVD, he's finding an enthusiastic new following.

{ LOST IN TRANSLATION }

Bill Murray's acting in Sofia Coppola's *Lost in Translation* (2003) is surely one of the most exquisitely controlled performances in recent movies. Without it, the film could be unwatchable. With it, I can't take my eyes away. Not for a second, not for a frame, does his focus relax, and yet it seems effortless. It's sometimes said of an actor that we can't see him acting. I can't even see him *not* acting. He seems to be existing, merely existing, in the situation created for him by Sofia Coppola.

Is he "playing himself"? I've known Murray since his days at Second City. He married the sister of a girl I was dating. We were never friends, I have no personal insights, but I can fairly say I saw how he behaved in small informal groups of friends, and it wasn't like Bob Harris, his character in the movie. Yes, he likes to remain low key. Yes, dryness and understatement come naturally to him. Sharing a stage at Second City with John Belushi, he was a glider in contrast to the kamikaze pilot. He isn't a one-note actor. He does anger, fear, love, whatever, and broad comedy. But what he does in *Lost in Translation* shows as much of a reach as if he were playing Henry Higgins. He allows the film to be as great as Coppola dreamed of it, in the way she intended, and few directors are so fortunate.

She has one objective: she wants to show two people lonely in vast foreign Tokyo and coming to the mutual realization that their lives are stuck.

Perhaps what they're looking for is the same thing I've heard we seek in marriage: a witness. Coppola wants to get that note right. There isn't a viewer who doesn't expect Bob Harris and Charlotte (Scarlett Johansson) to end up in love, or having sex, or whatever. We've met Charlotte's husband John (Giovanni Ribisi). We expect him to return unexpectedly from his photo shoot and surprise them together. These expectations have been sculpted, one chip of Hollywood's chisel after another, in tens of thousands of films. The last thing we expect is . . . what would probably actually happen. They share loneliness.

One of the strengths of Coppola's screenplay is that her people and everything they do are believable. Unlike the characters in most movies, they don't quickly sense they belong together, and they don't immediately *want* to be together. Coppola keeps them apart for a noticeably long time. They don't know they're the Girl and the Boy. They don't have a meet cute. We grow to know them separately.

We understand Charlotte loves her husband, and we understand how he wounds her, and why she cries on the phone. There's no possibility he will cheat on her with the Other Woman, the ditzy "star" Kelly, played by Anna Faris. John is simply a moth fluttering around her fame. That's what hurts Charlotte; he leaves her alone in the hotel for silly reasons that betray him as callow. We understand that Bob loves his wife and especially his children at home in America, but after years and years he knows and says that marriage and children are "hard." So they are. We know that. Few movie characters know it in the sense he means.

After they start talking, Johansson is instinctive in striking the right note of tentative friendliness. She knows Bob is a star, but doesn't care. Earlier their eyes met in the kind of telepathic sympathy strangers share when they know they're thinking the same thing about something happening in a room. Now they can't sleep and it's the middle of the night in a hotel bar. She isn't flirting, and she isn't not flirting. He isn't flirting. He's composed and detached. He doesn't give away one hint of emotion. Without making it a big deal, he's almost studiously proper, as if making it clear he's *not* coming on to her. Of course he finds her attractive. He did when he saw her in the elevator and she didn't notice him. Or are we simply assuming he'd feel the same way we'd feel? Maybe he noticed her because they were the two tallest people in the elevator.

I can't tell you how many people have told me they just don't get *Lost in Translation*. They want to know what it's about. They complain "nothing happens." They've been trained by movies that tell them where to look and what to feel, in stories that have a beginning, a middle, and an end. *Lost in Translation* offers an experience in the exercise of empathy. The characters empathize with each other (*that's* what it's about), and we can empathize with them going through that process. It's not a question of reading our own emotions into Murray's blank slate. The slate isn't blank. It's on hold. He doesn't choose to wear his heart on his sleeve for Charlotte, and he doesn't choose to make a move. But he is very lonely and not without sympathy for her. She would plausibly have sex with him, casually, to be "nice," and because she's mad at her husband and it might be fun. But she doesn't know as he does that if you cheat it shouldn't be with someone it would make a difference to.

There is wonderful comedy in the film, involving the ad agency's photo shoot for the Suntory Scotch commercial and Bob's guest shot on the "Japanese Johnny Carson." But Coppola remains firmly grounded in reality. The Japanese director seems to be spouting hysterical nonsense until you find a translation online and understand what he's saying and why. He's not without humor. The translator seems to be simplifying, but now we understand what she's doing. There's nothing implausible about the scene. Anyone who watches Japanese TV, even via YouTube, knows the TV show is straight from life. Notice the microscopic look Murray gives the camera to signal "just kidding."

What is lost in translation? John understands nothing of what Charlotte says or feels, nor does he understand how he's behaving. (Ribisi's acting in the scene where he rushes out saying he loves her is remorselessly exact.) Bob's wife and assistant don't understand how desperately indifferent he is to the carpet samples. And so on. What does get translated, finally, is what Bob and Charlotte are really thinking. The whole movie is about that act of translation taking place.

The cinematography by Lance Acord and editing by Sarah Flack make no attempt to underline points or nudge us. It permits us to regard. It is content to allow a moment to complete itself. Acord often frames Charlotte in a big window with Tokyo remotely below. She feels young, alone, and exposed. He often shows Bob inscrutably looking straight ahead (not at the camera; not at anything). He feels older, tired, patient, not exposed because he has a surer sense of who he is. That's what I read into the shots. What do you get? When he brings them together they are still apart, and there is more truth in a little finger touching the side of a foot than a sex scene.

Catherine Lambert, who plays the singer in the hotel bar, is every pretty good lounge act in the world. It's more or less a foregone conclusion that they will sleep with one another. It won't mean anything to either one of them. When Charlotte discovers the singer is in Bob's room, she's startled but not angry or heartbroken. Sex wasn't what she and Bob were about, and he made that clear. When they meet next, they step carefully around that glitch and resume their deeper communication.

So much has been written about those few words at the end that Bob whispers into Charlotte's ear. We can't hear them. They seem meaningful for both of them. Coppola said she didn't know. It wasn't scripted. Advanced sound engineering has been used to produce a fuzzy enhancement. Harry Caul of *The Conversation* would be proud of it, but it's entirely irrelevant. Those words weren't for our ears. Coppola (1) didn't write the dialogue, (2) didn't intentionally record the dialogue, and (3) was happy to release the movie that way, so we *cannot* hear. Why must we know? Do we need closure? This isn't a closure kind of movie. We get all we need in simply knowing they share a moment private to them, and *seeing* that it contains something true before they part forever.

MAKE WAY FOR TOMORROW

When I was still living in Urbana, I would often take my mother for a drive. If our way took us past the Champaign County Nursing Home, she'd invariably say, "There's where I'm going to end up." She saw herself old and lonely, abandoned by her only son. This was when she was only in her 50s. She said she'd been shaped by the Depression, when old people for the first time had to "live on the county."

Make Way for Tomorrow (1937) is a nearly forgotten American film made in the Depression. It tells the story my mother imagined for herself. A couple has lived happily together for 50 years. They lose their home to a bank. Their five grown children are sincerely sorry to hear this, but what can they do with them? One has moved to California and is rarely heard from. The others live closer but don't have the space to take in two people. It is decided that mother and father will stay with two different children, "for now." Their last night in their home is the last time they will sleep together in the same bed.

Oh, it's not that their children don't love them. It's that they're so— busy, you know. Their kids will find them a place "as soon as possible," but for a "few weeks" Lucy Cooper will share her granddaughter's room, and her husband Barkley will sleep on a son's living room sofa. He is in New York City, she is in a small country town.

They talk on the phone. They write. As time passes and they wear out their welcomes, Lucy (Beulah Bondi) discovers that her son George (Thomas Mitchell) and his wife Anita (Fay Bainter) are thinking of sending her to a rest home. It's decided that Barkley (Victor Moore) will take the train to California to stay with the unseen daughter. This is all "just for now," of course.

The movie is not a melodramatic tearjerker. It's so tough it might not be filmable today, when even Alzheimer's stories have happy endings. The director, Leo McCarey, made his name with laughter and uplift. He was the first to pair Laurel and Hardy, he directed the best Marx Brothers's movie (*Duck Soup*), he made those films our priest sent us to see, *Going My Way* and *Bells of St. Mary's*. In the same year as *Make Way for Tomorrow*, he made Cary Grant a star in *The Awful Truth*. When McCarey won the Best Director Oscar for the latter, Peter Bogdanovich tells us, he stood up and said, "You gave it to me for the wrong picture."

Make Way for Tomorrow is quietly observant about the social awkwardness of the situation. None of the children are cruel. They all speak with their parents kindly. There are no villains. But Anita holds bridge classes in her living room, for perhaps 20 students. When Lucy comes in to sit in a rocking chair, it creaks. The players are distracted. When she tries to make conversation, she talks about hearts, which she played instead of bridge. When Bark calls, everyone can hear her speaking into the phone, and what they hear is sad. Lucy means well. Anita knows she does. But it's not working out. If only she would stay in "her" room—which the young daughter feels territorial about. Anita and the daughter take turns trying to shift an overlarge portrait of Bark back and forth between the bedroom and living room. When your house has been "decorated," you don't want old-fashioned portraits.

At his son's expensive New York apartment, Bark develops a cold while sleeping on the sofa. A doctor is called, and his daughter-in-law quickly moves him into the couple's bedroom, tucking him in so the doctor won't learn the truth. He receives a visit from the only friend he's made, an old Jewish store owner (Maurice Moscovitch) who sizes up the situation and whose reaction is perfectly summarized by McCarey in one significant gesture only Bark can see.

The fact is, old people don't fit in the modern lifestyle. The fault is with the lifestyle, but there you have it. In traditional societies, families often lived in the same house, children taking over as their parents passed on. In my life and in my family I've seen this, but you don't see it much anymore. "Seniors" in TV ads are tanned, fit, and sexy, playing golf, happy they planned for their futures. If they're not struck by lightning on the golf course, they'll grow old and sick, health costs will melt away their savings, and they'll end up living in a "home," whether it's on the county or not. The happy stars of the seniors ads from the 1990s aren't so photogenic today.

Yet the movie plays fair, if you can call it that. When Lucy unsettles the students in the bridge class, Bondi doesn't make her cute or lovable. We catch ourselves thinking she really *is* a nuisance. She might get on our nerves, too. Of course we always identify ourselves with the children, not the parents. In our society we think it proper that children move out on their own, and we say empty nesters are at last free to enjoy their golden years. But what kind of a life is it when every nest is empty? Don't old ears need to hear chirps?

The great final arc of *Make Way for Tomorrow* is beautiful and heart-breaking. It's easy to imagine it being sentimentalized by a studio executive, being made more upbeat for the audience. That's not McCarey. What happens is wonderful and very sad. Everything depends on the performances. Beulah Bondi was not yet 50 when she played Lucy (with makeup by Wally Westmore) and Victor Moore was 61. In appearance, movement, and performance, they are very convincingly old. In the film they're around 70. That was thought a much older age in 1937 than it seems today.

Their children arrange for them to meet in the city before Bark gets on the train for California, where his daughter has "found a nice place for him." This is "only until they can get together again," of course. These lies make it possible for us to get through life. Often we're lying to ourselves. There's a family dinner planned for the evening, but Bark and Lucy make their own plans. What they do and how it makes us feel is a tribute to the artists. It isn't ramped up for easy smiles. It doesn't give us any consolation. They're happy, but not deceived. The Japanese might describe their hours together as *mono no aware*, which is roughly "a bittersweet sadness at the passing of all things."

It's said this film inspired Yasujiro Ozu's *Tokyo Story*, the only film that ever made my students cry. This one might do the same. Entertainment is about the way things should be. Art is about the way they are. The closing passages of *Make Way for Tomorrow* depend on deep empathy between the filmmakers and the characters. They respect them. These two people have spent a lifetime together, raised a family, and lived in their own home until Bark got laid off. They've maintained a mutual dignity and they're not about to turn sappy now.

Look at how gently, and with what respect, they treat each other. Observe how certain strangers, caught up in the business and pleasure of their own lives, observe this and glimpse for a second their own futures. See how strangers can be kind—for a moment, anyway, although they too may have parents they don't have room for.

What's so powerful about the film is its level gaze. It calmly, almost dispassionately, regards the situation and how it plays out. No spin. It is the same with *Tokyo Story*. The most powerful films often simply show you events without instructing you how to feel about them. It is remarkable that a film this true and unrelenting was made by Hollywood in 1937.

{ A MAN ESCAPED }

Robert Bresson's films are often about people confronting certain despair. His subject is how they try to prevail in the face of unbearable circumstances. His plots are not about whether they succeed, but how they endure. He tells these stories in an unadorned style, without movie stars, special effects, contrived thrills, and elevated tension. His films, seemingly devoid of audience-pleasing elements, hold many people in a hypnotic grip. There are no "entertainment values" to distract us, only the actual events of the stories themselves. They demonstrate how many films contain only diversions for the eyes and mind, and use only the superficial qualities of their characters.

Consider *A Man Escaped* (1956). Here is a movie about a man condemned to death in 1943 in Montluc, a Nazi prison camp in Lyon, inside German-occupied France. In a shot that comes even before the titles, we learn that 7,000 men were killed there during the war. Then we meet the captured Resistance fighter Fontaine (François Leterrier), who has every reason to believe he will be one of them. The character is based on a postwar memoir by André Devigny, who escaped from Montluc on the very day he was scheduled to die.

If you saw this man sit on his bunk and stare at the wall, or hold his head in his hands, you would not blame him. What are his options? His cell is small, the walls and door are thick, the prison walls are high, the Nazi guards are outside. He is in solitary confinement most of the day, although sometimes he can tap out messages in a code, or secretly exchange notes during washing-up time. During the period of his confinement another man he has "met" this way is shot trying to escape.

Fontaine's method is to use Bresson's own method: the close scrutiny of salient details. In his films there are no "beauty shots." No effects. No emphasis on the physical appearances of the actors. No fancy zooms or other shots that call attention. He uses the basic vocabulary of long, medium, close, and insert shots to tell what needs to be told about every scene. No shock cutaways. Reality-based, calm editing.

In this way, we watch Fontaine examine his cell. We know it as well as he does. We see how he stands on a shelf to look out a high, barred window. We see how the food plates enter and leave, and how the guards can see him through a peephole. We see the routine as prisoners are marched to morning wash-up.

What we don't see much of are the Nazi guards. Their figures appear in some shots, of course, but no point is made of them. None becomes a notable character. None has a name. Dialogue is disembodied. There are none of the usual clichés about the sadistic guard or the friendly guard. Even few of the other prisoners become very familiar to us; Fontaine sees them in passing. Although men are killed in the prison, it doesn't happen onscreen. No ominous set-ups. Just offscreen sounds.

Therefore most of what happens takes place in Fontaine's cell, as it must. By looking intently at every detail, Fontaine devises a way to get through the door, and then, he hopes, get over the wall. I won't tell you what he does, which is what the movie is largely about. He doesn't attempt his escape alone, but I won't describe the other man, except to observe that Fontaine feels he must either try to bring him along or kill him. By trusting him, Bresson has Fontaine demonstrate a faith in a fellow human that is central to what he has to say in the film. Indeed, if Fontaine had not brought him along, it's a good question whether his escape could succeed.

François Leterrier, playing Fontaine, is a man of ordinary appearance. Bresson did not choose to work with stars. Indeed, many stars might have been unhappy with his way of describing actors as "models." Their role in a Bresson film is to embody a character, perform the physical actions, look plausible, and not draw undue attention. He wanted no "acting." Whatever an actor did in bringing style or eccentricity to a role was unnecessary. It was all about the fact of the character, his situation and his behavior. Yes, we all love movie stars. But to some degree every shot they're in is about them. They don't get called back if nobody notices them. That's why even extras dream of little bits of "business." In theory, you should be able to see a Bresson film, go to dinner with the actor two days later, and not recognize him.

This has been an unusual movie review, mostly describing what *doesn't* happen. Is the film therefore a static bore? Few films have seemed more absorbing to me. A man will die, or escape. Here is his cell. He has the desire. He uses his mind. We follow him every second of the way. There is a sparse narration, presumably based on André Devigny's original book, but it describes only what actually happens and expresses no abstract thinking.

Watching a film like *A Man Escaped* is like a lesson in the cinema. It teaches by demonstration all the sorts of things that are not necessary in a movie. By implication, it suggests most of the things we're accustomed to are superfluous. I can't think of a single unnecessary shot in *A Man Escaped*.

If you removed the unnecessary shots from, say, Michael Bay's *Transformers: Revenge of the Fallen*, you would be left with two much shorter films: (1) a montage of the special effects action, which is all some people are interested in; (2) a montage of plot points and essential explanatory dialogue, which would be much shorter than (1). The entire film is a smash-up between those two little films.

What have you learned at the end of the Bay film? Nothing, because the characters and the robots are flatly impossible. There may be value in overcooked hyperaction, and I'm not saying there isn't. I've hugely enjoyed some action films for what they were. I admire *A Man Escaped* for what it is, for what it isn't, and for what I learned from it.

What was that? In a famous book by Paul Schrader, *Transcendental Style in Film*, three directors are considered: Yasujiro Ozu, Robert Bresson, Carl Dreyer. Schrader feels transcendentalism is embedded in their work. Rather than involve ourselves in a deep discussion of transcendentalism, we might profitably start at the kindergarten level. The simplest parable for existentialism can be found in Albert Camus's *The Myth of Sisyphus*. He takes only 120 pages, but we need only a paragraph:

Sisyphus was a man condemned to spend his life pushing a stone up a mountain and seeing it roll back down again. At the bottom of the mountain, I suggest, is death. Pushing the stone is life. It is tempting to give up on the bloody stone, but Camus (also a supporter of the Resistance) said that it was necessary to revolt. In Montluc, 7,000 men died, but Fontaine did not agree he need be one of them. Even if he were crushed by the stone rolling downhill over him, at least he tried. It is probably relevant to this film that Bresson himself was a member of the Resistance and was imprisoned by the Nazis.

THE MAN WHO SHOT
LIBERTY VALANCE

John Ford and John Wayne together created much of the mythology of the Old West we carry in our minds. Beginning with *Stagecoach* (1939), continuing from 1948 through 1950 with the Cavalry Trilogy (*Fort Apache, She Wore a Yellow Ribbon*, and *Rio Grande*), and finally to 1962 and *The Man Who Shot Liberty Valance*, together in 10 features they largely formed the templates of the Hollywood Western. Of these *Liberty Valance* was the most pensive and thoughtful.

The film takes place at that turning point in the West when the rule of force gave way to the rule of law, and when literacy began to gain a foothold. It asks the question: Does a man need to carry a gun in order to disagree or state an opinion? It takes place in the town of Shinbone, in an unnamed territory that is moving toward a vote on statehood. Farmers want statehood. Cattlemen do not. In a few characters and a gripping story, Ford dramatizes the debate about guns that still continues in many Western states. That he does this by mixing in history, humorous supporting characters, and a poignant romance is typical; his films were complete and self-contained in a way that approaches perfection. Without ever seeming to hurry, he doesn't include a single gratuitous shot.

Three men stand at the center of the story: Stoddard, Doniphon, and Valance. As the film opens, US Senator Ransom Stoddard (James Stewart) arrives in Shinbone by the new railroad with his wife Hallie (Vera Miles) to attend the funeral of a man named Tom Doniphon (John Wayne). The corpse is being held in a plain pine box, and when he views it Stoddard is angered to see the boots have been stolen. An old black cowboy named Pompey (Woody Strode) takes Hallie on a buckboard ride into the countryside where they regard the burned-out remains of Doniphon's cottage. It's clear they loved him.

In a long flashback involving most of the film, Ford recalls the events leading up to that day. Years ago Shinbone was held in a grip of terror by the sadistic Liberty Valance (played by Lee Marvin in a performance evoking savage cruelty). He had many murders on his conscience and much enjoyed using a leather bullwhip. Tom Doniphon is a local farmer, who observes, "Liberty Valance's the toughest man south of the Picketwire—next to me." Valance and his two sidekicks hold up a stagecoach on the way to town, and when one of the passengers, Ransom, stands up to him Liberty nearly whips him to death.

In town, he's nursed back to health by Nora and Peter Ericson, two recent Swedish immigrants who run the local chowhouse. We also meet Link Appleyard (Andy Devine), the drunken town marshal; Doc Willoughby (Ken Murray), the drunken town doctor; and Dutton Peabody (Edmond O'Brien), the editor of the paper. All three spend much of their time hanging out in the restaurant kitchen. Working in the restaurant is young Hallie.

Stoddard has come to town with a satchel full of law books and hangs out his shingle at the newspaper office. Liberty Valance cannot abide anyone standing up to him, and the shingle is an affront. Valance gives him a choice: leave town, or face him in a shootout on Main Street. Keeping to one side, Tom Doniphon observes everything but is slow to act; his strength is silently coiled. Besides, there is a complication. Tom has long considered Hallie "my girl," and is adding a room to his farmhouse that has a nice porch with a rocking chair in preparation for the day he has no doubt she will marry him. Now Hallie has started to like this lawyer-man from the East, who starts up a one-room schoolhouse to teach people how to read. His illiterate students include Hallie.

As a showdown between Stoddard and Valance begins to seem inevitable, Ford creates considerable tension. I will not go into details because the suspense should not be spoiled. Look instead at a debate that continues between the lawyer and the farmer about guns. Ransom Stoddard believes in the US Constitution, the rule by law, the trust in government. Tom Doniphon tells him that without a gun in his hand and the experience to use it, he will sooner or later certainly be killed by Valance. Stoddard believes so firmly in the law that he is willing to lose his life for his principles. The drunken marshal won't protect him. The newspaper editor prints the truth about Valance, and for his pains has his office trashed and is whipped nearly dead.

This is fascism against democracy: the tyranny of the strongman over the ordinary people. Everyone in Shinbone hates Liberty Valance, but they're powerless against him and his two sidekicks, one of them a giggling fool. Tom could stand up to Valance, but it would suit him to have Stoddard out of the way so that he could bring Hallie home to that porch with its rocking chair.

There is a purity to the John Ford style. His composition is classical. He arranges his characters within the frame to reflect power dynamics—or sometimes to suggest a balance is changing. His magnificent Western landscapes are always there, but as environment, not travelogue. He films mostly on sets, but we're not particularly aware. In a film with Lee Marvin's snarl, Andy Devine's squeaky voice, and the accent of the Swedes, John Wayne as usual provides the calm center, never trying for an effect. (One stylistic touch: in this film, he habitually calls Stoddard "Pilgrim," which expresses an insight into the lawyer's character.)

Ford's view of women is interesting. Shinbone is the only Western town I've seen in a movie with no prostitutes. Indeed Hallie and Nora Ericson (Jeanette Nolan) are the only two noticeable women in town; little wonder Tom's love for Hallie is intense. As played by Jimmy Stewart, Stoddard spends much of the film wearing an apron and washing dishes in the restaurant, sending a hardly ambiguous message about a man who doesn't wear a gun.

The way Ford employs the African-American Pompey is worth noting. The tall, confident Woody Strode appeared in five Ford pictures, all the way from *Stagecoach* to Ford's final film, *7 Women* (1966). It is made clear in *Liberty Valance* that segregation was the practice in the territory. When a meeting is held to vote on statehood, Pompey sits outside on the porch. When he walks into a bar to fetch Tom, the bartender won't serve him, and Tom slams hard on the bar: "Give him a drink." But Pompey won't drink. He is Tom's farmhand and seems to be his only confidant, a protective presence; he always has Tom's back. Ford isn't making an anachronistic statement on racism, but he's being sure we notice it.

There's a lot in the film if we care to notice. "*The Man Who Shot Liberty Valance*," the *New Yorker*'s Richard Brody writes, "is the greatest American political movie." He explains: "The Western is intrinsically the most political movie genre, because, like Plato's *Republic*, it is concerned with the founding of cities, and because it depicts the various abstract functions of government as direct, physical actions." This is all to be seen: the role of a free press, the function of a town meeting, the debate about statehood, the civilizing influence of education.

It's not saying too much to note that Ransom Stoddard is elected to the US Senate because he is "The Man Who Shot Liberty Valance." Yes, but there's more to it than that, and in John Ford's mind, gun ownership is very much an open question. The screenplay by James Warner Bellah and Willis Goldbeck contains one of the best-known lines of dialogue in any Ford movie, spoken to Stoddard years later by the town's new newspaper editor: "This is the West, sir. When the legend becomes fact, print the legend."

MAN WITH A
MOVIE CAMERA

In 1929, the year it was released, films had an average shot length (ASL) of 11.2 seconds. *Man with a Movie Camera* had an ASL of 2.3 seconds. The ASL of Michael Bay's *Armageddon* was—also 2.3 seconds. Why would I begin a discussion of a silent classic by discussing such a mundane matter? It helps to understand the impact the film made at the time. Viewers had never seen anything like it, and Mordaunt Hall, the horrified author of the *New York Times* review, wrote: "The producer, Dziga Vertov, does not take into consideration the fact that the human eye fixes for a certain space of time that which holds the attention." This reminds me of Harry Carey's advice in 1929 to John Wayne, as the talkies were coming in: "Stop halfway through every sentence. The audience can't listen that fast."

Man with a Movie Camera is fascinating for many better reasons than its ASL, but let's begin with the point Dziga Vertov was trying to make. He felt film was locked into the tradition of stage plays, and it was time to discover a new style that was specifically cinematic. Movies could move with the speed of our minds when we are free-associating, or with the speed of a passionate musical composition. They did not need any dialogue—and indeed, at the opening of the film he pointed out that it had no scenario, no intertitles, and no characters. It was a series of images, and his notes specified a fast-moving musical score.

There was an overall plan. He would show 24 hours in a single day of a Russian city. It took him four years to film this day, and he worked in three cities: Moscow, Kiev, and Odessa. His wife Yelizaveta Svilova supervised the editing from about 1,775 separate shots—all the more impressive because most of the shots consisted of separate set-ups. The cinematography was by his brother, Mikhail Kaufman, who refused to ever work with him again. (Vertov was born Denis Kaufman, and worked under a name meaning "spinning top." Another brother, Boris Kaufman, immigrated to Hollywood and won an Oscar for filming *On the Waterfront*.)

Born in 1896 and coming of age during the Russian Revolution, Vertov considered himself a radical artist in a decade where modernism and surrealism were gaining stature in all the arts. He began by editing official newsreels, which he assembled into montages that must have appeared rather surprising to some audiences, and then started making his own films. He would invent an entirely new style. Perhaps he did. "It stands as a stinging indictment of almost every film made between its release in 1929 and the appearance of Godard's *Breathless* 30 years later," the critic Neil Young wrote, "and Vertov's dazzling picture seems, today, arguably the fresher of the two." Godard is said to have introduced the "jump cut," but Vertov's film is entirely jump cuts.

There is a temptation to review the film simply by listing what you will see in it. Machinery, crowds, boats, buildings, production line workers, streets, beaches, crowds, hundreds of individual faces, planes, trains, automobiles, and so on. But these shots have an organizing pattern. *Man with a Movie Camera* opens with an empty cinema, its seats standing at attention. The seats swivel down (by themselves), and an audience hurries in and fills them. They begin to look at a film. This film. And this film is about—this film being made.

The only continuing figure—not a "character"—is the Man with the Movie Camera. He uses an early hand-cranked model, smaller than the one Buster Keaton uses in *The Cameraman* (1928), although even that one is light enough to be balanced on the shoulder with its tripod. This Man is seen photographing many of the shots in the movie. Then there are shots of how he does it—securing the tripod and himself to the top of an automobile or the bed of a speeding truck, stooping to walk through a coal mine, hanging in a basket over a waterfall. We see a hole being dug between two train tracks, and later a train racing straight towards the camera. We're reminded that when the earliest movie audiences saw such a shot, they were allegedly terrified, and ducked down in their seats.

Intercut with this are shots of this film being edited. The machinery. The editor. The physical film itself. Sometimes the action halts with a freeze-frame, and we see that the editor has stopped work. But that's later—placing it right after the freeze-frame would seem too much like continuity. If there is no continuity, there is a gathering rhythmic speed that reaches a crescendo nearer the end. The film has shot itself, edited itself, and now is conducting itself at an accelerating tempo.

Most movies strive for what John Ford called "invisible editing"—edits that are at the service of the storytelling, and do not call attention to themselves. Even with a shock cut in a horror film, we are focused on the subject of the shot, not the shot itself. Considered as a visual object, *Man with a Movie Camera* deconstructs this process. It assembles itself in plain view. It is about itself, and folds into and out of itself like origami. It was in 1912 that Marcel Duchamp shocked the art world with his painting *Nude Descending a Staircase*. It wasn't shocked by nudity—the painting was too abstract to show any. They were shocked that he depicted the descent in a series of steps taking place all at the same time. In a way, he had invented the freeze-frame.

What Vertov did was elevate this avant-garde freedom to a level encompassing his entire film. That is why the film seems fresh today; 80 years later, it *is* fresh. There had been "city documentaries" earlier, showing a day in the life of a metropolis; one of the most famous was *Berlin: Symphony of a Great City* (1927).

By filming in three cities and not naming any of them, Vertov had a wider focus: his film was about the City, and the Cinema, and the Man with a Movie Camera. It was about the act of seeing, being seen, preparing to see, processing what had been seen, and finally seeing it. It made explicit and poetic the astonishing gift the cinema made possible, of arranging what we see, ordering it, imposing a rhythm and language on it, and transcending it. Godard once said, "The cinema is life at 24 frames per second." Wrong. That's what life is. The Cinema only starts with the 24 frames—and besides, in the silent era it was closer to 18 fps. It's what you do *after* you have your frames that makes it Cinema.

The experience of *Man with a Movie Camera* is unthinkable without the participation of music. Virtually every silent film was seen with music, if only from a single piano, accordion, or violin. The Mighty Wurlitzer, with its sound effects and different musical voices, was invented for movies.

The version available in the United States is from Kino, and features a score by composer Michael Nyman ("The Piano"). It was performed by the Michael Nyman Band on May 17, 2002, at London's Royal Festival Hall. As the tempo mounts, it takes on a relentless momentum. Another score was created by the Cinematic Orchestra, and you can hear it while viewing nine minutes of the film here: http://www.youtube.com/watch?v=vv TF6B5XKxQ

A famous score was created by the Alloy Orchestra of Cambridge, Massachusetts, which devotes itself to accompanying silent cinema. To mark the 80th anniversary of the film, the Alloy obtained and restored a print from the Moscow Film Archive and performed their revised score in the city. They will tour with the print in 2010.

THE MATCH
FACTORY GIRL

This poor girl. I wanted to reach out my arms and hug her. That was during the first half of *The Match Factory Girl* (1990). Then my sympathy began to wane. By the end of the film, I think it's safe to say Iris gives as good as she gets.

The film begins with a big log. In documentary style, we see what happens to it. It has its bark stripped off. Blades shave thin sheets from it. These sheets are chopped into matchsticks and divided and stacked and dipped and arrayed and portioned into boxes, which are labeled, packed into larger boxes, and labeled again. That's where Iris comes in. At first we see only her hands, straightening labels, sticking them down, removing duplicates. Then we see her face, which reflects absolutely no emotion.

The Finnish director Aki Kaurismäki fascinates me. I am never sure if he intends us to laugh or cry with his characters—both, I suppose. He often portrays unremarkable lives of unrelenting grimness, sadness, desolation. When his characters are not tragic, he elevates them to such levels as stupidity, cluelessness, self-delusion, or mental illness. Iris, the match factory girl, incorporates all of these attributes.

She is played by the actress Kati Outinen, a Kaurismäki favorite who has often starred for him. Whatever it is she does, she is very good at it. His camera stares at her, and she stares back. She is a pale blonde, slender, with a receding chin and eyes set deep in pools of mascara. If she were to laugh, that would be as novel as when Garbo talked for the first time. It would be easy to describe her as "plain," but you know, she would have a pretty face if she ever animated it with a personality. In *The Match Factory Girl* she is deadpan and passive, a person who is accustomed to misery.

Her job at the match factory is boring and thankless. She is one of the few humans among the machines. She takes the tram home to Factory Lane, where a shabby alley door admits her to the two-room apartment she shares with her mother and stepfather. They sit in a stupor watching the news on TV. Her mother smokes mechanically, so listless long ashes gather on her cigarette. Iris cooks dinner, serves it, and sits down with them. A soup has pieces of meat in it, and her mother reaches out a fork and stabs a bite from Iris's plate. She is expected to do all the cleaning, sleep on the sofa, and pay rent.

In the evenings she goes out seeking companionship and is ignored. At a club, nobody asks her to dance. In a bar, she locks eyes with a bearded man. His gaze is aggressive, not affectionate. They sleep with one another. He never calls her again. She goes to his flat to indicate she cares for him. He tells her, "Nothing could touch me less than your affection." That's all he ever says to her. Her stepfather says less. "Whore," he calls her, after she spends some of her paycheck on a pretty red frock.

I watched hypnotically. Few films are ever this unremittingly unyielding. I found myself as tightly gripped as with a good thriller. I could hardly believe the litany of horrors. What made it more mesmerizing is that it's all on the same tonal level: Iris passively endures a series of humiliations, cruelties, and dismissals. This cannot be tragedy because she lacks the stature to be a heroine. It cannot be comedy because she doesn't get the joke. What can it be?

Kaurismäki has made many films with hapless characters. When I see each one it makes me eager for the next. I suppose my description makes this one sound depressing, but although it is about a depressed woman it is always challenging us, nudging, teasing our incredulity. When Kaurismäki has an entry in a film festival, I will make it my business to see it.

I've reviewed four of his other films: *Ariel* ("the character's lack of physical and social finesse is a positive quality"); *Lights in the Dusk* ("his characters are dour, speak little, expect the worst, smoke too much, are ill-treated by life, are passive in the face of tragedy"); *Drifting Clouds* ("he wants his characters to always seem a little too large for their rooms and furniture"); and *The Man Without a Past* ("He finds a community of people who live in shipping containers. There is a kind of landlord, who agrees to rent him one").

Not all of these films are as dour as *The Match Factory Girl*. Some of his characters are more resilient. I never get the idea he hates them; in fact, I think he loves them, and feels they deserve to be seen in his movies because they are invisible to other directors. In making them, he seems to be consciously resisting all the patterns and expectations we have learned from other movies. He makes no conventional attempt to "entertain." That's why he's so entertaining. He wants only to hold our interest. He wants us to decide why he chooses such misfits, loners, and outsiders, and to ask how they endure their lives. Even those who are not victims have a passive acceptance bordering on masochism. Life has dealt them a losing hand, and that's how it is.

Kaurismäki's camera work is meticulous. He composes without any eagerness to put elements in or leave elements out; his camera simply votes "present," and gazes with the same dispassionate eyes that Iris has. An image is there before us. We see it. There you have it. We can draw our own conclusions. He doesn't go in for reaction shots, or perhaps it would be more fair to say that every shot is a reaction shot. Asked at a film festival why he moves his camera so little, he explained: "That's a nuisance when you have a hangover."

He is often compared to Robert Bresson, who also made films about isolated, lonely characters (*Mouchette* about a village outcast; *Diary of a Country Priest* about a disliked and unsuccessful young priest; *Au Hasard Balthazar* about a mistreated donkey). Both directors use an objective gaze. Both move deliberately. (Told he must have been influenced by Bresson, Kaurismäki said, "I want to make him seem like a director of epic action pictures.") Actually few directors are more different. Bresson's films are deeply empathetic, spiritual, transcendental. Kaurismäki seems detached from his characters. Most of his films could open with the title card, "Here's another sad sack."

But there's something concealed beneath the attitude of detachment. He invites us to peer closely at these people he pins so precisely to the screen. What does it say that there can be such lives? How do people endure it? How do some of his characters even prevail? In *Drifting Clouds*, again starring Kati Outinen as a luckless waitress with a jinxed husband, there is actually dark humor in the way the clouds are always dark and rainy. As sad as her life is, the film is immensely amusing in its over the top bad luck. When her luck changes at the end, it's thanks to the Helsinki Workers' Wrestlers Association.

Growing up in Finland Kaurismäki would certainly have heard Hans Christian Andersen's story "The Little Match Girl." It told the story of a waif in the cold on Christmas Eve, trying to sell matches so her father will not punish her. To keep warm she lights one match after another, and they summon visions which give her comfort. She finally finds happiness of a heartbreaking sort.

In the early scenes of this film Iris doesn't smoke at all. When she finally lights a cigarette—with a match from her factory—it summons visions for her; ideas of revenge. We watch as she acts on these notions. Does she find happiness? That would be asking too much. But she finds . . . satisfaction.

The Match Factory Girl is the third film in Kaurismäki's Proletariat Trilogy. It follows Shadows in Paradise *(1986), about an aimless garbage collector, and* Ariel *(1988), about a coal miner who escapes his subterranean work by turning to crime.*

MON ONCLE
D'AMERIQUE

Three children are born in France. One, Rene, is the son of struggling farmers. One, Janine, a daughter of proletarians. The third son, Jean, is born in a manor house to wealthy bourgeois. These children grow up, are educated, find occupations often against the will of their parents, and enter relationships. They don't much think of themselves as laboratory rats, but they might be surprised how consistently their behavior is consistent with the involuntary responses of a rat. This observation is not intended as an insult to them, or to the rat.

Alain Resnais's *Mon oncle d'Amerique* (1980) is one the New Wave pioneer's best films, a winner of the Grand Prize at Cannes. It is audacious. Beginning with big stars of the time (Gerald Depardieu, Nicole Garcia, Roger Pierre), he tells the life stories of these three in a way that promises to be traditional narrative.

Then he introduces a fourth figure. This is the much older Henri Laborit, a physician, philosopher, and expert on evolutionary psychology. Laborit differs from the others in that he isn't fictional. He plays himself, he speaks directly to the camera, he explains his theories about human behavior and how it's often illuminated by tests involving laboratory animals. He had considerable influence on American market research 50 years ago.

His involvement in the film becomes its most intriguing element, elevating melodrama to the level of rather disturbing insight. We humans are much concerned with whether or not we truly have free will. There are two popular theories: (a) everything we do is predestined, either by God or as a result of the causes and effects of the physical laws of the universe; (b) yes, we have free will, and can do as we choose, within the limits of practical possibility.

I have no idea what Henri Laborit's ideas about God are. I think he believes that our free will is more controlled than we think by instructions from the lower levels of our brain. We do our basic survival functioning at levels formed during the reptilian period, from which we all descend. Our biological behavior is often determined by the conditioning of our mammalian brains, which involve hunger, lust, courtship, territorial competition, and so on. Then humans and to a lesser degree species like chimpanzees and orangutans have a level involving more developed cerebral cortexes. This is where we do our conscious thinking: *I choose to do this, but not that.*

We think we choose. To some degree, we may be preinclined to choose, or even forced to choose. Laborit narrates an experiment involving white rats in a lab. Cute little creatures. One is put in a cage divided in half by a doorway. When an alarm is sounded, the floor where it's standing will produce an electric shock in a few seconds. The rat quickly learns to scamper through the door to avoid the pain. Another alarm, another escape, back and forth. Simple. We would do the same.

Now the door is closed. The alarm sounds. The rat scrambles desperately to escape. No luck. The electric shock occurs. After a time, the rat gives up trying to escape. It crouches hopelessly, trembling slightly from the electrical current. It is passive, defeated, no longer thinking of a way to escape because there is none. Ah, but now it gets interesting. Two rats are placed in the same divided cage. They quickly learn to run back and forth. The door is closed. Both rats struggle to escape. No luck. Then what happens? Do they give up and crouch forlornly side by side? Not at all. *They begin fighting.*

Did you almost forget I was writing about a movie? Resnais shows his characters growing up in response and reaction to their childhoods. The farm child helps to support his family by going to work in a textile mill. He dreams of studying in Paris, but his girlfriend gets pregnant and he remains in the district, eventually becoming in charge of the mill. The girl, a fervent Young Communist, rebels against her parents and runs away to join the theater. Her career goes nowhere, she become the mistress of—the bourgeois boy, now a politician and the head of French national radio. That's also a rebellion against her youthful ideals. The bourgeois was a devout Catholic, but he leaves his wife and children to live with the mistress. Another rebellion. Oh, and when the worker is demoted and shunted to a distant job, he rebels in a refusal to play along with the corporate plans.

So by running away from home, wife, and job, each of the three has exercised free will, correct? Resnais is only getting started. In scenes which play much better than they may sound, he uses humans dressed as giant white rats in reruns of key scenes from other angles. And Resnais uses Laborit's narration to analyze other scenes. It begins to appear as if all three of these modern French citizens, from different social backgrounds, may have been acting instructions beamed in from their vestigial brain centers.

The genius of the film is that even without Laborit and his rats, *Mon oncle d'Amerique* would tell an entertaining story on its own. The characters are sympathetic (given what we know about them), the narrative is well-constructed, and we care. But consider one sequence. In itself it is perfectly absorbing. Then see how Resnais deconstructs it. Jean was raised by his grandfather on an island. He tells Janine he will take her there one day. Two years after they break up, they meet by chance on the island. They cross at low tide to a little nearby island. The tide returns, but as they're returning they pause to continue a fight, and are threatened with being stranded.

Hmm. Considering what we know about how they got together, and why and how they split up, and what each one knows and doesn't know, their behavior on this day, which seems so spontaneous, becomes almost compelled by the same conditioning process suffered by the rats. And then we cycle back through other events in the film, seeing those in a new light. I used the word "deconstruction." That can sometimes apply to the study of films in terms of story structure, conventional devices, social meanings, and so on. What Resnais seems to be hinting is that the characters in a movie, and the people who make it, and those who watch it, may all be acting to some degree on impulses imbedded untold millennia ago on the shores of lonely seas.

Alain Resnais was born in 1922 and as recently as May 2009 won the Special Jury prize for his new film, *Wild Grass*. At the dawn of the New Wave he gained fame for films such as *Hiroshima, mon Amour* and *Last Year at Marienbad*. He confessed once to me that he's crazy about comic books. He makes great and sometimes weighty films but is not lacking in a quixotic humor, and *Mon oncle d'Amerique* is in some ways a comedy. Also a film that has you discussing for long afterward, and not in the terms you use for most films.

And now my article is completed. It's about the right length, and I'll dispatch it to my editor in plenty of time. In all the years since I won my first newspaper job in high school, I've never missed a single deadline. I like to think that's because I choose not to. I wonder. And you, who are not very good about making deadlines, don't be too quick to blame yourself. Pin it on the turtles. By the way, the American uncle never shows up.

{ MONSIEUR HIRE }

Patrice Leconte's *Monsieur Hire* (1989) is a tragedy about loneliness and erotomania, told about two solitary people who have nothing else in common. It involves a murder, and the opening shot is of a corpse. Monsieur Hire is a scrawny, balding, middle-aged tailor who lives by himself. Alice is a beautiful, tender-hearted, 22-year-old blonde who lives alone across the courtyard from Hire in the same apartment building.

On the night of the murder, a slight man was seen by witnesses running toward the building. In his investigation among its residents, a police detective learns that nobody likes Hire. Hire is the first to agree. He admits he seems to strike people oddly. As a neighbor from across the hall peeks at him from his doorway, he asks, "Want a photo?" As he walks through his courtyard, white powder is dumped on his impeccable black suit.

Everything about Hire (Michel Blanc) is impeccable: his suit, his tie, the shine on his shoes, the fringe of his hair so neatly trimmed. Alice (Sandrine Bonnaire) is sunny, open-faced, with a warm smile. One night during a thunderstorm a flash of lightning reveals a man watching her from the shadows of the apartment opposite. This is Hire, who watches her for hour after hour, night after night: sleeping, waking up, dressing, undressing, ironing her clothes, making love with her lout of a boyfriend, Emile (Luc Thuillier).

What does she do when she discovers this? The screenplay is based on *Monsieur Hire's Engagement* by Georges Simenon, but it's nothing like his Inspector Maigret *policiers*, much more of a traditional novel with carefully observed behavior and details. Simenon was fascinated by peculiarities of human personality, which he described in elegant, simple prose, not unlike Leconte's controlled visual style here.

The film is in color, but Hire's world is black and white: his suits, shirts, the white mice he keeps in a little cage in his tailor shop. His skin is so pale he might never go outside in daytime. Alice, on the other hand, likes red: her clothing, her lipstick, the grocery bag of ripe tomatoes she "drops" on a staircase so they roll toward Hire as he opens his door. Does he leap to assist her? No, he simply stands and regards her. What is the purpose of her contrivance?

Another day, she knocks on his door, but he doesn't answer. He must know it's her because he never has visitors and he must realize she's just left her own apartment. She knocks the next day, and he invites her to visit a restaurant—in a train station, which may be a clue to certain of his thoughts. Eventually he confirms that, yes, he has seen her and her boyfriend making love. And he witnessed something else that he believes explains her sudden and unexpected friendliness toward him.

So it may, at first. But Alice's feelings for him grow more complicated, and she is touched by his declaration of love. Her boyfriend Emile, on the other hand, is a crude physical type whose idea of a perfect date is taking her to a boxing match and ignoring her. Later, when he needs to sneak out of a window quickly, he steps first in a cradle formed by her hands, and then on her shoulders. Hire shares his secrets with Alice. He makes considerable use of prostitutes, he tells her, and as he describes the process of a bordello her face reflects fascination, perhaps that a man like Hire could have such erotic experiences and describe them so sensuously. But he can never visit a prostitute again, he explains, because he has fallen in love with her.

Hire is a man with many secrets. One night in the course of the police inspector's investigation, he takes him along to a bowling alley, where he rolls strike after strike flawlessly, even backwards between his legs, even blindfolded, and is applauded by the regulars who have seen this before. He collects a payment from the owner, joins the cop at the bar, tosses back a shot, and says, "You see? I'm not disliked everywhere."

What's going on between Hire and Alice? For that matter, what are her feelings for the boyfriend, Emile? That relationship seems pretty standard for a film noir; he seems to be a witless small-time criminal, and only her loyalty can save him. Her devotion to him is pointless and undeserved, as far as we can see, and although sex figures between them, she's too complex for that to explain everything. She's never met a man whose love for her is more profound and devoted (and obsessive) than Hire's. Emile wouldn't even be able to understand it.

At the center of this film is great sadness, captured in a late fast-motion shot that slows for an instant to show a detail lingered on in heartbreaking slow motion. Then the ending wraps everything up, but not to everyone's satisfaction.

Patrice Leconte, born in 1947, is one of the most versatile of French directors. He switches styles and genres from film to film, and you may be a fan of his without realizing it. *Monsieur Hire* (1989) was his first considerable success, premiered at Cannes, which is where I saw it. He also made *Ridicule* (1996), about a provincial landowner during the reign of Louis XVI, who seeks to win the favor of the court by practicing the quick wit much loved by the king; *The Widow of Saint-Pierre* (2000), about a condemned killer awaiting death on a French-Canadian island until an executioner can be imported from Paris; *Man on the Train* (2002) with Jean Rochefort and Johnny Hallyday as a suave provincial gentleman's chance encounter with a thief; and another of my Great Movies, *The Hairdresser's Husband* (1990), again starring Rochefort as a man so enraptured by a small town hairdresser that he marries her, buys her a beauty parlor, and requires only that he be allowed to sit in it, day after day, adoring her.

"I don't think that a filmmaker is manipulating puppets," Leconte told me at the 2002 Toronto Film Festival. "On the contrary, I believe a filmmaker is more like a chemist. You mix elements that have nothing to do with each other and you see what will happen. The starting point for *The Man on the Train* was the meeting of the two actors. Put in a few drops of Johnny

Hallyday, a few drops of Jean Rochefort and look what happens. Sometimes it blows up in your face."

I asked him an obligatory question about the French New Wave and he said, "Well, I didn't know Truffaut at all. I never met him, because he died too early probably. One of the things that I loved most about Truffaut was that he loved movies. And I would like that on my tomb: *This man loved to make movies.*"

{ MULHOLLAND DR. }

It's well known that David Lynch's *Mulholland Dr.* (2001) was assembled from the remains of a cancelled TV series, with the addition of some additional footage filmed later. That may be taken by some viewers as a way to explain the film's fractured structure and lack of continuity. I think it's a delusion to imagine a "complete" film lurking somewhere in Lynch's mind—a ghostly director's cut that exists only in his original intentions. The film is openly dreamlike, and like most dreams it moves uncertainly down a path with many turnings.

It seems to be the dream of Betty (Naomi Watts), seen in the first shots sprawled on a bed. It continues with the story of how Betty came to Hollywood and how she ended up staying in the apartment of her aunt, but if we are within a dream there is no reason to believe that on a literal level. It's as likely she only dreams of getting off a flight from Ontario to Los Angeles, being wished good luck by the cackling old couple who met her on the plane, and arriving by taxi at the apartment. Dreams cobble their contents from the materials at hand, and although the old folks turn up again at the end of the film, their actual existence may be problematic.

The movie seems seductively realistic in several opening scenes, however, as an ominous film noir sequence shows a beautiful woman in the backseat of a limousine on Mulholland Drive—that serpentine road that coils along the spine of the hills separating the city from the San Fernando Valley. The limo pulls over, the driver pulls a gun and orders his passenger out of the car, and just then two drag-racing hot rods hurtle into view and one of them strikes the limo, killing the driver and his partner. The stunned woman (Laura Elena Herring) staggers into some shrubbery and starts to climb down the hill—first crossing Franklin Dr., finally arriving at Sunset. Still hiding in shrubbery, she sees a woman leaving an apartment to get into a taxi, and she sneaks into the apartment and hides under a table.

Who is she? Let's not get ahead of her. The very first moments of the film seemed like a bizarre montage from a jitterbug contest on a 1950s TV show, and the hot rods and their passengers visually link with that. But people don't dress like jitterbuggers and drag race on Mulholland at the time of the film (the 1990s), not in now-priceless antique hot rods, and the crash seems to have elements imported from an audition, perhaps, that will later be made much of.

I won't further try your patience with more of this mix-and-match. Dreams need not make sense, I am not Freud, and at this point in the film it's working perfectly well as a film noir. They need not make sense, either. Conventional movie cops turn up, investigate, and disappear for the rest of the film. Betty discovers the woman from Mulholland taking a shower in her aunt's apartment and demands to know who she is. The woman sees a poster of Rita Hayworth in *Gilda* on the wall and replies, "Rita." She claims to have amnesia. Betty now responds with almost startling generosity, deciding to help "Rita" discover her identity, and in a smooth segue the two women bond. Indeed, before long they're helping each other sneak into apartment #17. Lynch has shifted gears from a film noir to a much more innocent kind of crime story, a Nancy Drew mystery. When they find the decomposing corpse in #17, however, that's a little more detailed than Nancy Drew's typical discoveries.

What I've been doing is demonstrating the way *Mulholland Dr.* affects a lot of viewers. They start rehearsing the plot to themselves, hoping that if they retrace their steps they can determine where they are and how they got there. This movie doesn't work that way. Each step has a way of being like an open elevator door with no elevator inside.

Unsatisfied by my understanding of the film, I took it to an audience that hadn't failed me for 30 years. At the Conference on World Affairs at the University of Colorado at Boulder, I did my annual routine: showing a title on Monday afternoon, and then sifting through it a scene at a time, sometimes a shot at a time, for the next four afternoons. It drew a full house, and predictably a lot of readings and interpretations. Yet even my old friend who was forever finding everything to be a version of Homer's *Odyssey* was uncertain this time.

I gave my usual speech about how you can't take an interpretation to a movie. You have to find it there already. No consensus emerged about what we had found. It was a tribute to Lynch that the movie remained compulsively watchable while refusing to yield to interpretation. The most promising direction we tried was to delineate the boundaries of the dream(s) and the identities of the dreamer(s).

That was an absorbing exercise, but then consider the series of shots in which the film loses focus and then the women's faces begin to merge. I was reminded of Bergman's *Persona*, also a film about two women. At a point when one deliberately causes an injury to the other, the film seems to catch on fire in the projector. The screen goes black, and then the film starts again with images from the earliest days of silent film. What is Bergman telling us? Best to start over again? What is Lynch telling us? Best to abandon the illusion that all of this happens to two women, or within two heads?

What about the much-cited lesbian scenes? Dreams? We all have erotic dreams, but they are more likely inspired by desires than experiences, and the people in them may be making unpaid guest appearances. What about the film's material involving auditions? Those could be stock footage in any dream by an actor. The command about which actress to cast? That leads us around to the strange little man in the wheelchair, issuing commands. Would anyone in the film's mainstream have a way of knowing such a figure existed?

And what about the whatever-he-is who lurks behind the diner? He fulfills the underlying purpose of Lynch's most consistent visual strategy in the film. He loves to use slow, sinister sideways tracking shots to gradually peek around corners. There are a lot of those shots in the aunt's apartment. That's also the way we sneak up to peek around the back corner of the diner. When that figure pops into view, the timing is such that you'd swear he knew someone—or the camera—was coming. It's a classic BOO! moment and need not have the slightest relationship to anything else in the film.

David Lynch loves movies, genres, archetypes, and obligatory shots. *Mulholland Dr.* employs the conventions of film noir in a pure form. One useful definition of noirs is that they're about characters who have committed a crime or a sin, are immersed with guilt, and fear they're getting what they deserve. Another is that they've done nothing wrong, but it nevertheless certainly appears as if they have.

The second describes Hitchcock's favorite plot, the Innocent Man Wrongly Accused. The first describes the central dilemma of *Mulholland Dr.* Yet it floats in an uneasy psychic space, never defining who sinned. The film evokes the feeling of noir guilt while never attaching to anything specific. A neat trick. Pure cinema.

{ MYSTERY TRAIN }

At nights in the summertime I heard lonesome whistles blowing and dreamed of taking the train to the future. To romance. To the rest of my life. Or just simply out of town. Trains embody the fact of travel, the sense of moving through time and space and day and night. Airplanes are elevators whose doors close and then open in another city. The two Japanese kids in Jim Jarmusch's *Mystery Train* (1989) have the right idea. They're on a train to Memphis. With one suitcase suspended on a pole between them, they wander the bedraggled streets until passing by accident the door of the Sun Records studios, which is a shrine for them.

This is not a Memphis approved by the chamber of commerce. The city seems forlorn and deserted: vacant lots, boarded storefronts, hardly any traffic or pedestrians. I am sure Memphis, then and now, has pleasant outlooks. But Jarmusch isn't your man to look for them. His worldview is by Nelson Algren out of Edward Hopper, Elvis Presley by way of Screamin' Jay Hawkins. He hears the train a comin', it's rollin' 'round the bend, and he ain't seen the sunshine since he don't know when.

Can you already guess that *Mystery Train* is a romance? Not a romance between people, but about the romance of the big city and its obscure corners where outsiders, seekers, and the forlorn go to spend the night. I hope Charles Bukowski saw this film before he died. Then again, he didn't need to.

The film tells three stories, which are glancingly connected. The characters in all three check in, more or less by chance, at the same hotel. This hotel is on life support. It has no more furniture than a hotel in a Looney Tunes cartoon. People check in, look around, and say, "No TV." Just a bed, a couple of busted chairs, a night table, and a portrait of Elvis on the wall. The rooms are so small I'm sure the eyes of Elvis can't help following them as they walk around.

What brings these people to the hotel? Jun (Masatoshi Nagase) and Mitzuko (Youki Kudoh), about 20, from Yokohama, are on a rock-and-roll odyssey. They share earphones plugged into the same Walkman. She loves Elvis. He's a purist, and prefers Carl Perkins. She's lively, but he keeps a blank poker face; maybe he thinks that makes him look cool. His hair is combed in a meticulous pompadour. He parks a cigarette behind his ear. She speaks a little English, he less, and as the fast-talking guide at Sun Records recites a memorized spiel, they're baffled. Jarmusch lovingly recreates this quintessential Memphis scene, including the saucer-eyed Americans also on the studio tour. Jun and Mitzuko find the hotel and check in. Later, from another room, they hear a gunshot.

Luisa (Nicoletta Braschi) has come to Memphis from Italy to pick up a coffin containing her husband's dead body. She has to take the next day's flight. In an almost deserted Formica diner, a con artist (Tom Noonan) tries to panhandle her with that old story about the guy who picked up a hitchhiker outside of Memphis. A hitchhiker who wanted to be dropped off at . . . Graceland. You know the story. Then Luisa's followed on the street by three disturbing young men, and darts into the hotel. In the lobby she meets Dee Dee (Elizabeth Bracco), frightened, happy to share a room for the night. We find out later why she's scared and why she's heading for Nanchez in the morning. From another room, they hear a gunshot.

In the third story, set in a pool hall named Shades, a Brit named Johnny (Joe Strummer) cultivates his hair and sideburns so artfully that everyone calls him "Elvis." (Elvis would have been comfortable with Jarmusch's own hair style, if only it were black.) Johnny is getting drunk with his brother-in-law Will Robinson (Rick Aviles) and produces a gun. Terrified, Will calls Johnny's best friend Charlie (Steve Buscemi). You knew Buscemi had to turn up in this movie sooner or later. They all stop at a package store to get two more bottles and something bad happens that causes them to cruise the empty streets forever, it seems; Jarmusch shows them coming and going and coming and going until finally they arrive at the hotel.

A thread from the beginning has involved the deadpan interplay between the desk clerk (Screamin' Jay Hawkins himself) and the bellboy (Cinque Lee, with a little Philip Morris hat worn at a rakish angle). They're sleepy and bored. The clerk has seen everything. The bellboy seems to be experiencing everything for the first time. Elvis sings "Blue Moon" on the radio. It's heard during all three stories, which are possibly happening at the same time. The bellboy observes, "At the time of his death, if he were on Jupiter, Elvis would've weighed six hundred and forty-eight pounds." The clerk says, "Damn!" Screamin' Jay Hawkins has the innate authority to make this, and everything else he says, sound like the final word on the subject.

Elvis is called The King at one time or another by nearly everyone in the film. His shadow falls over the nighttime streets. His ghost appears in one of the hotel rooms. There is every reason to believe this is a real ghost. He does what most ghosts do: he manifests his presence. Making him visible is the least Jarmusch can do. Elvis's legend permeates Memphis and everyone in the film. Many of the black rhythm and blues artists whose music he learned from were also here in Memphis, and in a sense they also appear as ghosts, as the camera pans past the boarded-up studio of Stax Records. No pilgrims there. The pool hall is in a black neighborhood, which the Buscemi character is uneasily aware of. Although there's no overt danger, watch his body language as he tries not to bump into anyone. There is other history in Memphis than rock and roll, and everybody knows it except possibly the Japanese.

Several times in the film, Jarmusch shows trains roaring through town. With the exception of the ones boarded by characters, none of them stop. One in particular roars close above a scene of great desperation. But the movie isn't an embrace of misery. It's more an evocation of how the personal styles of the characters help them cope with life, or not. Jun, Luisa, and Will Robinson will survive. The others in one way or another are shaping their fates. The desk clerk and the bellboy will endure, and are still there in the lobby, for all I know.

Mystery Train premiered at Cannes 1989, was a great success, and confirmed the promise Jarmusch showed when *Stranger than Paradise* premiered there in 1984. His influence in the 1980s resurgence of indie filmmaking is incalculable. He differs from some indies, however, in the formal calculation that goes into his composition and editing. Jarmusch is in no hurry to get anywhere. He chews before swallowing. He will rest on a shot to allow it to reveal itself; shots aren't the impatient hurrying along of a story. Notice how some of his traveling shots in *Mystery Train* seem to dictate the movements of characters, rather than following them. See how he isolates a portion of an interior rather than "establishing" a whole location. Notice the unobtrusive manipulation of time when the drunks are riding around in a pickup.

After *Stranger than Paradise*, Jarmusch returned to Cannes in 1986 with *Down by Law*, with Tom Waits, who was born to be a Jarmusch star; John Lurie, the musician who began with Jarmusch in his first student film; and Roberto Begnini, who was soon to be famous, but arrived as from another planet. Sometimes his further reaches of style try my patience, as they did in *The Limits of Control* (2009). More often he delights me with the level, almost objective gaze he directs at goofballs and outsiders. He found an unsurprising rapport with Bill Murray in *Broken Flowers* (2005), with Murray seeking out the former loves of his life. His *Night on Earth* (1991) was five stories set entirely in taxis. *Coffee and Cigarettes* (2003) had poetically peculiar conversations and situations. His *Dead Man* (1995), with an amazing cast ranging from Johnny Depp to Robert Mitchum, didn't work for me, but was so highly praised I need another look.

In his work there is a deep embedding of comedy, nostalgia, shabby sadness, and visual beauty. *Mystery Train* tells of a long night that's very hard on some of the characters. But the sun comes up, and a morning train is pulling out. Jun from Yokohama is having a great trip. "We saw Graceland, and tomorrow in New Orleans we get to see Fats Domino's house!"

{ NIGHT MOVES }

Arthur Penn's *Night Moves* (1975) is about an old-fashioned private eye who says and does all the expected things while surrounded by a plot he completely fails to understand.

Harry Moseby is played by Gene Hackman as a man who, in 1975 Los Angeles, still seems to be taking his cues from old film noir movies. The glass on his office door says:

> *Moseby*
> *Confidential*

. . . and there is an understated romanticism in that curt wording that fits with his battered desk and the arched window that looks down, no doubt, on mean streets. His wife is always after him to join a big detective agency and enter the modern world, but he likes the life of a freelancer, tooling around in his aging Mustang, jotting down license plate numbers in his little spiral notebook.

As the movie opens, he is summoned to the kind of client who would be completely at home in a Sam Spade or Philip Marlowe story. Arlene Iverson (Janet Ward) is a onetime B-movie sweater girl who married a couple of rich guys—one dead, the other ex—and must be lonely, because she greets Harry dressed as if she's hired him to look at her breasts. Her 16-year-old daughter, Delly, has run away from home, and she wants Harry to find her, although if Harry wants to have a drink with Arlene first, that would be nice.

Harry takes the job but first does a little sleuthing on his own time. His wife, Ellen (Susan Clark), asks if he wants to go see *My Night at Maud's*, but he tells her, "I saw a Rohmer film once. It was kinda like watching paint dry." Then he stakes out the theater and sees her meeting a man Harry doesn't know. Out comes the spiral notebook. The man is Marty Heller (Harris Yulin), who lives out in Malibu, and later Harry confronts him, although in a curiously lukewarm way: "How serious is it?" When his wife finds out he knows, she makes it his fault: "Why didn't you ask me first?" He leaves town to work on the case as a sort of therapy.

His trail leads first to a movie location, where he meets a mechanic (James Woods) who once dated Delly, and then a stunt pilot (Anthony Costello) who took her away from the mechanic, and then a stunt pilot who says Delly is probably in Florida with her stepfather, the charter pilot Tom Iverson (John Crawford). In Florida, Moseby finds her (played by Melanie Griffith in her movie debut) living with Tom and Tom's lover, Paula (Jennifer Warren).

Now we have most of the characters on board, and I will stop describing the plot, not so much because I fear giving it away as because I fear I cannot.

It is probably true that if you saw *Night Moves* several times and took careful notes, you could reconstruct exactly what happens in the movie, but that might be missing the point. I saw it a week ago with an audience at that holy place of the cinema, George Eastman House in Rochester, New York, and then I was joined in a discussion with Jim Healy, the assistant curator—we talked for an hour with a room full of moviegoers and we were left with more questions than we started with.

Of course, we could fall back on the old film critic ploy, "we're not supposed to understand the plot." That worked for *Syriana*. But in *Night Moves*, I think it's a little trickier. The plot can be understood, but not easily, and not on first viewing, and besides, the point is that Moseby is as lost as we are. Something is always turning up to force him to revise everything he thought he knew, and then at the end of the film he has to revise everything again, and there is a shot where one of the characters, while drowning, seems to be desperately shaking his head as if to say—what? "I didn't mean to do this"? "I didn't know who was in the boat"? "In the water"? "You don't understand"?

Harry doesn't understand, that's for sure, and the last shot in the film, taken from high above, shows him in a boat that is circling aimlessly in the Gulf Stream, a splendid metaphor for Harry's investigation.

I was reminded of another Gene Hackman character named Harry. That would be Harry Caul, from Francis Ford Coppola's *The Conversation* (1974). Caul is a high-tech investigator who bugs people and eavesdrops on conversations and is fanatic and paranoid and, like Moseby, not nearly as clever as he needs to be. Harry Caul has his workplace invaded by a competitor, he's fooled by a hidden microphone in a ball-point pen, he gets calls on his unlisted number, his landlord walks right past the security system in his apartment, and although he has a tape recording of a crucial conversation, he has no idea what it means.

Moseby is as helpless as Caul. He vaguely understands that most of the people he meets in his investigation are connected in one way or another—even people who should not know each other. He figures out that they're up to more than selling antiques, making movies, or chartering boats and airplanes. He sees some of the romantic connections and gets himself involved in others. Delly, who has a disconcerting way of taking off her clothes, is perhaps interested in Harry—but in seducing him, or just rattling his walnuts? Harry falls hard for Paula, and she seems attracted to him, too. They have one of those conversations where two people talk in the abstract about important things that are code for, "Do you want to sleep with me?" The screenplay by Alan Sharp is literate and elliptical all the way through:

"Where were you when Kennedy got shot?"
"Which Kennedy?"

Paula lights some candles and talks about how her nipples misbe-have in intriguing situations, and otherwise gives Harry reason to believe he may be getting somewhere. Then he and Paula and Delly take the glass-bottomed boat out in the middle of the night and Delly goes scuba-diving and by accident finds a plane on the ocean floor with a skeleton in it and those are fish where were once his eyes. Whose skeleton is it? At this stage of decomposition it's hard to say, but I thought it belonged to the James Woods character, and I was wrong.

I was wrong again and again, but so was Harry. There is a profound disconnect between his investigation and what is really happening, and es-sentially the movie shows him acting like a private eye while the case un-folds independently in front of him. When the movie was released, there was a lot of discussion about a second plane crash and the identity of the person in that plane, but at Eastman House it was very clear who the per-son was. Left unanswered, however, is what he was doing in the plane, how he was able to fly it with a machine gun in one hand and the other arm in a cast, and what he was trying to tell Harry, who watches through the glass-bottomed boat as he drowns. Those are very good questions.

Night Moves came after a lull in Arthur Penn's career; he and Hack-man worked together in *Bonnie and Clyde* (1967) and then Penn made *Alice's Restaurant* (1969) and *Little Big Man* (1970). For Hackman, it was a period of astonishing work in such films as *I Never Sang for My Father* (1970), *The French Connection* (1971), and *The Conversation*. What he brings to *Night Moves* is crucial; he must be absolutely sure of his identity as a freelance gumshoe, even while all of his craft is useless and all of his hunches are based on ignorance of the big picture. Maybe the movie is saying that the old film noir faith is dead, that although in Chandler's words "down these mean streets a man must go who is not himself mean, who is neither tar-nished nor afraid," when this man goes down those streets he is blindsided by a plot that has no respect for him.

{ NOSFERATU THE VAMPYRE }

There is a quality to the color photography in Werner Herzog's *Nosferatu the Vampyre* (1979) that seeps into your bones. It would be inadequate to call it "saturated." It is rich, heavy, deep. The earth looks cold and dirty. There isn't a lot of green, and it looks wet. Mountains look craggy, gray, sharp-edged. Interiors are filmed in bold reds and browns and whites—whites, especially, for the faces, and above all for Count Dracula's. It is a film of remarkable beauty, but makes no effort to attract or visually coddle us. The spectacular journey by foot and coach to Dracula's remote Transylvanian castle is deliberately not made to seem scenic.

There is often something fearful and awesome in Herzog's depiction of nature. It is not uplifting so much as remorseless. Clouds fall low and drift like water. Peaks tower in intimidation. Shadows hint at horrors. The simple peasants that Jonathan Harker encounters on his journey are not colorful and friendly, but withdraw from him. Herzog takes his time before allowing us our first sight of Dracula; his stage has been set by words and the looks in eyes of people who cannot believe he is seeking the Count.

Herzog follows the structure of F. W. Murnau's famous *Nosferatu* (1922), one of the greatest of all silent films. That was based on Bram Stoker's 1897 novel *Dracula*. Murnau changed the character names for copyright reasons, and Herzog was free to use the originals: Dracula (Klaus Kinski), the land agent Jonathan Harker (Bruno Ganz), his wife Lucy (Isabelle Adjani), Dr. Van Helsing (Walter Ladengast), and he of the maniacal laugh, Renfield (Roland Topor).

The film opens with Renfield offering Harker a large commission to travel to Dracula's castle and sell him an isolated property in town. Harker wants the money because he thinks his wife deserves a nicer house. Renfield's spasmodic laughter doesn't deter him. His journey takes a great deal more time than in the many other movies based on this famous story. There is an ominous scene at an inn where he mentions Dracula's name and the entire room falls silent, simply staring at him. Herzog takes his time building up anticipation before Dracula's entrance.

No coach will take Harker to the castle. No one will sell or rent him a horse. Renfield continues on foot, walking narrow pathways above cruel chasms. Finally Dracula's coach comes out to fetch him. It looks like (because it is) a hearse. The door to the castle creaks open and we regard Dracula. In creating the vampire, Herzog follows the striking art direction of the Murnau film, making the count look more like an animal than a human being. None of your handsome, sleek vampires played by Tom Cruise. The head is shaved. The face and skull are clown white. The fingernails are spears. The ears are pointed like a bat's. The eyes are sunken and rimmed in black and red. Most extraordinary of all are the two prominent fangs in the center of the mouth, placed like a bat's, unconcealed. In most movies Dracula's teeth are up and to the sides, more easily concealed. Here there can be no mistaking them.

Many famous details are paid homage. The line, "Listen. The children of the night make their music." The Count's barely controlled lust when Harker cuts his thumb with a bread knife. The meals mysteriously appearing without servants. Then the race as Dracula goes by sea and Harker by land to the city of Bremen, where Lucy is in danger.

Herzog is the most original of filmmakers, not much given to remakes. His only other one, *The Bad Lieutenant: Port of Call New Orleans* (2009), was so different from the original that only the idea of a corrupt cop was kept. Why was he drawn to remake one of the most famous and least dated of German silent films?

I think it was partly because of love—for Murnau, and for the film, which suits the macabre strain in some of his own work. It was partly in homage. And I suspect it was above all because he had the resource of Klaus Kinski. He had first laid eyes on Kinski when he was still a boy, and the fierce-eyed actor lived in the same building. "I knew at that moment," he told me, "that it was my destiny to make films, and direct Kinski in them." The two developed an almost symbiotic relationship, which led at times to death threats against each other, and also to such extraordinary work as *Aguirre, the Wrath of God* and *Fitzcarraldo*. Kinski of all actors could most easily create the driven and the mad.

To say of someone that they were born to play a vampire is a strange compliment, but if you will compare the two versions of Nosferatu you might agree with me that only Kinski could have equaled or rivaled Max Schreck's performance. Opposite him Herzog cast Isabelle Adjani, a French beauty who is used here not only for her facial perfection but for her curious quality of seeming to exist on an ethereal plane. Adjani does not easily play ordinary women. Her skin always seems unusually white and smooth, as is porcelain. Here she provides a pure object for Dracula's fangs.

The other masterstroke of casting is Roland Topor, as the Bremen realtor. Topor did a fair amount of acting, but was principally an author and artist, the cofounder of the Panic Movement with Alejandro Jodorowsky (*El Topo*). Herzog recalls watching a trivial German TV show on which Topor's weird high-pitched giggle seemed to evoke perfect madness. Here it is used to suggest the unwholesome nature of his relationship with Dracula.

Nosferatu the Vampyre cannot be confined to the category of "horror film." It is about dread itself, and how easily the unwary can fall into evil. Bruno Ganz makes an ideal Harker because he sidesteps any temptation to play a hero, and plays a devoted husband who naively dismisses alarming warnings. He is loving, then resolute, then uncertain, then fearful, then desperate, and finally mad—lost.

Although I don't believe *Nosferatu* had a particularly large budget, its historical detail looks unfaked and convincing. Herzog travels much in search of arresting imagery; the mummies at the start are from Mexico, the mountains are the Carpathian, the castles and castle ruins are in the Czech Republic, Slovakia, and Germany, and I believe the city with canals is in the Netherlands.

That said, Herzog told me that some shots were set up to use the same locations that Murnau used, and often had similar compositions. Once I asked him why he took a crew far into the South American rain forests to shoot *Aguirre* and *Fitzcarraldo*, and he said he believed in "the voodoo of locations." A rain forest forty miles away from a city would have *felt* wrong. The actors would project a different energy if they knew they truly were buried in a wilderness. We would be able to sense it. In the same spirit, I suppose, Kinski standing where Murnau's actor Max Schreck stood would generate an energy. This film is haunted by the earlier one.

I wonder if Kinski himself believed this was a role he was born to play. Famously temperamental, his emotions on a hair trigger, he endured four hours of makeup daily without complaining. The bat ears had to be destroyed in removal and constructed again every morning. It's as if he regarded Schreck's performance and wanted to step in and claim the character as partly his own.

One striking quality of the film is its beauty. Herzog's pictorial eye is not often enough credited. His films always upstage it with their themes. We are focused on what happens, and there are few "beauty shots." Look here at his control of the color palate, his off-center compositions, of the dramatic counterpoint of light and dark. Here is a film that does honor to the seriousness of vampires. No, I don't believe in them. But if they were real, here is how they must look.

{ THE ONLY SON }

Why was I thinking about flower arrangement while watching *The Only Son* (1936), the first sound film made by the Japanese master Ozu? It must have involved the meticulous and loving care he used with his familiar visual elements. In Japan in 1984 I attended a class at the Sogetsu School, which teaches ikebana, the Japanese art of flower arranging. I learned quickly that sorting a big bunch of flowers in a vase was not ikebana. One selected just a few elements and found a precise way in which they rested together harmoniously.

If you think that ikebana has nothing to do with film direction, think again. The Sogetsu School was then being run by Hiroshi Teshigahara, the director of *Woman in the Dunes*, who left filmmaking to become the third generation of his family to head the school. After he died in 1991, his daughter became the fourth. I gathered that the Teshigaharas believed when you studied ikebana you studied your relationship with the material world.

Now turn to Yasujiro Ozu, who is one of the three or four best filmmakers in the world, and certainly the one who brings me the most serenity. I've seen 14 of his films, four of them with the shot-by-shot approach. That doesn't make me an expert, but it makes me familiar with his ways of seeing. In the films I've seen, he has a few favorite themes, subjects, and compositions, and carefully arranges and rearranges them. Some say "he makes the same film every time." That's like saying "all people are born with two eyes." What matters is how you see with them.

Over an opening frame of *The Only Son* (1936), we read a quotation by the writer Akutagawa: "Life's tragedy begins with the bond between parent and child." So do most of Ozu's films. Again and again, he focuses on parents and their children, and often on their grandchildren. A typical plot will involve sacrifice by a parent or a child for the happiness of the other. It is not uncommon for both parent and child to make sacrifices in a mistaken belief about what the other desires. The issues involved are marriage, children, independence for the young, care for the old, and success in the world.

He tells these stories within a visual frame so distinctive that I believe you can identify any Ozu film after seeing a shot or two, sometimes even from a still. How he came upon his approach I don't know, but you see it fully mature even in his silent films. For Ozu, all depends on the composition of the shot. He almost never moves his camera. He usually shoots from the eye level of a person seated on a tatami mat. He often begins shots before characters enter, and holds them after they leave. He separates important scenes with "pillow shots" of exterior architectural or landscape details. He uses evocative music, never too loud. I have never seen him use violence. When violence occurs, people commit it within themselves.

Parents and children, then families, are his chosen subjects. He tells each story with his familiar visual strategy, which is pure and simplified, never calling attention to itself. His straight-on shots are often framed on sides and back and with foreground objects. His exteriors and groups of two or more characters are usually at oblique angles. Is this monotonous? Never, because within his rules he finds infinite variation. A modern chase scene is much more monotonous, because it gives you nothing to think about.

In *The Only Son*, there is a remarkable moment when we have a great deal of time to think. The story is about the son of a widowed mother who works in a provincial silk spinning mill. This is hard and spirit-crushing work, but she does it to put her son through high school and set him on his road in life. After graduating, he follows an admired teacher to seek his future in Tokyo. Four years pass. His mother comes to visit him, unannounced. They are happy to see one another, they love one another, but he has a surprise: he has a wife and an infant child. Why didn't he tell her? We gather he didn't want to create an occasion for her to visit Tokyo and find that he is very poor, has a low-paying job, teaching geometry in a night school, and that he lives in a desolate district in view of the smokestacks of the Tokyo garbage incinerators.

The rest of the plot you can discover. It leads to a conversation in which he shares his discouragement and tells her she may have wasted her sacrifice. She encourages him to persevere. He thinks he's had a bad roll of the dice. There is no place for him in Tokyo. Simple mill worker that she is, what can she reply to this? She sits up late, sleepless. He awakens, and they talk some more. She weeps. In a reframed shot, his wife weeps. Then Ozu provides a shot of an unremarkable corner of the room. Nothing much there. A baby bottle. A reproduction of a painting. Nothing. He holds this shot. And holds it. And holds it. I feel he could not look at them any longer, and had to look away, thinking about what has happened. Finally there is an exterior pillow shot of the morning.

If Ozu returns to characteristic visuals, he also returns to familiar actors. In *The Only Son*, the small but important role of the hero's teacher is played by Chishû Ryû—the teacher who, after moving to Tokyo, fails to realize his own dreams and, as the son bitterly tells his mother, is "reduced to frying pork cutlets." This was Ryû's seventh film for Ozu. In all he was to appear in 52 of Ozu's 54 films, between 1929 and 1962. He is the old father in *Tokyo Story* (1953).

Ryû is an actor who we recognize from body language. He exudes restraint, courtesy. He smokes meditatively. He said Ozu directed him as little as possible: "He had made up the complete picture in his head before he went on the set, so that all we actors had to do was to follow his directions, from the way we lifted and dropped our arms to the way we blinked our eyes."

Ryû is the ideal actor for Ozu because he never seems to be trying. He is the canvas. By not "acting," he invites us to look inside him and find a world there. I care deeply for his characters and remembering them, each looking similar, each distinctive. Acting like his doesn't win prizes like the Oscar; Brando drove that kind of acting out of Hollywood, rarely to return.

I really do feel as if Ozu is looking at his films along with me. He isn't throwing them up on the screen for me to see by myself. Together we look at people trying to please, and often failing, and sometimes redeeming. What finally gives the mother hope in this film would sound sentimental if I described it, but it's very serious.

A reminder that we're watching along with Ozu is his little teapot. In every film of his I've seen, a small teapot appears here or there in most of the interior scenes. It has a way of moving around, not that you'd notice that. A little unremarkable teapot. In his first color film, we discovered it was red. Of course it was. On a Japanese scroll, red is the color of the artist's mark.

{ PALE FLOWER }

At the center of *Pale Flower* (1964) stands a very quiet man, closed within himself, a professional killer. He works for a gang in the Yakuza, the Japanese mafia, and as the film begins he has returned to Tokyo after serving a prison sentence for murder. He did the prison time as the price to be paid for committing a murder, but although we see his gang boss several times, even in a dentist's chair, there is no effort to make him seem worthy of such loyalty. He is an ordinary older man. Muraki (Ryo Ikebe), the yakuza, seems loyal more to the ideal of loyalty, a version of the samurai code. It is his fate to be a soldier and follow orders, and he is the instrument of that destiny. He thinks his crime was "stupid," but he is observing, not complaining.

Pale Flower is one of the most haunting noirs I've seen, and something more; in 1964 it was an important work in an emerging Japanese New Wave of independent filmmakers, an exercise in existential cool. It involves a plot, but it is all about attitude. Muraki, elegantly dressed, his hair in a carefully stylized cut, his eyes often shielded by dark glasses, speaking rarely, revealing nothing, guards his emotions as if there may be no more where they came from. He glides through nights and an underworld of high-stakes gambling clubs and hooker bars, but lives in a rude and shabby room as if it is merely a cave for sleeping.

After his first night back in his familiar world, he goes to a clock shop where Shinko (Chisako Hara), his young lover, lives and works. She clings to him abjectly, and they have sex without ceremony. He betrays no affection. He advises her to find a husband and start a family. He returns to the customary life of the gang without ceremony, as if dwelling on the prison term would be unseemly.

He likes to gamble. The movie began with a gambling sequence, there are several more of them, and visually they're as elegantly composed as a scene by Ozu. The director of *Pale Flower* is Masahiro Shinoda, whose visual choice is widescreen black and white and whose characters move with the grace of Antonioni's at about the same time. That Shinoda worked as an assistant to Ozu may explain some of his precise framing. The gamblers play the Flower Card game involving thick cardboard chips that click when they touch; listen carefully to the sound track by Toru Takemitsu, the masterful composer who, Shinoda says, told him "record all the sounds and I will use them." He segues from the clicking of the cards to recorded tap-dancing and then to discordant chords, as if the rhythm of the game gives way to angular interior emotions.

Seated across from Muraki is a beautiful women, very young, who gambles with the same recklessness she uses to meet his eyes. This is Saeko (Mariko Kaga). Like Muraki, she has no small talk and betrays no emotions. She seems equally indifferent if winning or losing. There is a man at the games who does not play. He is Yoh (Takashi Fujiki), said to be a new employee of the boss. He sits against the wall, regarding the room with aggressive objectivity. Shinoda uses a series of shots in which Muraki leans back to regard this man, who returns his gaze as if to say, "I would kill you or anyone else without a second thought."

Saeko asks Muraki if he knows of a game with bigger stakes. She seems addicted to excitement. She betrays emotion only twice, when after a high-speed drag race on empty city streets she begins to giggle almost orgasmically, and again when she giggles after they are almost caught in a police raid. She says that "Yoh," the malevolent newcomer, seems "exciting." Perhaps she finds it exciting, too, that Muraki is a murderer.

Shinoda chose Ryo Ikebe as his star when the actor was at a low ebb, having been fired from a play for freezing onstage. In an interview included with the new Criterion edition of the film, the director recalls Ikebe, depressed, asking, "Why do you want me? I'm just a ham actor." But Shinoda had seen him in Ozu's *Early Spring* (1956) and other films, where he was sleekly handsome, and he says he wanted to feel the quality of a man down on his luck. In this film, Ikebe reminds me of the also handsome Alain Delon in Jean-Pierre Melville's *Le Samourai* (1967), another film about a detached hit man. Here the performance depend on Ikebe's ability to maintain a Charles Bronson–like impassivity. It is the quality of a man wary of emotion, and the story depends on how he helplessly becomes fascinated by Saeko because she seems even more distant and guarded than he is.

He warns her against drugs. One night she tells him she has shot up. She says a friendly doctor gave her the shot. But Yoh has the skin and the aura of a drug addict. What does Muraki think? He never reveals. But when the boss asks for a volunteer to murder the boss of a rival gang, Muraki says he'll do it. He doesn't have to. The boss has already given him an exemption because he's just finished one prison term. If you meditate on why Muraki volunteers, I think you will close in on his motivation, and find the theme.

In his interview, Shinoda shows himself familiar with avant garde art. He was chafing at working within the studio system, and even though *Pale Flower* was produced by the major studio Shochiku he considers it an independent film, and so, apparently, did the studio. "After the screening, the writer said it wasn't the film he had written," he recalls, "and that was the excuse the studio needed." At a loss for how to deal with it, Shochiku shelved it for months, although when it was finally released it was a great success, no doubt because it captured the sense of both film noir and the emerging European art films.

The writer, Masaru Baba, began with a novel by Shintaro Ishihara. His approach was apparently conventional, and he disagreed sharply with Shinoda about the gambling scenes. "We just write 'they gamble,'" he told the director. Shinoda nodded, kept his peace, and used the novel as a basis for shooting the extraordinary card games. The film makes no effort to explain how the game is played, but is visually acute about the details: the goading rhythm of the croupier, the ritual of a card withdrawn from concealment and folded within a cloth, the placing of bets. Shinoda gives great attention to the implacable faces of Muraki, Saeko, and (at a greater distance) Yoh. The gambling scenes are not about the game but about the emotional signals being exchanged by these three; Shinoda has little interest in the other players.

Not many scenes take place in daytime. The film is shot mostly indoors, or outdoors on sometimes rainy streets. The opening establishes Tokyo, but Shinoda shot mostly in Yokohama, where an older look and many narrow lanes gave him a feeling he was looking for, of the night pressing down on Muraki. One cat-and-mouse foot chase through empty streets and shadows is particularly well done.

Although the tone of the film is set by Toru Takemitsu's discordant score, a late climactic killing is scored by an aria from Henry Purcell's opera, *Dido and Aeneas*. It goes to slow motion and is intercut with unexpected stained-glass windows. What is happening here, as you will understand when you see the film, is the equivalent of an orgasm created by Muraki for Saeko.

Film noir is almost always about a central figure who is destroyed by his flaws. This figure often tries to live by a code, even a criminal code, but is defeated by some kind of moral weakness. In noir the fact that you've killed someone may not be a moral failing, but simply an expression of the duties of your milieu. Muraki has schooled himself to not feel, and to not care for Shinko, who cares for him. But by her very inapproachability, the mysterious Saeko defeats his defenses and sets in motion those decisions that cause him to kill again, and trap himself. At the end of the film, he discovers what his choices have left him with. It is an ending of bleak sadness and empty destiny.

⎰ PINK FLOYD: THE WALL ⎱

The rock opera *Pink Floyd: The Wall*, first performed in 1978, came at a time when some rock artists were taking themselves very seriously indeed. While the Beatles and Stones had recorded stand-alone songs or themed albums at the most, The Who produced *Tommy* in 1969 and *Quadrophenia* in 1973. David Bowie and Genesis followed, and *Pink Floyd: The Wall* essentially brought a close to that chapter.

This isn't the most fun to listen to and some viewers don't find it too much fun to watch, but the 1982 film is without question the best of all serious fiction films devoted to rock. Seeing it now in more timid times, it looks more daring than it did in 1982 when I saw it at Cannes. Alan Parker, a director who seemed to deliberately choose widely varied projects, here collaborates with Gerald Scarfe, a biting British political caricaturist, to make what is essentially an experimental indie. It combines wickedly powerful animation with a surrealistic trip through the memory and hallucinations of an overdosing rock star. It touches on sex, nuclear disarmament, the agony of warfare, childhood feelings of abandonment, the hero's deep unease about women, and the lifestyle of a rock star at the end of his rope.

What it doesn't depict is rock performance. There are no actual concert scenes, although there are groupies and limousines and a personal manager. Or perhaps there are concert scenes, and they're disguised as an extended portrait of a modern fascist dictator whose fans morph into an adoring populace. I don't believe this dictator is intended as a parallel to any obvious model like Hitler or Stalin; he seems more a fantasy of Britain's own National Socialists led by Oswald Mosley.

Pink Floyd: The Wall was written almost entirely by Roger Waters, the band's intellectual, self-analytical, sometimes tortured lead singer. Its central character, named Pink, is played by Bob Geldof, of all people, who could not be less like Pink. The credits say he is being "introduced." He's onscreen more than anyone else, goes through punishing scenes, and even sings at times, although this isn't a performance film but essentially a 95-minute music video. Geldof morphs through several standard rock star looks, all familiar from other stars: the big-haired sex god, the attractive leading man, the haunted neurotic, the cadaverous drug victim. In his most agonizing scene, he shaves off all his body hair in a bloody reprise of Scorsese's famous short "The Big Shave."

There's also a scene where he trashes a hotel room; he must have carefully studied the room destruction in *Citizen Kane*. The scene involves a terrified groupie (Jenny Wright) who flees around the room and cowers behind furniture but inexplicably doesn't flee immediately into the corridor. More frightening is that although Pink narrowly misses her with a wine bottle and a piece of furniture, he doesn't seem really aware that she's there.

The girl is earlier portrayed as concerned about him, and rather sweet. That sets her aside from the other females in the movie. There is Pink's mother, so devastated by her husband's death in war that she becomes smothering and domineering toward her son. Then Pink's wife, alienated by his zombie-like disconnection from life, turning finally to an antiwar lecturer to cheat with a man who cares about something. These are both at least recognizable women. The most grotesque female figure in the film is created by Scarfe's animation.

This is a flower so gynecological that Georgia O'Keefe might have been appalled. The bloom seduces a male flower, ravishes him, plunders him, and ultimately devours him. Perhaps she reflects Pink's terror of castration.

Scarfe distorts the flower into other shapes for disquieting transformations, as a dove becomes a screaming eagle and then a warplane, landscapes are devastated and walls and goose-stepping hammers march across the land.

As you have gathered, I'm not describing what we think of as a "musical." This is a bold, relentless visualization of Waters's despair. It incorporates a theme that resonates with British audiences, an educational system ruled by stern, kinky headmasters. The opera's most famous song becomes its best scene. As Parker visualizes "Another Brick in the Wall," students on a conveyor belt are fed into blades that extrude them as ground meat. In the process, the students lose their faces behind blank masks, which are seen again in the faces of the dictator's followers. Message: Education produces mindless creatures suitable as cannon fodder or the puppets of fascists. I gather Waters wasn't keen on attending the reunions of his old school.

There is a narrative, although *Pink Floyd: The Wall* doesn't underline it. It suggests that Pink has vivid images of his father's ordeal under fire, is raised too protectively, was incapable of a successful marriage, took no pleasure in casual sex, and finally disappeared into psychological catatonia under the influence of drugs. The opening scene returns later, suggesting all of the action in the film takes place in Pink's head in that hotel room in more or less the film's running time.

The best audience for this film would be one familiar with filmmaking techniques, alert to directorial styles, and familiar with Roger Waters and Pink Floyd. I can't imagine a "rock fan" enjoying it very much on first viewing, although I know it has developed a cult following. It's disquieting and depressing and very good. No one much enjoyed making it. I remember Alan Parker being somewhat quizzical at the time; I learn from Wikipedia that he fought with Waters and Scarfe and considered the film "one of the most miserable experiences of my creative life." Waters's own verdict: "I found it was so unremitting in its onslaught upon the senses, that it didn't give me, anyway, as an audience, a chance to get involved with it."

So it's difficult, painful, and despairing, and its three most important artists came away from it with bad feelings. Why would anybody want to see it? Perhaps because filming this material could not possibly have been a happy experience for anyone—not if it's taken seriously. I believe Waters wrote out of the dark places in his soul, fueled by his contempt for rock stars in general, himself in particular, and their adoring audiences. He was, in short, composing not as an entertainer but as an artist. Sir Alan Parker is a cheerful man, although not without a temper, and there is no apparent thread to connect this film with his credits such as *The Commitments*, *Fame*, *Bugsy Malone*, or even such heavier films as *Shoot the Moon* and *Angela's Ashes*. I can't say I really know Parker, but I've spent enough time around him to sense he wasn't congenitally drawn to this material.

Those tensions and conflicts produced, I believe, the right film for this material. I don't require that its makers had a good time. I'm reminded of my favorite statement by François Truffaut: "I demand that a film express either the joy of making cinema or the agony of making cinema. I am not at all interested in anything in between."

{ THE PLEDGE }

Sean Penn's *The Pledge* (2001) begins when it seems his protagonist's career is ending. Jack Nicholson plays Jerry Black, a Nevada police detective whose retirement party is interrupted by news of the brutal murder of a young girl. Across the noisy room he senses a shift in tone, and joins a conversation between his chief and the man who will be taking over his job. Then he goes along to the murder scene, perhaps out of habit or because he hasn't officially retired. The little girl in a red coat is a pitiful sight with her blood staining the snow.

Jerry is angered at the poor preservation of the crime scene, and at the general reluctance of the cops to notify the girl's parents. Hell with it. He'll do it himself. We see him slowly approach them across a floor covered with agitated turkey chicks. Penn holds his camera at a distance as Jerry breaks the news to the parents, whose anguish is apparent. Later, inside their house, he reassures them the killer will be found. The mother (Patricia Clarkson) holds up a crucifix made by her daughter, and asks for his solemn pledge. He gives it. He will not rest until then.

The scene plays exactly like that. But later, thinking back to it, perhaps we sense a deeper level. Jerry Black is twice-divorced, childless, a career cop who now allegedly looks forward to spending the rest of his life fishing. But he was drawn to the news of the murder, drawn to the crime scene, drawn to be the one who informs the parents, and now he vows to solve the crime. What happened to his fishing trip? This is a man who is holding onto his identity with a desperate grip.

That determination is at the core of *The Pledge*, which seems to follow the form of a police procedural and then plunges deeper into the mysteries of innocence, evil, and a man's need to validate himself. At some point we realize that retirement, for Jerry, is a form of defeat and death. When the girl's mother says, "There can't be such devils out there," look at his eyes as he tells her, "There *are* such devils." He has been working against them for his entire life, and now he must find this one to save himself.

He looks through the one-way glass at the interrogation of the prime suspect, a retarded American Indian named Toby (lank-haired Benecio Del Toro). The questions come from Krolak (Aaron Eckhart), who will take over Jerry's job. He coaxes and coos in Toby's ear, seducing a confession, and when he gets one he throws up his hands in victory like a football coach. Jerry is appalled: the Indian clearly has no idea what he is saying. And then, a few seconds later, Toby kills himself and the case seems closed.

The Pledge may be Nicholson's finest performance. Here are none of the familiar signals of his more popular performances, none of the relish of characterization, none of the sardonic remove. We see a lonely man, aging, whose attempts to go through the motions of retirement fail. He stays on the case. After leaving the force he uses a map to triangulate three crime scenes where, over a period of years, young girls, all of them wearing red, have been killed. At a crossroads he finds a small country store and gas station with an apartment upstairs. He walks in and makes the owner (Harry Dean Stanton) an offer too good to refuse.

If the three crimes were committed by the same man, that man must pass here. From a friend of the murdered girl, he obtained a drawing of a man she has met, a "giant," who gave her "porcupines" and drove a big black car. He grows intense every time a black car pulls in. At a local tavern, he becomes friendly with Lori, the barmaid (Robin Wright Penn), and when she turns up battered one day, he takes her in. She and her young daughter can live with him. No strings attached.

We are afraid to draw an obvious conclusion. Is Jerry going to use the little girl as bait? Is one child to be put at risk in his determination to avenge another one? Sean Penn never underlines this. Indeed, his film is so intimately involved with the daily details of life that there's a good stretch when we aren't really focusing in those terms. We fall into the rhythms of life in rural Nevada, outside Reno. We fall into the routine of the new household that has been formed. Jerry, who never had a child, reveals himself as a good father, reading bedtime stories, keeping a cautious eye on the girl. He never informs Lori of the murder case, but uses his background as a cop to explain his deep concern for the girl's safety.

Sean Penn shows himself in this film as a sure-handed director with great empathy for performance. He peoples his cast with great actors (Helen Mirren, Vanessa Redgrave, Tom Noonan, Michael O'Keefe, Mickey Rourke, Lois Smith, Sam Shepard, Del Toro, Stanton, Clarkson, Eckhart). That he and Nicholson were able to attract such names for small roles speaks for itself. But Penn uses them for what he knows about them, not for their face value, and the presence of actors with real weight brings importance to roles that are "supporting" but not minor. Robin Wright, then Penn's wife, is pitch-perfect as a weary working woman who seeks safety and affection for herself and her child.

Penn and his cinematographer, Chris Menges, fill the frame with so many local details that the film doesn't seem to be insisting on an agenda. It emerges from the situation. A scene set at a local crafts fair, for example, involves people we know, others we don't know, and then a shot that reminds us of Hitchcock: a single pink balloon, floating free above the crowd. A later scene, of a police stakeout in the woods, is staged and acted with cold precision, although we can hardly believe what we're seeing.

Penn relentlessly draws the focus closer to the Jerry Black character. The edges of the frame tighten on him. The film hasn't been about murder but about need. Everything he has seen and everything he has done has been driven by his need to prove himself still a good detective. Still a man.

The Pledge was Penn's third film as a director. *The Indian Runner* (1991) starred David Morse and Viggo Mortensen as brothers—one a deputy sheriff, the other a troubled hothead. *The Crossing Guard* (1995) starred

Nicholson as a man whose daughter has been killed by a drunk driver. He confronts his ex-wife (Anjelica Huston), and her new husband vows that now that the driver (David Morse) is out of prison, he will find him and kill him. He shouts at Mary's new husband: "Man to man—when she picks up the paper and reads that he is dead—look at her face and see if you don't see pride and relief. Pride. And relief." Freddy's motivation is not revenge, but the need to impress his former wife.

These three films are not really about the events in the plot. They are about the need of a central character to persevere in the face of failure and even madness to complete a task he has set himself.

Now consider Penn's fourth film, *Into the Wild* (2007), the American Film Institute's film of the year. Emile Hirsch gave a powerful performance that evoked our growing dread. He played a 20-year-old who rebelled against his parents and his life, and started driving west and north until he disappeared into the Alaskan wilderness. He was not seeking death. He wanted to prove he could live off the land and survive.

This film, too, showed Penn embedding his protagonist in a cast of stars in small roles: Vince Vaughn, Catherine Keener, Hal Holbrook, Marcia Gay Harden, William Hurt, Jena Malone, Kristen Stewart. These are never "cameos," but require the actors to do their very best work in a short time.

All of these films show a man determined to prove something, at whatever cost. He is not proving it to others. He is proving it to himself. Penn wrote the screenplays for all but *The Pledge*; for *Into the Wild*, he began with a true-life book by Jon Krakauer. What does the theme mean for Penn? I would not venture to say. He is not only as good as any living actor, he has also steadily been growing as a great director of actors. One of the reasons *The Pledge* is so important is that he asked his friend Jack Nicholson to follow him into the wild, and they proved something.

{ RED BEARD }

Told in the world of early nineteenth-century Japan, Akira Kurosawa's *Red Beard* (1965) is a passionate humanist statement, almost the last he would make about an exemplary human being. After completing its two years of filming in 1965, the master would turn to flawed and damaged characters—one of them, the hero of *Ran* (1985), inspired by Shakespeare's King Lear. Dr. Kyojô Niide would be the closest he ever came to creating a man moral and good in every respect. In the film you can sense Kurosawa's best nature shining.

In the second act of his career he would allow discouragement and doubt to show through, ending with *Rhapsody in August* (1991), about the devastation of Nagasaki, and *Madadayo* (1993), about an old professor beloved by his students. The title is a word meaning "not yet!" The professor recites it at the birthday parties thrown by those he mentored. He was not dead—not yet. Kurosawa, who perhaps saw some of himself in the professor, died in 1995.

The man called Red Beard is the doctor in charge of a century-old village clinic treating the poor and the penniless. He is played by Toshiro Mifune, in the sixteenth and last time the two would work together. After such films as *Rashomon*, *The Seven Samurai*, *Yojimbo*, and *High and Low*, what a long way they had come, and what a serene note to part on. Dr. Niide is not even seen in the opening scenes of the film, but his presence pervades the clinic, a spartan but spic-and-span building in a humble neighborhood (Kurosawa built a traditional village to surround it).

The film is not really the story of Red Beard at all, but of Noboru Yasumoto (Yuzo Kayama), an ambitious young man who has graduated from a Dutch medical school in Japan and fancies himself on a fast track to join the shogun's household. He interns at the clinic resentfully, having heard tales of its autocratic director and "smelly" clientele. He suspects family intrigues may have been behind his obscure posting.

The clinic seems to permit a certain amount of democracy among the patients and the loud, energetic nursing and kitchen staffs. They all have opinions on everything. Some patients, like the saintly Sahachi (Tsutomu Yamazaki), are not exactly dying but seem to have moved in permanently, and we find that Red Beard's method is to indirectly treat soul along with body. In some aspects the clinic is a settlement house.

The newcomer Yasumoto declines to cooperate. Surely he is in this backwater unfairly. He refuses even to wear his medical uniform. Kurosawa establishes an omniscient but invisible presence for Red Beard, and then finally introduces him seen from behind, abruptly turning to face the young intern after a delay. Here and later Mifune invests Red Beard with gruff inscrutability; the doctor believes in teaching through object lessons and experience, not through lectures.

His first assignment simply involves watching by an old man's side as he dies. Yasumoto finds he is barely equal to the task. It is too real, too painful. There is a method to Red Beard's lesson. Yasumoto thinks of medicine as a career path, not an interaction with the sick. He is warned away from the beautiful patient known as The Mantis (Kyôko Kagawa), who is notorious for killing her husbands and is held in isolation. But she is seductive, and he nearly loses his life in trying to help her. Watch here how Kurosawa uses his compositions of the two characters enclosed in a room to concentrate the danger.

The saintly man draws close to death. He has spent his days making products to sell on behalf of his fellow patients. A mudslide shakes the clinic, and a skeleton is unearthed. The old man knows the skeleton belongs to his wife. No, he didn't kill her. It is more tragic than that. He tells his listeners the story in an evocative flashback which includes an earthquake, and notice how well Kurosawa photographs it through a cloud of dust, with foreground action and a line of people fleeing at the top of the frame.

The second act begins with Red Beard and Yasumoto visiting a brothel to treat for syphilis. There they find the traumatized 12-year-old Otoyo (Terumi Niki), who obsessively scrubs the wooden floor. Her mother died outside the brothel, the crass madam "gave her a home," and she is essentially a sex slave. Red Beard announces that she has a fever and he will take her away to live at the clinic. The madam refuses and summons her guards.

In a scene that stands amusingly outside the film's mood, Red Beard expertly uses martial arts and his knowledge of bones to break the arms and legs of all the guards, leaving them littered about the courtyard. Then he takes Otoyo away. As they leave, he apologizes to Yasumoto for his use of violence. This is a theme through the film: Red Beard's criticism of his own faults. A doctor must never harm others, he informs his pupil, as his victims lie moaning.

The story of Otoyo supplies the emotional heart of *Red Beard*. I will not tell too much. Experience it. But observe (after Red Beard orders Yasumoto to keep Otoyo in his room for observation and treatment) that she awakens behind him in darkness and sits upright with a cry. She is in shadow, except for a pinpoint of light that picks out her eyes, glowing fiercely like a tiger's. She turns away and is a dark silhouette. Then lowers herself and her eyes shine again from the dark. The choreography for camera here must have been meticulous.

Red Beard's philosophy seems to be that the sick grow better by helping others. Two centuries ago, he has a wise and instinctive understanding of psychology: he doesn't lecture patients or help them "talk through" their problems. He places them in practical situations where they are able to take inventory of themselves and focus on the troubles of others. That is the cure. It works for Otoyo and Yasumoto both.

Otoyo, broken in mind and spirit, notices a little thief half her age trying to steal gruel. Still almost catatonic, she rouses herself to offer him some food and becomes involved in his life. In telling the thief's story, Kurosawa has a magnificent composition where the screen is crossed by clotheslines of drying sheets or kimonos. In foreground, Yasumoto and a nurse listen as, in top background, the thief relates his story. As I describe this, it must be difficult to imagine. How can top and bottom and foreground and background be composed in that way? Kurosawa does it with simple elegance.

For me, the most unforgettable scene in the film takes place after the little boy seems about to die. A dreadful mourning sound comes from outside. What can it be? It is the sound of the cooks, crying the thief's name down into the well, which is believed to penetrate to the center of the earth where souls go. They are calling him back. Otoyo runs out and joins them. What seems to be a single shot looks up at them calling into the well, and pans down its walls to look down at their reflections. How this was accomplished I have no idea.

Another example of the cinematography comes with the passage of the seasons. Rain and snow are both notoriously difficult to photograph. Both are done with great effect. We know Kurosawa awaited a real snowfall. Did he also wait for it to really rain? I've never seen wetter rain in another movie.

Red Beard is a long and deliberate film, as it must be, because the lessons of the great doctor cannot be ticked off in vignettes. Doctors need to watch awhile at deathbeds and learn about the patients. We need to observe how a man who thinks of himself as flawed can be wholly good. And how a man who has an unearned high opinion of himself can learn goodness through humility. I believe this film should be seen by every medical student. Like Kurosawa's masterpiece, *Ikiru* (1952), it fearlessly regards the meanings of life, and death.

{ RICHARD III }

Was ever there a villain such as Richard the Third? Murderer of his brother Henry VI; of Prince Edward; later of Edward's wife Anne; of his own brother Clarence; of Anne's brother Rivers; of his henchmen Grey and Vaughn; of Lord Hastings; of his own two young nephews; of Lady Anne; and finally of his long-loyal retainer Buckingham. All had to make way for Richard's overwhelming ambition to rise to the throne. All died in vain, as Richard was unmounted in battle and uttered the famous cry, "A horse, a horse, my kingdom for a horse!"

Or so Shakespeare has it, and his Richard III is the version that has been popularly accepted for centuries. English history tells a different story, depriving Richard even of his most famous crime, the execution of his two nephews. Richard, in fact, may not have been entirely evil at all, but as John Ford has a character say many years later, "When the legend becomes fact, print the legend." Certainly Richard III is one of the most memorable characters in all of Shakespeare.

His Richard is vile and without merit, universally loathed, loathing himself. A hunchback, he looks in the mirror on the play's first scene and described what he sees: *Deformed, unfinished, sent before my time into this breathing world, scarce half made up, and that so lamely and unfashionable that dogs bark at me as I halt by them.* The historical Richard was of perfectly average proportions, but Shakespeare's invention has given countless actors an embellishment to be grateful for.

Harold Bloom argues in his book *Shakespeare: The Invention of the Human* that the bard all but invented human character in drama and fiction by creating characters who were self-aware and shared their feelings with the audience. In the same opening scene, Richard, who is pathologically secretive, openly shares his plans with us: *. . . therefore, since I cannot prove a lover . . . I am determined to prove a villain.* Throughout the play he casts an eye at the audience and reveals his inner thoughts.

Bloom thought Sir Ian McKellen was the greatest Richard III he had ever seen, and Richard Loncraine's 1995 film is based on McKellen's famous 1990 National Theater performance. It sets the play in an England of an alternate timeline, which clearly evokes 1930s fascism. In recent London, Shakespeare's language remains the same; I imagine the playwright himself would have cared little about the sets and costumes of a staging so long as his words were respected.

This is a film with a dread fascination. McKellen occupies it like a poisonous spider in its nest. Lurching sideways through his life, smoking as if it's as necessary to him as breathing, seductive when he wants to be, when angered Richard reveals the predator within. As he makes a great show of loving his little nephews, one of them jumps playfully on his deformity and he snarls and bares his teeth like a jackal. When a retainer gives him an apple to feed to a pig, he throws it at the animal, nodding with quiet satisfaction at its squeal.

Yet this Richard has a reptilian charm. One of the most audacious proposals in all of literature occurs when Richard, who in the play has caused the death of Henry VI and his son Edward, follows Edward's widow Anne (Kristin Scott Thomas) as she accompanies the corpse of her husband through the streets. He confides in us: he plans to marry her and congratulates himself on his boldness:

Was ever woman in this humour woo'd?
Was ever woman in this humour won?
I'll have her; but I will not keep her long.
What! I, that kill'd her husband and his father,

To take her in her heart's extremest hate,
With curses in her mouth, tears in her eyes . . .

Years in fact passed between the murder and their wedding, but never mind; notice a small touch added by Loncraine and McKellen. After softening her up, Richard offers her a ring, which she accepts. All very well. But he removes the ring from his own finger by sticking it in his mouth and lubricating it with saliva, so that as he slips it on her finger she cannot help but feel the spit of her husband's murderer.

Such extra measures of repulsive detail scuttle through the entire film, making this *Richard III* perversely entertaining. When I saw it with a large audience, it chuckled almost the way people did during *Silence of the Lambs*; Richard, like Hannibal Lector, is not only a reprehensible man, but a smart one, who is in on the joke. He relishes being a villain; it is his revenge on the world.

From the start the film gives us the sense of being privileged insiders, knowing Richard better than any of the characters. The famous opening lines ("Now is the winter of our discontent") begin in public glory, and then conclude in private, standing at a urinal, speaking directly to the camera.

This Richard has an uncanny power to control men. His close aides and confidants know full well the enormity of his crimes and the innocence of his victims. Yet smoothly, without question, they nod at his commands and cry them out. The chief of the admirers is Lord Buckingham (Jim Broadbent), his hair slicked back, his face always in judicious neutrality, quick to smile and agree. We are reminded of the words of Shakespeare's Julius Caesar:

Let me have men about me that are fat;
Sleek-headed men and such as sleep o' nights

He, too, will eventually fall to Richard's paranoia, so that at the end, fallen in battle, Richard is alone, all alone. He goes to bed uneasy:

I have not that alacrity of spirit,
Nor cheer of mind, that I was wont to have.

Then follows the dreadful nightmare during which he is visited by the accusing ghosts of all his victims. He awakes trembling:

It is now dead midnight.
Cold fearful drops stand on my trembling flesh.
What do I fear? myself? there's none else by:
Richard loves Richard; that is, I am I.
Is there a murderer here? No. Yes, I am:
Then fly. What, from myself?

Yes, from himself, the final evil he cannot flee.

Richard III, written in about 1591, is said to be Shakespeare's first great play. We can only speculate about the effect it had on its first audiences. The Elizabethan drama was a great popular art form, created not for royal courts but for poor groundlings who paid a penny to stand in the pit beneath the stage, or bourgeois such as Pepys, who paid a little more to be sure of a seat and a good view.

What Shakespeare and his contemporaries were creating was, if you will, an early form of the gutter press, in which the misdeeds of the great were presented for the entertainment of the commoners. Yet they were written in sublime verse and contained profundities we are still awed by; at the dawn of the English language, that was an age of genius, and at its summit stood Shakespeare, the most extraordinary artist in any medium in human history.

McKellen has a deep sympathy for the playwright. In London I saw his one-man show *Acting Shakespeare*, in which he effortlessly commands many of Shakespeare's great characters, evoking period, setting, and character with only his gift and some lighting. On the stage McKellen has also played Hamlet, King John, Lear, Romeo, Macbeth, Coriolanus, and Othello. Here he brings to Shakespeare's most tortured villain a malevolence we are moved to pity. No man should be so evil and know it. Hitler and others were more evil, but denied out to themselves. There is no escape for Richard. He is one of the first self-aware characters in the theater, and for that distinction he must pay the price.

{ R I O   B R A V O }

Howard Hawks didn't direct a film for four years after the failure of his *Land of the Pharaohs* in 1955. He thought maybe he had lost it. When he came back to work on *Rio Bravo* in 1958, he was 62 years old, would be working on his forty-first film, and was so nervous on the first day of shooting that he stood behind a set and vomited. Then he walked out and directed a masterpiece.

To watch *Rio Bravo* (1959) is to see a master craftsman at work. The film is seamless. There is not a shot that is wrong. It is uncommonly absorbing, and the 141-minute running time flows past like running water. It contains one of John Wayne's best performances. It has surprisingly warm romantic chemistry between Wayne and Angie Dickinson. Dean Martin is touching. Ricky Nelson, then a rival of Elvis and with a pompadour that would have been laughed out of the Old West, improbably works in the role of a kid gunslinger. Old Walter Brennan, as the peg-legged deputy, provides comic support that never oversteps.

Wayne and the other men and the gambling lady inhabit a town that is populous and even crowded, but not a single citizen, except for an early victim, a friendly hotel owner and his wife, and of course the villain, ever says a word to them. The shadows are filled with hired killers with $50 gold pieces in their pockets—"the price of a human life." All that buys

Wayne and his deputies a stay of execution is the prisoner they precariously hold as a hostage. In a film with suspenseful standoffs and looming peril, even a scene where Wayne and Martin walk down Main Street after nightfall is frightening.

The story situation was fashioned by Jules Furthman and Leigh Brackett, two veterans who wrote Hawks's great film *The Big Sleep* (1946). It centers on four men holed up inside a sheriff's office: a seasoned lawman, a drunk, an old coot, and a kid. This formula would prove so resilient that Hawks would remake it in *El Dorado* (1966), John Carpenter would remake it as *Assault on Precinct 13* (1976), and directors from Scorsese to Tarantino to Stone would directly reference it. It is a Western with all the artifice of the genre, but the characters and their connections take on a curious reality; within this closed system, their relationships have a psychological plausibility.

Wayne, as Sheriff John T. Chance, plays what he himself called "the John Wayne role." He even wears the same hat, now battered and torn, that he had worn in Westerns ever since John Ford's *Stagecoach* (1939). Yet here he calls upon the role and his own history to bring nuance and depth to the character. Grumpy old Ford, seeing Hawks's *Red River*, said, "I never knew the big son of a bitch could act."

Wayne is effective above all when he simply stands and regards people. "I don't act, I react," he liked to say, and here you see what he meant. His Chance doesn't feel it necessary to impose himself, apart from the formidable fact of his presence. He never sweet-talks Feathers (Dickinson), indeed tends to be gruff toward her, but his eyes and body language speak for him. There is a moment when he is angered that she didn't get on the stage out of town, stalks upstairs to her hotel room, barges through the door, and then—in the reverse shot—sees her and transforms his whole demeanor. Can you say a man "softens" simply by the way he holds himself? With the most subtle of body movements, he unwinds into the faintest beginning of a courtly bow. You don't see it. You feel it.

Dickinson was 27, looked younger, when she made the film—her first significant feature role after bit parts and TV. Wayne was 51. No matter. They fit together. They liked each other. They make this palpable without throwing themselves at each other. If you will go to chapter 21 of the DVD, you will see a romantic scene so sweet and unexpected, it may make you hold your breath. Dickinson absolutely holds the screen against the big man. Her carriage and deep, rich voice project a sense of who she is—not a saloon floozy but a competent professional gambler accustomed to sparring with men.

She was the type of woman Hawks liked and returned to time and again: Lauren Bacall, Katharine Hepburn, Carole Lombard, Jean Arthur, Rosalind Russell, indeed the future studio executive Sherry Lansing. He loved to use again what had worked for him earlier; when Dickinson asks Wayne to kiss her a second time, because "it's even better when two people do it," there's an echo of Bacall in *To Have and Have Not*, telling Bogart, "It's even better when you help." Peter Bogdanovich notices this in a supplement on the DVD and praises the long opening sequence in *Rio Bravo*, which runs, he says, five minutes without dialogue. And no wonder: Hawks used the business of a coin thrown into a spittoon in the silent film *Underworld* (1927), for which he wrote the scenario. And where might Hawks have found inspiration for the scene where Wayne lifts Dickinson in his arms and carries her upstairs?

Much of the strength of the Chance character comes from the way he holds himself in reserve, not feeling the need to comment on everything. His delicate relationship with Dean Martin's alcoholic character Dude involves a minimum of lectures and a lot of simply waiting to see what Dude will do. When Dude and old Stumpy (Brennan) get in a loud argument, Hawks holds Chance in center background, observing, not interfering. Chance is always the unspoken source of authority, the audience the others hope to impress.

The score by Dimitri Tiomkin evokes a frontier spirit when it wants to but also helps deepen the film, which rarely for a Western marks the passage of days with sunsets and sunrises, and makes the town streets seem lonely and exposed. There is also the introduction of a theme known to the Mexicans as "The Cutthroat Song," which the villain Burdette (John Russell) orders the band to play. Chance reads it as a message: "No quarter taken." The song haunts the film.

There is another use of music that some will question. In a lull in the action, the men relax inside the barricaded sheriff's office, and Martin, resting on his back with his hat shielding his eyes, begins to sing about a cowboy's loneliness. Nelson picks up his guitar and accompanies him. Then Ricky sings an uptempo song of his own, with Martin and even Brennan in harmony. Does this scene feel airlifted in? Maybe, but I wouldn't do without it. Martin and Nelson were two of the most popular singers of the time, and the interlude functions well as an affectionate reprise for the men before the final showdown. Needless to say, Sheriff Chance doesn't sing along.

The brave sheriff takes a stand against the outlaws who threaten a town. It is a familiar Western situation, which may remind you of *High Noon* (1952). In 1972, I interviewed Wayne on the set of his *Cahill, U.S. Marshal* in Durango, Mexico. *High Noon* came up, as it will when Westerns are being discussed.

"What a piece of you-know-what that was," he told me. "I think it was popular because of the music. Think about it this way. Here's a town full of people who have ridden in covered wagons all the way across the plains, fightin' off Indians and drought and wild animals in order to settle down and make themselves a homestead. And then when three no-good bad guys walk into town and the marshal asks for a little help, everybody in town gets shy. If I'd been the marshal, I would have been so goddamned disgusted with those chicken-livered yellow sons of bitches that I would have just taken my wife and saddled up and rode out of there."

{ SENSO }

Visconti's *Senso* (1954) opens in an opera house and in a way never leaves it. This is a passionate and melodramatic romance, with doomed lovers, posturing soldiers, secret meetings at midnight, bold adultery, and dramatic deaths. That it mostly takes place in Venice is appropriate—Venice, that city where every view is a backdrop for an aria.

The opening sequence brings all the characters on stage and sets up their stories of doom. Visconti films on location inside the city's La Fenice, that beloved music box of an opera house, destroyed by fire in 1836 and 1996, rebuilt both times. The tiers of boxes are unusual in that they rise straight up one above another, so the patrons are all fully on display. La Fenice is known for more intervals than most houses; in the winter opera season the regulars often know one another and love to mingle and gossip. As they kept track of the comings and goings in other boxes and followed each other's eyes, the theater must have worked in earlier centuries like Facebook.

It is 1866. Intrigue is afoot. The best orchestra seats up front are filled by officers of the occupying Austrian army, dressed in showy whites. In the galleries, patriots distribute leaflets, and these shower down upon the foreigners as, in Verdi's *Il Trovatore*, the hero cries, "To arms! To arms!" The leaflets call for an end to the Austrian presence and the unification of Venice with Italy, then in the making by Garibaldi.

In the melee, sharp words are exchanged between an Austrian soldier and a young Venetian partisan. A duel is set for the following morning. This is observed from a box by Countess Livia Serpieri, whose wealthy
husband is one of the aristocracy. Her favorite cousin, Marquis Roberto
Ussoni, was the offended partisan. She summons an Austrian officer so she
can beg mercy for her cousin. And now all the parts of the tragedy are in
motion.

The countess is played by Alida Valli, who we remember as Harry
Lime's loyal mistress in *The Third Man*. She was a great but reserved beauty;
the critic David Thompson said he couldn't remember her smiling in a film.
Her detachment serves her well here, because the countess will need to de-
ceive, betray, and act entirely selfishly. The Austrian, Lt. Franz Mahler, is
played by Farley Granger, handsome and charming in an insubstantial way.
She appeals to him to forbid the duel. She doesn't know the rat has betrayed
her cousin to the authorities and Marquis Ussoni is already behind bars.

Alida Valli and Farley Granger were not Visconti's first choices for
the roles; he preferred Maria Callas at first, and then Ingrid Bergman and
Marlon Brando. His film would have the biggest budget in Italian history,
and he wanted star names (like all Italian films for many years, it would be
dubbed into all the necessary languages). Brando even tested for the role, but
he fell out, Bergman was troubled in her controversial marriage to Roberto
Rossellini, and Count Luchino Visconti settled for Valli, an important European star, and Granger, a lesser but well-known star from America.

Was that a loss to the film? I don't think so. Bergman made her her-
oines sympathetic and warm, and Livia is neither. Brando was an imposing
masculine presence, and Mahler needs to be a faithless coward. In terms of
the requirements of the roles, the movie was ideally cast, and Granger, who
usually made a second-rate hero, made a first-rate cad.

Visconti takes his time moving the action from La Fenice, and
when we finally glimpse Venice it is only a distant canal seen from the
cavernous vestibule of Count Serpieri's palazzo. But we will see a great deal
of the city as the Countess and the Lieutenant meet apparently by accident,
he offers to escort her through a dangerous quarter, and they end up walking and talking all night. Visconti's filming is richly atmospheric; anyone

who knows Venice will recognize every location because, minus advertising signs and shop windows, Venice doesn't change.

Count Serpieri is a powerful man but understands that his trophy wife will not take orders from him. He foolishly believes her word, and his wife succumbs to Mahler's sexual hypnosis. What's clear to us, in part because of Farley Granger's very presence, is that he is a heartless opportunist. Mesmerized by him, she betrays not only her husband and her patriot cousin, she pays for Mahler to bribe a doctor to declare him unfit for military service.

More plot details can be left alone. What fascinates Visconti is the extremes to which sexual passion drives her; like the hero of his *Death in Venice* (1970), she is helplessly in love, forced to a rendezvous with doom. She stays out night after night. Although she must be famous in the small Venetian community, she risks identification by boldly calling at Mahler's quarters even in daytime. She doesn't or won't comprehend clear warnings and unmistakable insults to her character. The only difference between her and the heroine of an opera is that she doesn't sing. As for Mahler, how invisible does he think he is at night with his flamboyant white uniform and its sweeping cape?

Senso has obvious associations with another great Visconti film, *The Leopard* (1963). Both are set at about the same time, in the early 1860s, and both involve aristocrats faced with social upheaval. Visconti was the Count of Lonate Pozzolo, descendant from a medieval Milanese ruling family; born rich, he was a Marxist, yet in both these films he was concerned more with individuals at a moment of historical change than with political and economic issues. The difference is that *The Leopard* has affection for the traditions that are ending, and *Senso*, made nine years earlier, shows only contempt for the ruling class.

Senso is lush, broadly emotional, and beautifully photographed, but it has always ranked below *The Leopard* in popularity, perhaps because its leading characters are rotten to the core. Only the cousin, Roberto Ussoni, is heroic; he fights in Garibaldi's campaign for Italian unification and land reform. It's significant that the character of Ussoni was invented by Visconti and wasn't present in the novella he and Suso Cecchi d'Amico adapted, by

Camillo Boito. The added character was invaluable in allowing Visconti to show the revolution betrayed by the aristocracy, but the betrayal is more a matter of Livia's character than of her class.

In any event, Visconti's love of opera was more important here than his Marxism. He directed Maria Callas five times at La Scala between 1954 and 1957, and indeed she was his first choice for Livia but her schedule had no room for a film. He directed some 25 operas in all, and in his cowriting of *Senso* you sense the larger than life emotions, the grand scale. What's surprising is that this film itself hasn't been adapted for an opera.

Senso has had a checkered history. Italian censors forced Visconti to reshoot the ending, saying his original version was an insult to the Italian army in showing soldiers mistreating the forlorn and pathetic heroine. Despite the alleged star power of Valli and Granger, the film was shortened for markets outside Italy, and seen in England and America in an English-language version named variously *Livia* and *The Wanton Countess*, with both leads speaking their own English.

The rich Technicolor won the admiration of Martin Scorsese, whose Film Foundation paid for the restoration of this new version, released in February 2011 in the Criterion Collection. A disk of extras includes *The Wanton Countess*.

SEVEN

It is almost always raining in the city. Somerset, the veteran detective, wears a hat and raincoat. Mills, the kid who has just been transferred into the district, walks bare-headed in the rain as if he'll be young forever. On their first day together, they investigate the death of a fat man they find face-down in a dish of pasta. On a return visit to the scene, the beams of their flashlights point here and there in the filthy apartment, picking out a shelf lined with dozens of cans of Campbell's tomato sauce. Not even a fat man buys that much tomato sauce.

This grim death sets the tone for David Fincher's *Seven* (1995), one of the darkest and most merciless films ever made in the Hollywood mainstream. It will rain day after day. They will investigate death after death. There are words scrawled at the crime scenes; the fat man's word is on the wall behind his refrigerator: *Gluttony*. After two of these killings Mills realizes they are dealing with a serial killer, who intends every murder to punish one of the Seven Deadly Sins.

This is as formulaic as an Agatha Christie whodunit. But *Seven* takes place not in the genteel world of country house murders, but in the lives of two cops, one who thinks he has seen it all and the other who has no idea what he is about to see. Nor is the film about detection; the killer turns himself in when the film still has half an hour to go. It's more of a

BALTIMORE COUNTY
PUBLIC LIBRARY

Cockeysville Branch
410-887-7750
www.bcpl.info

Customer ID: **********8275

Items that you checked out

Title: How to draw cute stuff around the world
ID: 31183206490051
Due: Monday, April 1, 2024

Title: Magpie murders
ID: 31183212952987
Due: Monday, April 1, 2024

Title: Talking pictures : how to watch movies
ID: 31183186240179
Due: Monday, April 1, 2024

Title: The beautiful poetry of Donald Trump
ID: 31183194075591
Due: Monday, April 1, 2024

Title: The great movies IV
ID: 31183183694980
Due: Monday, April 1, 2024

Total items: 5
Account balance: $0.00
Checked out: 11
Messages:
Patron status is ok.
3/11/2024 1:43 PM

Free Be to All In
Late fees no longer assessed for over due
items
Ask for details or visit bcpl.info
Shelf Help 410-494-9063

character study, in which the older man becomes a scholar of depravity and the younger experiences it in a pitiable and personal way. A hopeful quote by Hemingway was added as a voice-over after preview audiences found the original ending too horrifying. But the original ending is still there, and the quote plays more like a bleak joke. The film should end with Freeman's "see you around." After the devastating conclusion, the Hemingway line is small consolation.

The enigma of Somerset's character is at the heart of the film, and this is one of Morgan Freeman's best performances. He embodies authority naturally; I can't recall him ever playing a weak man. Here he knows all the lessons a cop might internalize during years spent in what we learn is one of the worst districts of the city. He lives alone, in what looks like a rented apartment, bookshelves on the walls. He puts himself to sleep with a metronome. He never married, although he came close once. He is a lonely man who confronts life with resigned detachment.

When he realizes he's dealing with the Seven Deadly Sins, he does what few people would do, and goes to the library. There he looks into Dante's *Inferno*, Milton's *Paradise Lost*, and Chaucer's *Canterbury Tales*. It's not that he reads them so much as he references them for viewers; it is often effective in a horror film to introduce disturbing elements from literature as atmosphere, and Fincher provides glimpses of Gustav Dore's illustrations for Dante, including the famous depiction of a woman with spider legs. Somerset sounds erudite as he names the deadly sins to Mills, who seems to be hearing of them for the first time.

What's being used here is the same sort of approach William Friedkin employed in *The Exorcist* and Jonathan Demme in *The Silence of the Lambs*. What could become a routine cop movie is elevated by the evocation of dread mythology and symbolism. *Seven* is not really a very deep or profound film, but it provides the convincing illusion of one. Almost all mainstream thrillers seek first to provide entertainment; this one intends to fascinate and appall. By giving the impression of scholarship, Detective Somerset lends a depth and significance to what the killer apparently considers moral statements. To be sure, Somerset lucks out in finding that the killer has a library card, although with this killer, thinking back, you figure he didn't get his ideas in the library and checked out those books to lure the police.

The five murders investigated by the partners provide variety. The killer has obviously gone to elaborate pains in planning and carrying them out—in one case, at least a year in advance. His agenda in the film's climactic scene, however, must have been improvised recently. *Seven* draws us relentlessly into its horrors, some of which are all the more effective for being glimpsed in brief shots. We can only be sure of the killing methods after the cops discuss them—although a shot of the contents of a plastic bag after an autopsy hardly requires more explanation. Fincher shows us enough to disgust us and cuts away.

The killer obviously intends his elaborate murders as moral statement. He suggests as much after we meet him. When he's told his crimes will soon be forgotten in the daily rush of cruelty, he insists they will be remembered forever. They are his masterpiece. What goes unexplained is how, exactly, he is making a statement. His victims, presumably guilty of their sins, have been convicted and executed by his actions. What's the lesson? Let that be a warning to us?

Somerset and Mills represent established fiction formulas. Mills is the fish out of water, they're an odd couple, and together they're the old hand and the greenhorn. The actors and the dialogue by Andrew Kevin Walker enrich the formulas with specific details and Freeman's precise, laconic speech. Brad Pitt seems more one-dimensional, or perhaps guarded; he's a hothead, quick to dismiss Freeman's caution and experience. It is his wife Tracy (Gwyneth Paltrow) who brings a note of humanity into the picture; we never find out very much about her, but we know she loves her husband and worries about him, and she has good instincts when she invites the never-married Somerset over for dinner. Best to make an ally of the man who her husband needs and can learn from. Watching the film, we assume the Tracy character is simply a placeholder, labeled Protagonist's Wife and denied much dimension. But she is saving her impact until later. Thinking back through the film, our appreciation for its construction grows.

The killer, as I said, turns himself in with 30 minutes to go and dominates the film from that point forward. When *Seven* was released in 1995 the ads, posters, and opening credits didn't mention the name of the actor, and although you may well know it, I don't think I will either. This actor has a big assignment. He embodies Evil. Like Hannibal Lecter, his character must be played by a strong actor who projects not merely villainy but twisted psychological complexities. Observe his face. Smug. Self-satisfied. Listen to his voice. Intelligent. Analytical. Mark his composure and apparent fearlessness. The film essentially depends on him and would go astray if the actor faltered. He doesn't.

Seven (1995) was David Fincher's second feature, after *Alien 3* (1992), filmed when he was only 29. Still to come were such as *Zodiac* (2007) and *The Social Network* (2010). In his work he likes a saturated palate and gravitates toward sombre colors and underlighted interiors. None of his films is darker than this one. Like Spielberg, he infuses the air in his interiors with a fine unseen powder that makes the beams of flashlights visible, emphasizing the surrounding darkness. I don't know why the interior lights in *Seven* so often seem weak or absent, but I'm not complaining. I remember a shot in Murnau's *Faust* (1926) in which Satan wore a black cloak that enveloped a tiny village below. That is the sensation Fincher creates here.

{ SHADOW OF A DOUBT }

No one would ever accuse Alfred Hitchcock's *Shadow of a Doubt* (1943) of being plausible, but it is framed so distinctively in the Hitchcock style that it plays firmly and never breaks out of the story. Later you question the absurdity of two detectives following a suspect from New York to California, apparently without being sure of how he looks, and hanging around idly outside his residence for weeks while chatting up the suspect's niece; one of them eventually even proposes marriage. Nor are we convinced that the niece, believing her uncle is a killer of old ladies, would allow him to buy her silence by promising to leave town (because his guilt would "destroy her mother").

One of Hitchcock's favorite subjects was the Innocent Man Wrongly Accused. In *Shadow of a Doubt*, there's no possibility of innocence. It's clear from the outset that Uncle Charlie (Joseph Cotten) is the notorious "Merry Widow Killer," and more than once Hitchcock cuts to nightmarish fantasies of (presumably) merry widows waltzing. We first see Charlie lying on top of his bed, smoking a cigar, when told by his landlady two men had been asking for him. He sees them standing on the corner downstairs, packs a bag with cash, leaves the house, and boldly walks right past them. This demonstrates they don't know what he looks like, but not why they wouldn't be interested in *any* man leaving the boarding house. The incompetence, and apparently unlimited expense account, of these two cops is one reason the action can span several weeks.

Charlie's peppy niece Charlotte (Teresa Wright), nicknamed "Young Charlie" after her uncle, has idolized him for years and complains to her family that life wouldn't be so dull if he paid them a visit. Amazingly, that day they receive a telegram telling them to expect him. In a well-known shot Hitchcock shows Charlie's train arriving beneath an ominous cloud of black smoke. He has arrived in Santa Rosa, California, a paragon of small towns that could have modeled for Norman Rockwell's *Saturday Evening Post* covers.

The town and the Newton family play major roles in the film and may reveal Hitchcock's own inner feelings. He shot in late 1941 and early 1942, at the outset of World War II, at a time when he was unable to visit his dying mother in London because of wartime restrictions. He later credited the friendliness of the town for making this the most pleasant of all his film locations. His emphasis on the comfy Newton home, a chatty neighborhood, a corner cop who knows everyone's name, the nightly meals around a big dining table—all add up to a security that both he and Uncle Charlie were seeking, and Charlie rhapsodizes about the joys of home and family. The visiting uncle is so quickly embraced by the town there is even a ceremony in his honor.

What we begin with, then, is the innocent Newton family and the sinister uncle, who moves into Young Charlie's room at the top of the stairs. Also in the family are her father Joseph (Henry Travers), her mother Emma (Patricia Collinge), and her young sister Ann (Edna May Wonacott) and brother Roger (Charles Bates). Travers was in his late 60s and Collinge around 50 when the film was made, and they look on the old side for Ann and Roger's parents but about right for the movie's apple pie symbolism. The next door neighbor, who drops in without knocking, is Herb (Hume Cronyn, in his movie debut). He and Joseph are crime buffs and spend much time in debates about methods of committing a perfect murder. Their asides are funny in themselves, and more so because of Uncle Charlie's discomfiture. His preferred method is strangulation with his bare hands.

So now everyone is onstage. The uncle, the family, the neighbor, the cops (notably the good-looking younger detective Jack, played by Macdonald Carey, who falls in love with Young Charlie). With Uncle Charlie seemingly content to spend the rest of his life in Santa Rosa, Hitchcock needed something to create a shadow of a doubt, and I suppose his Mac-Guffin this time is a story in the newspaper about the Merry Widow Killer. This story might have passed unnoticed if Uncle Charlie didn't unwisely and unsuccessfully try to conceal it. That triggers Young Charlie's growing suspicion that there must be more to her uncle than it appears. Charlie has a dark side to his nature, a way of narrowing his eyes and seeming threatening, that is later, somewhat awkwardly, accounted for by a head injury when he was young.

The engine of the plot then involves Young Charlie's suspicion and her uncle's paranoia and clumsy attempts to murder her—as if that would accomplish anything more than confirming the suspicions of Jack the cop. As plots go, this one is not a Hitchcock masterpiece, but it works because it generates suspense; how close to the truth will the niece come before she's killed or proven right? During the running length of the film the elements all mesh efficiently; it's later that the weaknesses grow evident.

Much of the film's effect comes from its visuals. Hitchcock was a master of the classical Hollywood compositional style. It is possible to recognize one of his films after a minute or so entirely because of the camera placement. He used well-known camera language just a little more elegantly. See here how he zooms slowly into faces to show dawning recognition or fear. Watch him use tilt shots to show us things that are not as they should be. He uses contrasting lighted and shadowed areas within the frame to make moral statements, sometimes in anticipation before they are indicated. I found while teaching several of his films with the shot-by-shot stop-action technique that not a single shot violates compositional theory.

Not many directors were fonder of staircases than Sir Alfred. They impose a hierarchy of power and weakness. A character at the top of the stairs can seem to loom or be in danger of toppling, depending on whether the POV is high or low. The flow at the house goes up the sidewalk, onto the porch, through the door, and directly up the stairs. There are outside stairs in the back, and both staircases are used for tight little sequences of threat and escape. Notice how many variations of camera angles and lighting Hitchcock uses with the stairs. He considered them an ideal device for introducing imbalance into otherwise horizontal interiors. So important were they to him, so memorably used, that I can name some of his titles and if you've seen them you will instantly recall the stairs: *Notorious*, *Psycho*, *Strangers on a Train*, *Frenzy*, and of course *Vertigo*.

Joseph Cotten and Teresa Wright do all the heavy lifting in the acting department. The other characters are bundles of clichés. One of Hitchcock's inspirations for the film was Thornton Wilder's *Our Town*, inflaming his yearning for domesticity at a time when Britain was already at war. In a way there are two movies here: a Hitchcock, and a nostalgic small town fantasy. So innocent is the town that Uncle Charlie walks into the bank where Joseph Newton is president, deposits tens of thousands of dollars in bills from his briefcase, and Joseph never asks a question. The Newtons aren't given much to suspicion. The two detectives at one point cook up a harebrained story that they're working on a national survey that requires them to photograph the rooms Americans live in. Of course they hope to begin with the Newton residence, and Uncle Charlie's room. The front and back stairs come much into use here. How many bankers' families would believe that story?

Cotten has one of the best scenes of his career in a dinner table conversation. His dark side takes over, and he finds himself saying these extraordinary words: "The cities are full of women, middle-aged widows, husbands dead, husbands who've spent their lives making fortunes, working and working. And then they die and leave their money to their wives, their silly wives. And what do the wives do, these useless women? You see them in the hotels, the best hotels, every day by the thousands. Drinking the money, eating the money, losing the money at bridge. Playing all day and all night. Smelling of money. Proud of their jewelry but of nothing else. Horrible, faded, fat, greedy women. . . . Are they human or are they fat, wheezing animals, hmm? And what happens to animals when they get too fat and too old?" I think that may be the most eloquence Hitchcock ever allowed a killer.

$\left\{\text{ S H O A H }\right\}$

For more than nine hours I sat and watched a film named *Shoah* (1985), and when it was over, I sat for a while longer and simply stared into space, trying to understand my emotions. I had seen a memory of the most debased chapter in human history. But I had also seen a film that affirmed life so passionately that I did not know where to turn with my confused feelings. There is no proper response to this film. It is an enormous fact, a 550-minute howl of pain and anger in the face of genocide. It is one of the noblest films ever made.

They talk and talk. *Shoah* is a torrent of words, and yet the overwhelming impression, when it is over, is one of silence. Lanzmann intercuts two kinds of images. He shows the faces of his witnesses. And then he uses quiet pastoral scenes of the places where the deaths took place. Steam engines move massively through the Polish countryside, down the same tracks where trains took countless Jews, gypsies, Poles, homosexuals, and other so-called undesirables to their deaths. Cameras pan silently across pastures, while we learn that underneath the tranquility are mass graves. Sometimes the image is of a group of people, gathered in a doorway, or in front of a church, or in a restaurant kitchen.

Lanzmann is a patient interrogator. We see him in the corners of some of his shots, a tall, lanky man, informally dressed, chain-smoking. He wants to know the details. He doesn't ask large, profound questions about the meaning of the extermination of millions of people. He asks little questions. In one of the most chilling sequences in the film, he talks to Abraham Bomba, today a barber in Tel Aviv. Bomba was one of the Jewish barbers ordered to cut off the hair of Jewish women before they were killed in Treblinka. His assignment suggests the shattering question: How can a woman's hair be worth more than her life? But Lanzmann does not ask overwhelming and unanswerable questions like this. These are the sorts of questions he asks:

You cut with what? With scissors?

There were no mirrors?

You said there were about 16 barbers? You cut the hair of how many women in one batch?

The barber tries to answer. As he talks, he has a customer in his chair, and he snips at the customer's hair almost obsessively, making tiny movements with his scissors, as if trying to use the haircut as a way to avoid the questions. Their conversation finally arrives at this exchange, after he says he cannot talk any more:

A. I can't. It's too horrible. Please.

Q. We have to do it. You know it.

A. I won't be able to do it.

Q. You have to do it. I know it's very hard. I know and I apologize.

A. Don't make me go on, please.

Q. Please. We must go on.

Lanzmann is cruel, but he is correct. He must go on. It is necessary to make this record before all of those who were witnesses to the Holocaust have died.

His methods in obtaining the interviews were sometimes underhanded. He uses a concealed television camera to record the faces of some of the old Nazi officials whom he interviews, and we look over the shoulders of the TV technicians in a van parked outside the buildings where they live. We see the old men nonchalantly pulling down charts from the wall to explain the layout of a death camp, and we hear their voices, and at one point when a Nazi asks for reassurance that the conversation is private, Lanzmann provides it. He will go to any length to obtain this testimony.

He does not, however, make any attempt to arrange his material into a chronology, an objective, factual record of how the "Final Solution" began, continued, and was finally terminated by the end of the war. He uses a more poetic, mosaic approach, moving according to rhythms only he understands among the only three kinds of faces we see in this film: survivors, murderers, and bystanders. As their testimony is intercut with the scenes of train tracks, steam engines, abandoned buildings, and empty fields, we are left with enough time to think our own thoughts, to meditate, to wonder.

This is a long movie but not a slow one, and in its words it creates something of the same phenomenon I experienced while watching *My Dinner with Andre*. The words themselves create images in the imagination, as they might in a radio play. Consider the images summoned by these words, spoken by Filip Muller, a Czech Jew assigned to work at the doors of the gas chambers, a man who survived five waves of liquidations at Auschwitz:

A. You see, once the gas was poured in, it worked like this: It rose from the ground upwards. And in the terrible struggle that followed—because it was a struggle—the lights were switched off in the gas chambers. It was dark, no one could see, so the strongest people tried to climb higher. Because they probably realized that the higher they got, the more air there was. They could breathe better. That caused the struggle. Secondly, most people tried to push their way to the door. It was psychological; they knew where the door was; maybe they could force their way out. It was instinctive, a death struggle. Which is why children and weaker people and the aged always wound up at the bottom. The strongest were on top. Because in the death struggle, a father didn't realize his son lay beneath him.

Q. And when the doors were opened?

A. They fell out. People fell out like blocks of stone, like rocks falling out of a truck.

The images evoked by his words are unutterably painful. What is re-markable, on reflection, is that Muller is describing an event that neither he nor anyone else now alive ever saw. I realized, at the end of his words, that a fundamental change had taken place in the way I personally visualized the gas chambers. Always before, in reading about them or hearing about them, my point of view was outside, looking in. Muller put me inside.

That is what this whole movie does, and it is probably the most important thing it does. It changes our point of view about the Holocaust. After nine hours of *Shoah*, the Holocaust is no longer a subject, a chapter of history, a phenomenon. It is an environment. It is around us. Ordinary people speak in ordinary voices of days that had become ordinary to them. A railroad engineer who drove the trains to Treblinka is asked if he could hear the screams of the people in the cars behind his locomotive.

A. Obviously, since the locomotive was next to the cars. They screamed, asked for water. The screams from the cars closest to the locomotives could be heard very well.
Q. Can one get used to that?
A. No. It was extremely distressing. He knew the people behind him were human, like him. The Germans gave him and the other workers vodka to drink. Without drinking, they couldn't have done it.

Some of the strangest passages in the film are the interviews with the officials who were actually responsible for running the camps and mak-ing the "Final Solution" work smoothly and efficiently. None of them, at least by their testimony, seem to have witnessed the whole picture. They only participated in a small part of it, doing their little jobs in their little corners; if they are to be believed, they didn't personally kill anybody, they just did small portions of larger tasks, and somehow all of the tasks, when added up and completed, resulted in people dying. Here is the man who scheduled the trains that took the Jews to die:

Q. You never saw a train?

A. No, never. We had so much work, I never left my desk. We worked day and night.

And here is a man who lived 150 feet from a church where Jews were rounded up, held, and then marched into gas vans for the trip to the crematoriums:

Q. Did you see the gas vans?
A. No . . . yes, from the outside. They shuttled back and forth. I never looked inside; I didn't see Jews in them.

What is so important about *Shoah* is that the voices are heard of people who did see, who did understand, who did comprehend, who were there, who know that the Holocaust happened, who tell us with their voices and with their eyes that genocide occurred in our time, in our civilization.

There is a tendency while watching *Shoah* to try to put a distance between yourself and the events on the screen. These things happened, after all, 40 or 45 years ago. Most of those now alive have been born since they happened. Then, while I was watching the film, came a chilling moment. A name flashed on the screen in the subtitles, the name of one of the commandants at Treblinka death camp. At first I thought the name was "Ebert"—my name. Then I realized it was "Eberl." I felt a moment of relief, and then a moment of intense introspection as I realized that it made no difference what the subtitle said. The message of this film (if we believe in the brotherhood of man) is that these crimes were committed by people like us, against people like us.

But there is an even deeper message as well, and it is contained in the testimony of Filip Muller, the Jew who stood at the door of a crematorium and watched as the victims walked in to die. One day some of the victims, Czech Jews, began to sing. They sang two songs: "The Hatikvah" and the Czech national anthem. They affirmed that they were Jews and that they were Czechs. They denied Hitler, who would have them be one but not the other. Muller speaks:

A. That was happening to my countrymen, and I realized that my life had become meaningless. (His eyes fill with tears.) Why go on living? For what? So I went into the gas chamber with them, resolved to die. With them. Suddenly, some who recognized me came up to me. . . . A small group of women approached. They looked at me and said, right there in the gas chamber . . .

Q. You were inside the gas chamber?

A. Yes. One of them said: "So you want to die. But that's senseless. Your death won't give us back our lives. That's no way. You must get out of here alive, you must bear witness to our suffering and to the injustice done to us."

And that is the final message of this extraordinary film. It is not a documentary, not journalism, not propaganda, not political. It is an act of witness. In it, Claude Lanzmann celebrates the priceless gift that sets man apart from animals and makes us human, and gives us hope: the ability for one generation to tell the next what it has learned.

Smiles of a
Summer Night

Adultery was the great subject of many of Ingmar Bergman's films and much of his life. He was married five times, and not very faithfully, because he also had fairly public relationships with the actresses Harriet Andersson, Bibi Andersson, and Liv Ullmann, and was married during all of those affairs. He was far from a libertine, experienced a great deal of guilt during his liaisons, and returned to the subject repeatedly in his films. He wrote *Sunday's Children* (1994), directed by his son Daniel, about how Bergman's clergyman father created a household where public piety was joined with private anguish. His screenplay *Private Confessions* (1996) was about his mother's moral struggles.

It is necessary to conclude that both films draw directly from a personal history that Ullmann experienced first hand. The idea of commitment, marriage, betrayal, and guilt formed for Bergman a moral circle, and indeed in 2000, when he was 82 and felt he was too old to direct, he enlisted Ullmann to direct *Faithless* from his final screenplay. They remained close friends before, during, and after their romantic involvement, and had a daughter together, the actress Linn Ullmann. Perhaps it was the closeness and trust he felt with Ullmann that acted as a muse, because in so many of his films there is a need to confess guilt and seek redemption.

Faithless was the final chapter of his moral autobiography. It tells the story of an old man who evokes an imaginary actress (played by Lena Endre) to help him recreate scenes from his life which puzzle and shame him. He asks her to help him recreate her past. As she does, flashbacks show her cheating on her husband with a character named David, who is "Bergman" as a young man. Wheels within wheels. The old man wants to see her adultery through her own eyes. Did he lead her into sin? Did he lie to her? Did he lie to himself? The film was perhaps as autobiographical for her as for him.

"I've known him as long as anyone except my sister," she told me one afternoon at Cannes. "We worked so closely together and then we were friends so much longer; we did two films when we loved and now this and then we have a daughter together and we are still friends. You lose and you love and then lose again, and this has been a relationship where we never lost.

"Maybe he sees this story as his life, and he's told it, and it's over. If he writes something again maybe it will be about endless love. He cannot forgive himself. I told him two years ago: 'You have to forgive yourself for whatever betrayal you have committed.' 'I cannot forgive myself,' he said. That's why I made a scene where he appears with himself as a young man, and forgives that young man, even if he can't forgive himself as an old one."

I have chosen this indirect way of backing into a look at *Smiles of a Summer Night* (1955), a film that acted as an artistic and professional turning point. He had been directing films since *Torment* in 1944, with uneven results; *Summer with Monika* (1953) had some success, oddly, as soft-core porn, although it didn't qualify. He was financed by the Swedish Film Institute, which took a bet on *Smiles* and bankrolled it for $100,000—said to be the largest amount ever spent on a Swedish film. It was a resounding international success, and it won the European Film Award and something called the Award for Best Poetic Humor at Cannes. He says in an introduction included on the Criterion DVD that after *Smiles* he never again had to scramble for financing. He moved immediately into the first ranks of filmmakers, making *The Seventh Seal* (1957) and *Wild Strawberries* (1957).

The film is entirely about adultery. Most unusual for Bergman, it is a comedy. It flirts at times with screwball, but chooses more decisively to use the kind of verbal wit that Shaw and Wilde employed. One of its lines ("I can tolerate my wife's infidelity, but if anyone touches my mistress, I become a tiger") sounds like Wilde to begin with, and even more when it appears later in a different form ("I can tolerate my mistress's infidelity, but if anyone touches my wife, I become a tiger").

The speaker is Fredrik Engerman (Gunnar Björnstrand), a 50ish attorney who is in the second year of marriage to Anne (Ulla Jacobsson), a sensuous 19-year-old. He and his son Henrik (Björn Bjelfvenstam), a theology student, share the same household with Petra (Harriet Andersson), a saucy maid who flirts shamelessly with both of them. Fredrik for several years was the lover of Desiree Armfeldt (Eva Dahlbeck), a celebrated actress, and one night he takes his young wife to see her in a play.

Anne is alerted, because on the afternoon before the play they took a nap, and he unwisely said Desiree's name in his sleep. That night after the play, he and Anne go to bed and we discover that she is still a virgin. This causes him frustration, although he doesn't want to "hurry" her. After she falls asleep, Fredrik slips out for a rendezvous with Desiree, worldly and witty, who teases him about his young wife, and the possibility that she may become attracted to the young Henrik.

Fredrik slips and falls into a puddle on his way into Desiree's house, and she supplies him with a dressing gown belonging to her current lover, Count Malcolm (Jarl Kulle). Not long after the Count himself arrives, demands an explanation, and mentions a duel. The Machiavellian Desiree—certain she is finished with the Count, belongs back with Fredrik, and Anne belongs with the idealistic theologian—arranges for her wealthy mother to throw a dinner party involving all the players, as well as the Count's wife, Charlotte (Margit Carlqvist). Petra accompanies the Engermans and cheerfully flirts with Mrs. Armfeldt's groom (Naima Wifstrand). Old Mrs. Armfeldt has also done her time as a mistress. Asked by Desiree why she doesn't write her memoirs, she replies coyly, "My dear daughter, I was given this estate for promising not to write my memoirs."

We are meant to understand that everyone's sensibilities are erotically alert because it is one of those endless northern days where night is but a finger dragging the dusk between one day and the next. What happens during the course of the long night involves smiles and a great deal more, including a providential bed that slides through a wall from one bedroom to the next. You see that I mentioned slapstick. Everyone has been affected by the wine they shared at dinner, which is described by Desiree's worldly mother: "My dear children and friends. According to legend, the wine is pressed from grapes whose juice gushes out like drops of blood against the pale grape skin. It is also said that to each cask filled with this wine was added a drop of milk from a young mother's breast and a drop of seed from a young stallion. These lend to the wine secret seductive powers. Whoever drinks hereof does so at his own risk and must answer for himself."

It is difficult to imagine Bergman writing such dialogue, but those who knew him said he had a sense of humor that was the equal of his periods of depression and despair. Even this film has some dark moments, as when the Count's wife Charlotte has a bleak monologue about males: "Men are horrible, vain, and conceited. They have hair all over their bodies." That speech occurs at a point before the wine kicks in.

The film's photography was by Gunnar Fischer, who with Sven Nykvist was one of the two cinematographers Bergman almost always worked with. Both of them appreciated Bergman's lifelong custom of directing opera and theater every winter, while meanwhile writing a new screenplay he would start filming every spring. The diffused light of the long evenings provides the characteristic visual clarity of many of Bergman's scenes.

Pauline Kael called this a nearly perfect film. Having not seen it for most of a lifetime, I was startled by how quickly it beguiled me. There is an abundance of passion here, but none of it reckless; the characters consider the moral weight of their actions, and while not reluctant to misbehave, feel a need to explain, if only to themselves. Perhaps here, in an uncharacteristic comedy, Bergman is expressing the same need.

{ SOULS FOR SALE }

In the 1920s, the golden age of silent films, millions of Americans bought tickets every week to see movies like *Souls for Sale*. It isn't on any list of great movies I've ever seen, possibly because hardly anyone had seen it for more than 75 years. When it has played over the last few years on Turner Classic Movies, it's possible more people saw it than in all the decades since it was released in 1923.

This is a prime example of the mid-range entertainment Hollywood was producing so skillfully at the time. Filled with actors who were then stars, fast-moving, entertaining, with a spectacular circus action sequence at the climax, it is drama, melodrama, romance, and satire all at once—wrapped up in a behind-the-scenes look at how a desperate young woman fell into the movie business by accident and became a star.

The story involves the memorably named Remember Steddon, played by Eleanor Boardman as a wide-eyed girl from a rural town who literally leaps off the train on her honeymoon to escape her new husband (Lew Cody). He swept her off her feet in a whirlwind courtship, we learn, but now he fills her with loathing; and no wonder, because he's a snaky operator with a skinny mustache and a history of marrying women and killing them for their insurance money.

Produced by Samuel Goldwyn, obviously not on a limited budget, it's also an exploitation of the national fascination with Hollywood and its transgressions. The Fatty Arbuckle scandal of 1921 would have been in audience minds as they saw the milk-fed maiden venturing into the den of iniquity. Remember's father is a preacher who lectures on the sins of the movies, and she believes what she hears.

But what is a girl to do? Stranded in the California desert after escaping from the train, she staggers under the burning sun and is close to death when she's rescued by a sheik on horseback. Is he a mirage? Not at all. He's an actor making a film. Poking fun at Valentino, a title card notes: "The usual sheik led the usual captive across the usual desert." The girl is nursed back to life by the filmmakers and taken to Los Angeles.

Already two of the movie men are in love with her: Richard Dix, as the film's director, and Frank Mayo, as the actor on the camel. But Remember is mindful of her father's warnings and stays clear of the movies until desperation drives her to seek a job. This sets in motion a fascinating backstage story in which we follow her as she gets past the studio gates, is rebuffed by a casting director, is befriended by the director, and gets work as an extra.

Goldwyn must have called in a lot of favors, because there are cameo roles showing Charles Chaplin directing a scene while puffing furiously on a cigarette, Erich von Stroheim allegedly working on *Greed*, and such other stars as Barbara La Marr, Jean Hersholt, Chester Conklin, and Claire Windsor.

Remember is given a screen test, miserably fails, weeps when it is screened, and is told by Dix: "If you could only cry that well on camera." Of course, she can. He also gives her some very modern advice: "Don't try to act funny. Just *feel* funny. The camera photographs exactly what you are thinking of." He then helpfully promises her: "I'll make an actress of you if I have to break your heart and every bone in your body."

Eleanor Boardman is a spirited screen presence, a big star in the decade, who married the important director King Vidor and starred in his masterpiece *The Crowd* (1928). Her female costar in *Souls for Sale* is another silent legend, Mae Busch, who appeared in 131 roles between 1912 and 1947, most notably with Laurel and Hardy in *Sons of the Desert* (1933). Here her character's tragedy provides Boardman's big break: the newcomer takes over her starring role after a heavy overhead lamp falls on her: "She may not walk for a month—if ever!"

The movie was written and directed by Rupert Hughes, who was the uncle Howard Hughes so fatefully decided to visit in Hollywood. He adapted it from his own novel, which was serialized in *Redbook* magazine, and judging by his title cards, he was well aware of how absurd his plot was. After the treacherous husband discovers his wife has disappeared from the train, he returns to his seat and—goes to sleep. "Why didn't he tell the conductor and stop the train?" a title card asks, not unreasonably. Indeed, there are times when the titles seem to be doing the work of "MST 3000," providing a sardonic commentary on the action. One card observes: "That seasick camel is a regular osteopath."

Souls for Sale provides a pointed commentary on Hollywood's practice of putting the schedule above all other considerations. The climactic scene takes place during the filming of a circus scene. A violent storm is planned to threaten the Big Top, and a huge mounted propeller is brought in to generate wind. If the director warns people not to walk into that fan once, he does it three times. Then a real storm blows up, lightning strikes the crew's generator, the circus tent catches fire, Remember's evil husband turns up from his refuge in Egypt (she's afraid her lovers will discover she's already married, not knowing he was a bigamist), and the wind machine becomes a lethal weapon. But the animals in the menagerie are saved.

"Keep cranking until the flames grow too hot!" the director tells his camera crew. The Big Top goes up in a spectacular conflagration, there is a violent death (preceded by a heartfelt speech), and then, can you believe, with an ambulance hauling the deceased away, the heartless director asks Remember if she could possibly act in one more scene. She can. What a trouper. You can't tell me Rupert Hughes wasn't grinning when he wrote this.

He also seems to have had an open mind about camera possibilities. In a scene involving the setup for a studio scene, he hurries along with little jump cuts. His framing is fairly standard, but he doesn't overuse close-ups, and the editing is brisk. The titles, when they come, are not used only for dialogue or information, but also sometimes seem to supply Hughes's own comments as he looks at his picture.

There's one little moment I'm curious about. Like so many silent films, *Souls for Sale* is not all in black and white, but uses a great deal of color tinting. Red for the desert, sepia for indoors, blue for night, a little yellow hand-painted in for the flames of the circus tent. When Remember and the wife killer are on the rear observation platform of the speeding train, the scene is tinted for night, but when he decides they should go inside, there's a quick shot of him, still outside, tinted sepia. Why's that there? Foreshadowing?

Souls for Sale, popular on its release, was thought to be lost for many years. A few prints were discovered, and when the IMDb user "wmorrow59" saw one at the Museum of Modern Art, it was "badly tattered in places, with a confusing turn in the plot at one point, which suggested that a chunk of footage must be missing."

Since then the film has been restored; its first DVD version was released by Warner Bros. and Turner Classic Movies and looked remarkably good, considering its perilous survival. A new score has been added by Marcus Sjowall, part of TCM's Young Composers Competition, and the result is a lively and funny experience, enriched by the backstage rags-to-riches story; we see lots of sets, props, costumes, cameras, crew members, and, of course, that one unfortunate overhead light.

Title cards near the end reflect the blessing of Sam Goldwyn, if not his penmanship, in praising the toilers of Hollywood for their dedication in bringing our dreams to the screen. And despite the town's reputation, Remember Steddon will be a virgin on her wedding day.

{ THE SPIRIT OF THE BEEHIVE }

In a vast Spanish plain, harvested of its crops, a farm home rests. Some distance away there is a squat building like a barn, apparently not used, its doors and windows missing. In the home lives a family of four: two little girls named Ana and Isabel, and their parents, Fernando and Teresa. He is a beekeeper, scholar, and poet who spends much time in his book-lined study. She is a solitary woman who writes letters of longing and loss to men not identified. The parents have no conversations of any consequence.

It's an exciting day in the village. A ramshackle truck rattles into town announced by scampering children who shout, "The movies! The movies!" A screen and projector are set up in the public hall, and an audience of kids and old women gather to see *Frankenstein* (1931).

For the children, the movie had might as well only be about the monster, so tellingly performed by Boris Karloff. The creature comes upon a farmer's young daughter tossing flowers into a pond to watch them float. Perhaps because of censorship, the film cuts directly from this to the monster mournfully carrying the child's drowned body through the village. Perhaps because of censorship, we don't see that he did not drown her, but threw her in with delight, thinking she would float as well. For the two girls, especially Ana (Ana Torrent), this makes a dramatic impression.

Her misunderstanding of the scene will shape the events to follow in Victor Erice's *The Spirit of the Beehive* (1973), believed by many to be the greatest of all Spanish films. Although the time is not specified, it would have been clear to Spanish audiences that the film is set soon after the end of the Spanish Civil War, which began Franco's long dictatorship—so soon after that the same day, a wounded opponent of the regime takes refuge in the barnlike outbuilding.

Only a few years separate Ana and Isabel (Isabel Telleria), but they form that important divide where Ana depends on her big sister to explain mysteries. The little girl runs carefree all over the farmlands, and in the barn she discovers the wounded soldier. That night, her eyes wide open in the dark, she asks Isabel to explain why the creature drowned the little girl. "Everything in the movies is fake," she's told. "It's all a trick. Besides, I've seen him alive. He's a spirit." That of course serves for Ana as a possible explanation for the wounded man, and the next day, she sneaks him some food and water and her father's coat.

What follows is considered a coded message about Franco's fascist regime, but it's not for me to connect the dots. I relate to it more strongly as a poetic work about the imagination of children and how it can lead them into mischief and sometimes rescue them from its consequences.

The Spirit of the Beehive is one of only three features and a short subject directed by Erice (born 1940). Like such films as Charles Laughton's *The Night of the Hunter* (1955), it is a masterpiece that can only cause us to wonder what we lost because he didn't work more. It is simple, solemn, and in the casting of young Ana Torrent, takes advantage of her open, innocent features. We can well believe her when she accepts her sister's explanation, which goes far to account for her behavior later in the film.

This is one of the most beautiful films I've seen. Its cinematographer, Luis Cuadrado, bathes his frame in sun and earth tones, and in the interiors of the family home, he creates vistas of empty rooms where footsteps echo. The house doesn't seem much occupied by the family. The girls are often alone. The parents also, in separate rooms. Many of the father's poems involve the mindless churning activity of his beehives, and the house's yellow-tinted honeycomb windows make an unmistakable reference to beehives. Presumably this reflects on the Franco regime, but when critics grow specific in spelling out the parallels they see, I feel like I'm reading term papers.

More rewarding is to read the surface of the film. When Ana's good intentions to the "spirit" are misinterpreted, and when she is linked to the wounded man by her father's pocket watch, this sets up a situation that could be dangerous for both father and daughter. When she runs away and inspires a search—the lanterns of volunteers bobbing through the night—we feel how the behavior of innocent children can lead them into trouble. In a later scene when Ana plays a trick on Isabel, the older child also discovers how her myth-making has repercussions.

Ana Torrent starred in another notable Spanish film, Carlos Saura's *Cria Cuervos* (1976). She has gone on to a successful career, making 45 films and TV series, including Saura's *Elisa, My Life* (1977), his first film after Franco's fall. But child actors are often bathed in a glow of enchantment that no later role will quite capture.

{ SPIRITED AWAY }

Viewing Hiyao Miyazaki's *Spirited Away* (2001) for the third time, I was struck by a quality between generosity and love. On earlier viewings I was caught up by the boundless imagination of the story. This time I began to focus on the elements in the picture that didn't need to be there. Animation is a painstaking process, and there is a tendency to simplify its visual elements. Miyazaki, in contrast, offers complexity. His backgrounds are rich in detail, his canvas embraces space liberally, and it is all drawn with meticulous attention. We may not pay much conscious attention to the corners of the frame, but we know they are there, and they reinforce the remarkable precision of his fantasy worlds.

Spirited Away is surely one of the finest of all animated films, and it has its foundation in the traditional bedrock of animation, which is frame-by-frame drawing. Miyazaki began his career in that style, but he is a realist and has permitted the use of computers for some of the busywork. But he personally draws thousands of frames by hand. "We take handmade cell animation and digitize it in order to enrich the visual look," he told me in 2002, "but everything starts with the human hand drawing."

Consider a scene in *Spirited Away* where his young heroine stands on a bridge leading away from the magical bathhouse in which much of the movie is set. The central action and necessary characters supply all that is actually needed, but watching from the windows and balconies of the bathhouse are many of its occupants. It would be easier to suggest them as vaguely moving presences, but Miyazaki takes care to include many figures we recognize. All of them are in motion. And it isn't the repetitive motion of much animation, in which the only idea is simply to show a figure moving. It is realistic, changing, detailed motion.

Most people watching the movie will simply read those areas of the screen as "movement." But if we happen to look, things are really happening there. That's what I mean by generosity and love. Miyazaki and his colleagues care enough to lavish as much energy on the less significant parts of the frame. Notice how much of the bathhouse you can see. It would have been quicker and easier to show just a bridge and a doorway. But Miyazaki gives his bathhouse the complexity of a real place, which possesses attributes whether or not the immediate story requires them.

The story of *Spirited Away* has been populated with limitless creativity. Has any film ever contained more different kinds of beings that we have never seen anywhere before? Miyazaki's imagination never rests. There is a scene where the heroine and her companion get off a train in the middle of a swamp. In the distant forest they see a light approaching. This turns out to be an old-fashioned light pole that is hopping along on one foot. It bows to them, turns, and lights the way on the path they must take. When they arrive at a cottage, it dutifully hangs itself above the gate. The living light pole is not necessary. It is a gift from Miyazaki.

His story involves a 10-year-old girl named Chihiro, who isn't one of those cheerful little automatons that populate many animated films. She is described by many critics as "sullen." Yes, and impatient and impetuous, as she's stuck in the backseat during a long drive to a house her parents want to examine. Her father loses the way in a dark forest, and the road seems to end at the entrance to a tunnel. Investigating it, they find it leads to an abandoned amusement park. But at dusk, some of the shops seem to reopen, especially a food shop whose fragrances steam into the cool air. Her parents fall eagerly upon the counter jammed with food and stuff their mouths. Chihiro is stubborn and says she isn't hungry. Her parents eat so much they double or triple in size. They eat like pigs, and they become pigs. These aren't the parents of American animation, but parents who can do things that frighten a child.

The amusement park leads to a gigantic floating bathhouse, whose turrets and windows and ledges and ornamentation pile endlessly upon themselves. A friendly boy warns her to return, but she is too late, and the bathhouse casts off from the shore. Chihiro ventures inside and finds a world of infinite variety. She cannot find her way out again. The boy says everyone must have a job, and sends her to Kamaji, an old bearded man with eight elongated limbs, who runs the boiler room. He and a young girl advise her to apply to Yubaba, who owns the bathhouse. This is a fearsome old witch who exhales plumes of smoke and a cackling laugh.

This is the beginning of an extraordinary adventure. Chihiro will meet no more humans in the bathhouse. She will be placed under a spell by Yubaba, who steals her name and gives her a new one, Sen. Unless she can get her old name back again, she can never leave. One confusing space opens onto another in the bathhouse, whose population is a limitless variety of bizarre life-forms. There are little fuzzy black balls with two eyeballs, who steal Sen's shoes. Looming semi-transparent No Faces, who wear masks over their ghostly shrouds. Three extraordinary heads without bodies, who hop about looking angry and resemble caricatures of Karl Marx. There is a malodorous heap of black slime, a river creature whose body has sopped up piles of pollution. Shape-shifting, so common in Japanese fantasy, takes place here, and the boy who first befriended her is revealed as a lithe sea dragon with fierce fangs.

Sen makes her way through this world, befriended by some, shunned by others, threatened by Yubaba, learning as she goes. She never becomes a "nice girl," but her pluck and determination win our affection. She becomes determined to regain her name and return to the mainland on a daily train (which only runs one way). She wants to find her parents again.

Miyazaki says he made the film specifically for 10-year-old girls. That is why it plays so powerfully for adult viewers. Movies made for "everybody" are actually made for nobody in particular. Movies about specific characters in a detailed world are spellbinding because they make no attempt to cater to us; they are defiantly, triumphantly, themselves. As I watched the film again, I was spellbound as much as by any film I consider great. That helps explain why *Spirited Away* grossed more than *Titanic* in Japan and was the first foreign film in history to open in the United States having already made more than $200 million.

I was so fortunate to meet Miyazaki at the 2002 Toronto Film Festival. I told him I love the "gratuitous motion" in his films; instead of every movement being dictated by the story, sometimes people will just sit for a moment, or sigh, or gaze at a running stream, or do something extra, not to advance the story but only to give the sense of time and place and who they are.

"We have a word for that in Japanese," he said. "It's called 'ma.' Emptiness. It's there intentionally." He clapped his hands three or four times. "The time in between my clapping is 'ma.' If you just have nonstop action with no breathing space at all, it's just busyness."

I think that helps explain why Miyazaki's films are more absorbing than the frantic action in a lot of American animation. "The people who make the movies are scared of silence, so they want to paper and plaster it over," he said. "They're worried that the audience will get bored. But just because it's 80 percent intense all the time doesn't mean the kids are going to bless you with their concentration. What really matters is the underlying emotions—that you never let go of those.

"What my friends and I have been trying to do since the 1970s is to try and quiet things down a little bit; don't just bombard them with noise and distraction. And to follow the path of children's emotions and feelings as we make a film. If you stay true to joy and astonishment and empathy you don't have to have violence and you don't have to have action. They'll follow you. This is our principle."

He said he has been amused to see a lot of animation in live-action superhero movies. "In a way, live action is becoming part of that whole soup called animation. Animation has become a word that encompasses so much, and my animation is just a little tiny dot over in the corner. It's plenty for me."

It's plenty for me, too.

SPRING, SUMMER, FALL, WINTER . . . AND SPRING

Rarely has a movie this simple moved me this deeply. I feel as if I could review it in a paragraph, or discuss it for hours. The South Korean film *Spring, Summer, Fall, Winter . . . and Spring* (2003) is Buddhist, but it is also universal. It takes place within and around a small house floating on a small raft on a small lake, and within that compass, it contains life, faith, growth, love, jealousy, hate, cruelty, mystery, redemption . . . and nature. Also a dog, a rooster, a cat, a bird, a snake, a turtle, a fish, and a frog.

The one-room house serves the function of a hermitage, or a monk's cell. As the film opens, it is occupied by a monk (Oh Young Soo) and a boy (Seo Jae Kyung) learning to be a monk. The monk rises, wakes the boy, bows and prays to a figure of the Buddha, and knocks on a hollow bowl that sends a comfortable resonance out into the forest. We gather that the daily routine rarely changes.

Before I describe the action any further, let me better set the scene. The lake is surrounded on all sides by steep walls of forest or stone, broken here and there by ravines. It is approached through two large, painted wooden doors, which swing open to introduce each season of the movie and frame the floating house. These doors do not keep anyone out, because one would only have to walk around them to find the rest of the shoreline open and free. But they are always respected.

223

It is the same inside the house. The master and the boy sleep on pallets on either side of the room. At the foot of each sleeping area is a door. The area is otherwise open to the room and always visible. But when the monk awakens the boy, he is careful to open the door and enter, instead of simply calling out to him or stepping around the door. Several people will occupy these sleeping spaces during the movie, and they will always treat the door as if it had a practical function . . . except sometimes.

What do we learn from these doors that close nothing out or in? They are not symbols, I think, but lessons. They teach the inhabitants that it is important to follow custom and tradition, to go the same way that others have gone, to respect what has been left for them.

Perhaps embedded cultural ideas make this idea persuasive to us. We have a conception, idealized and romanticized, of the ancient wisdom of the Orient. We accept the notion of a monk living in seclusion for decades—meditating in a mountain cave, for example. If a modern Westerner—an American or German—lived in solitude on a raft in a lake with a small child whom he expected to continue there after his death, how would that seem to us? It would seem unwholesome. It would seem equally strange to Kim Ki Duk, its director, I suspect.

But that kind of thinking never invades our minds while watching a film like this. We fall easily into its premise. We are moved and comforted by its story of timelessness, of the transcendence of the eternal. To live on a lake raft through a cold winter would not be pleasant. In this film it is a passage on the wheel of the seasons. The film in its beauty and serenity becomes seductive and fascinating. We accept the lake as the center of existence.

Its shore is reached by an old but beautifully painted rowboat. The boy often goes ashore to collect herbs, which his master teaches him about. One day the boy rows to shore and plays in some little ponds. Inspired to mischief, he ties a string around a fish, and a small stone to the other end, to make it hard for the fish to swim. He burbles with laughter. Then he plays the same cruel trick on a frog and a snake. He does not know that the master has followed and is watching him.

And we do not know how the master got to shore without the rowboat, although more than once, he seems to be able to do that. The rowboat seems to moor itself next to an ancient tree in the lake, without tether or anchor, and on one occasion, seems to float toward the master at his bidding, but there is no hint earlier that the boat returned for the master. And the movie makes no point at all of the master's inexplicable materialization; some viewers may not notice it. It is at that level of mysticism where you wonder if you really did see something out of the corner of your eye.

The next morning when the boy awakens, he finds a stone tied to his back. The master orders him to return to shore and free the fish, the frog, and the snake. "If one of them has died, you will always carry that stone in your heart."

End of spring. I will not spoil the film's further unfolding, other than to note that when a girl comes to the hermitage to be cured, she and the boy (now a young man) fall in love. The monk thinks sex might be part of her cure, but warns of anger: "Lust awakens the desire to possess. And that awakens the intent to murder."

There is always an animal on the raft to keep the monk company (the dog is glimpsed only briefly at the beginning). The monk feeds them, pets the cat because it is the requirement of cats to be petted, and otherwise simply shares the space, as he does with his student. The lake, the raft, the house, the animals, the forest are there for them, and will be there after them, and the monk accepts the use of them.

The film is by Kim Ki Duk, or in the Korean style, Ki-duk Kim, born in 1960. We see him briefly at the end, playing another monk who has come to the island. I first became aware of his work at Sundance 2000, where he showed *The Isle*, probably the most viscerally violent film I have ever seen. No, it doesn't have explosions or shootings, but what it does with fish hooks is unspeakable.

Strange that the same director made both films. I note that some Korean directors have an inclination toward extreme violence and frank sexuality in their films, although it is usually represented as behavior, in a long shot, instead of being insisted upon in close-up. The nudity and sexuality in *Spring . . .* is context, not subject.

There must be something about floating isolation that fascinates this director. *The Isle* was about fishermen each occupying a small floating fishing shack on a large lake, their only contact with shore an unspeaking woman who rows out to them and supplies food, drink, supplies, and prostitutes. His *The Bow* (2005) involves a starting situation something like *Spring* . . . An old man lives on his boat with a girl he has raised since infancy. He expects (as the monk apparently expects of his student) that the arrangement will continue indefinitely. In both films, a visitor the same age as the protege comes aboard and introduces the possibility of carnality.

Kim Ki Duk avoids one practice: in his films that I have seen (also including *Three-Iron*, 2004, not a golf picture), he doesn't make his message manifest. There is little or no dialogue, no explanations, no speeches with messages. He descends upon lives that have long since taken their form. If conflict comes, his characters will in some way bring it upon themselves, or within themselves. That causes us to pay closer attention. How inferior a film like *Spring* . . . would be if it supplied a rival monk or visiting tourists or land developers. The protagonist in this film is life, and the antagonists are time and change. Nor is it that simple, because to be alive, you must come to terms with both of those opponents.

{ STAGECOACH }

Stagecoach (1939) is a film in which two great careers were renewed. Although he had appeared before in many films, as an extra, a stuntman, and then an actor in B films, this was John Wayne's first starring role in a film by John Ford. For Ford, it was a return after some years to a genre about which his ideas had grown—the genre in which he would make many of his greatest films. With Ford's clout as a director and Wayne's clout as a star, they would make iconic films and establish themselves as one of the legendary partnerships in cinema.

They came together at a propitious moment in Ford's career. He was 45. He had directed his first silent films (10 of them!) in 1917. He had tasted great success and won an Academy Award for directing *The Informer* in 1936. But now came his years of triumph. No director of the sound era made more great films more quickly than Ford did when he followed *Stagecoach* with *Young Mr. Lincoln* and *Drums along the Mohawk*, all three in 1939, and then made *The Grapes of Wrath* and *The Long Voyage Home* in 1940 and *Tobacco Road* and *How Green Was My Valley* in 1941, collecting in that period three nominations and two Oscars for directing.

Ford had his eye on John Wayne from the days when he was called Marion Morrison, nicknamed Duke, and was a football player from USC, working summers at 20th Century-Fox. In the decade before *Stagecoach*

Wayne worked in some 40 Westerns, from an extra to a lead, without distinguishing himself. Ford thought he had the makings of a star and decided Wayne was right for the key role of the Ringo Kid in *Stagecoach*. The studio was adamantly opposed to the casting; it demanded a name actor. "Pappy" Ford imperiously insisted. And Wayne made an impression that would change his life and one day win him a place on a US postage stamp.

Seen today, *Stagecoach* may not seem very original. That's because it influenced countless later movies in which a mixed bag of characters are thrown together by chance and forced to survive an ordeal. The genre is sometimes called the Ark Movie. The film at times plays like an anthology of timeless clichés. You will see a woman going into labor as a doctor orders, "Boil water! Hot water! And lots of it!" You will meet a prostitute with a heart of gold, and an evil banker, and a shifty gambler, and a pure-hearted heroine, and murderous Apaches, and a sultry Indian wife, and a meek little traveling man, and a chase scene with a stagecoach driver going hell for leather. You will see saloons, corrals, vast landscape, camp fires, and the US Cavalry—which sounds the charge before riding to the rescue.

Despite the familiarity of these conventions, *Stagecoach* holds our attention effortlessly and is paced with the elegance of a symphony. Ford doesn't squander his action and violence in an attempt to whore for those with short attention spans, but tells a *story*, during which we learn to know the characters and become invested in them. He doesn't give all the key scenes to the same big star. Top billing went to Claire Trevor, as Dallas, the lady of pleasure. ("Dallas?" One is reminded of Marlene Dietrich: "I didn't become Shanghai Lil in one night.")

Trevor was a star, but Ford gave nearly equal weight to the other passengers in the stagecoach, all played by actors who would have been familiar to movie audiences: squeaky-voiced Andy Devine as the driver, John Carradine as the elegant gambler, Thomas Mitchell as the alcoholic Doc Boone, Louise Platt as the pregnant soldier's wife, and Donald Meek as the effeminate Mr. Peacock, a traveling salesman who improbably wears a checkered deerstalker hat in the Old West. As they line up facing each other, the Ringo Kid sits on the floor between them, but Ford somehow never frames him to seem lower.

Confined for a good deal of the film inside the stagecoach, these gifted actors create a fascinating community as they gradually reveal their hidden reasons for traveling in great discomfort though hazardous Indian territory. The Ringo Kid, Wayne's character, is a wanted murderer being taken to prison by a US Marshall (George Bancroft). As the others pointedly shun the prostitute Dallas, he insists on her being given a drink of water and a place at the table, and his courtliness is manly and good-hearted. Of course he falls in love with her, and it inspires one of the great scenes:

> Ringo Kid: I still got a ranch across the border. There's a nice place—a real nice place . . . trees . . . grass . . . water. There's a cabin half built. A man could live there . . . and a woman. Will you go?
> Dallas: But you don't know me—you don't know who I am.
> Ringo Kid: I know all I wanna know.

The way Wayne says that embodies his effortless authority. He says it and you don't doubt he means it. Indeed, the impression he makes here suggests he was perhaps lucky to avoid such a high-visibility role earlier in his career. He was 32 when he made this film, tall and slim, and had outgrown the almost improbable boyish beauty of his youth. He could growl and take a position and hold his ground and not talk too much, and he always sounded like he meant it.

Simon Callow writes in his biography of Orson Welles that Welles saw *Stagecoach* 40 times before he made *Citizen Kane*. The two films are hardly similar. What did Welles learn from it? Perhaps most of all a lean editing style. Ford made certain through casting and dialogue that the purpose of each scene was made clear, and then he lingered exactly long enough to make the point. Nothing feels superfluous. When he deliberately slows the flow, as for a song performed by Yakima (Elvira Rios), the wife of an outpost boss, we understand it as the calm before a storm. (Howard Hawks uses a quiet song by Dean Martin in the same way in *Rio Bravo*.)

Ford never makes the mistake of cutting so quickly that the sense and context of an action sequence is lost. The extended stagecoach chase always makes sense, and he allows his camera to be clear about the stunt work.

Consider this extraordinary stunt: An Apache leaps from his own horse onto the stagecoach team, straddling the lead horses. He is shot. He falls between the horses to the ground, and the horses and stagecoach pass entirely over him. No CGI here; he risks his life.

Wayne is the hero of the film, but not an "action hero." He was manifestly a bad man; the "Ringo Kid" doesn't get his picture on Wanted posters for nothing. But he never suggests evil and seems prepared to be taken to prison even though he has many opportunities to escape. There is the suggestion he stays with the stagecoach because he is needed to protect its passengers, especially the two women. We see here Wayne's extraordinary physical grace and capacity for tenderness, and understand why Ford later cast him as "The Quiet Man."

Two scenes in particular. Wayne in left foreground, leaning against a wall as he watches Dallas walk away from him down a corridor. Observe his body language. The way he looks after her and then straightens up and follows her. And later, look at Ford's lighting and composition as Dallas, in foreground in the moonlight next to a fence, stands alone and the Ringo Kid, in background, the smoke from his cigarillo back-lighted as a backdrop, approaches her.

That was a studio shot. But much of the movie is shot on location in Ford's beloved Monument Valley, its prehistoric rock pillars framing the smallness of men. Ford returned again and again to the valley, where his casts and crews lived in tents and were fed from a chuck wagon; he valued the distance from meddling studio executives. He was a dictator, and in that vastness his word was law.

The film's attitudes toward Native Americans are unenlightened. The Apaches are seen simply as murderous savages; there is no suggestion the white men have invaded their land. Ford shared that simple view with countless other makers of Westerns, and if it was crude in 1939 it was even more so as late as *The Searchers* (1956), the greatest Ford/Wayne collaboration. Only in his final film, *Cheyenne Autumn* (1964), did he come around to more humane ideas.

Perhaps because of his long association with Wayne, Ford is often seen as a conservative. In fact he was an outspoken liberal, the standard bearer against Cecil B. DeMille's attempt to force a loyalty oath upon the Directors' Guild during the McCarthy witch-hunt. Ford was not a racist, nor was Wayne, but they made films that were sadly unenlightened. Within *Stagecoach*, however, beats a humanitarian heart: none of the occupants of the coach is taken for granted or dismissed casually. They are all given full weight in their mutual dependence. This is a very civilized Western.

{ SUPERMAN }

The first time we see Superman in his red, blue, and yellow uniform is nearly an hour into *Superman*. Perhaps the filmmakers agreed with Spielberg's famous statement that *Jaws* would work better the longer he kept the shark off the screen. That means the film doesn't open like most superhero movies or James Bonds with a sensational pre-title sequence. To be sure, it opens on the planet Krypton with his father Jor-El preparing him to be launched into space. But those aren't action scenes; they provide weight to the origin story every superhero requires.

In fact, Richard Donner's *Superman* (1978) is surprisingly slow-starting. The scenes of young Clark Kent's boyhood and adolescence might seem pointless if we didn't know, "and someday . . . that child will grow up to be Superman." The high school football scene, where the future Man of Steel gets bullied and has a cute girl snatched away from him, pay off later in establishing Clark Kent as a shy and, yes, mild-mannered reporter. But they also raise the intriguing question: Who is this being, anyway?

He is clearly not human. His body is not from our world. It's probable he can't reproduce here, or perhaps even have sex with the cute girl—or Lois Lane. Toward the end, when Lex Luthor's girlfriend kisses him, his response (before flying off to stop an earthquake) is positively Vulcan-like; he wonders why she kissed him before, and not after, freeing him from the Kryptonite.

Christopher Reeve, who must have spent his career in a love-hate relationship with the character, does a more nuanced acting job than he's usually credited for. As Clark Kent he's not *merely* mild-mannered, but performs with a wink to the audience because we know who he really is. Much of his dialogue is double entendre. Pushing his glasses up on his nose, looking like an undertaker in his blue suit, his hair coated with greasy alderman stuff, he may be 6-foot-4 and have the physique of a god, but Margot Kidder's Lois Lane doesn't take the bait. Perhaps she senses there's something . . . off . . . about Clark. She swoons for Superman and literally flies away with him, but then how could anyone think Superman looked like Clark Kent? Superman doesn't wear glasses. Is she seduced more by the superpowers than by the personality?

Probably. As Clark Kent, Reeve deliberately channeled a touch of Cary Grant in *Bringing Up Baby*. As Superman, he goes to some pains to have no personality at all. It would be fatal to play Superman as a hero, and Reeve and Donner understand that. He had no personality in the comic books and has none here. He exists as a fact.

Young Clark Kent is saddened when his human foster father (Glenn Ford) has died of a heart attack. His foster mother (Phyllis Thaxter) has been warm to him in their grief. But soon Clark leaves her (walking off straight through a field), and explains that he must be about his father's business. He's apparently unmoved that the widow will be left alone on the farm. Mrs. Kent takes it well: "I knew this day would come."

How did she know that? The Kents knew Clark was *sui generis*, but was it discussed? He was advised to keep his powers under wraps, but why? In the original screenplay there was a scene of Jor-El explaining why he would need to keep his powers secret. The scene is missing here, and it occurs to me that there never was a good reason why Clark Kent and Superman needed dual identities. It's also a question why Clark waits to flaunt his superpowers. He walks all the way to Metropolis, where he demonstrates he can fly, stop a helicopter and a 707 from falling, and so on. Did he always know he could do that? How did he know? Did it take practice?

The wisdom of the comic books and the movie is that no attempt is made to explain too much. The device of the deadly Kryptonite is necessary because a superhero must have at least one weakness to give him interest. Other astonishments are simply designed to be accepted, as children do when told a story. He is Superman, he fights for Truth, Justice, and the American Way, and that's that.

More recent superhero movies are top-heavy with special effects and wall-to-wall action. *Superman* is more restrained in its telling, but doesn't seem slow, probably because it tells a good story rich in archetypes. It started something. "It is to the superhero genre what *Snow White* is to animation," writes the young Indian critic Krishna Shenoi. "It is literally the film that started the superhero film genre. Without it, there would be no *Batman*, no *X-Men*, no *Iron Man*."

Superman pointed the way for a B picture genre of earlier decades to transform itself into the ruling genre of today. When the flamboyant producer Alexander Salkind announced his film and signed Marlon Brando and Gene Hackman for millions, the industry thought he was crazy. Comic books weren't being called graphic novels back then, and the emergence of the Marvel superhero stable was still ahead.

Superman's most influential element is probably its special effects. Superman did lots of stunts in his earlier incarnations in movie serials and on TV, but rarely had effects like these been linked to the genre. Some of his heroics are frankly laughable, as when he descends to the bottom of a rift in the earth caused by an earthquake and literally pushes the earth back up into place. Or when he flies into the exhaust of a missile and tilts it off course. And in the height of absurdity, he flies so fast around the planet that he reverses time and saves Lois Lane's life. The problems of logic presented by that stunt beggar the imagination.

But the point is, these effects on a vast scale are done well, and they upped the ante in the superhero genre. They are done traditionally, with back projection, traveling matte shots, blue screen, optical printers, and all the other tools rendered obsolete by CGI. Is it only my imagination that the old-fashioned effects seem to have more weight and presence?

The subterranean lair of Lex Luthor (Gene Hackman) is an example of classical set construction, probably combined with some effects. Luthor and his assistant Otis (Ned Beatty) and mistress Eve Teschmacher (Valerie

Perrine) lead a bizarre existence in what seems to be a subterranean train terminal. The film lacks the usual vista of Bond-style minions laboring at giant machines; instead, Hackman perhaps outsources his villainy. His plan to trigger the San Andreas Fault, drop California into the sea, and end up in possession of the new seacoast is rather glorious, I think.

Schemes no less absurd were plotted in Superman comic books, and in Bond movies. But *Superman* pushes on into the realm of comedy. Donner pulls off a balancing act involving satire, action, romcom clichés, and of course a full serving of clichés from hard-boiled newspaper movies. What's admirable is that Salkind and Donner realized they had to make a comedy. The film came in an era of disaster movies that took themselves with dreadful earnestness, and they knew the essential element of Superman was fun. Superheroes who came later to big budget movies, notably Batman and Iron Man, would be burdened with angst. But Superman was above that sort of thing. Above it, or emotionally incapable of it, or whatever.

Flashback: Alexander Salkind, his son Ilya, and his wife Berta held a press dinner at the Majestic Hotel in Cannes to celebrate *Superman.* Toasts were given, speeches were made, and then Berta rose majestically and shattered a glass on the floor. Silence fell. She was the great love of his life, a flamboyant Mexican woman.

"Alexander Salkind says he produced this film," she proclaimed. "He did not produce *Superman.* My son Ilya produced *Superman.* And I produced *Ilya!*" She then started throwing plates, glasses, bottles, vases, and pitchers around the room. The guests dove beneath their tables.

The headwaiter summoned aid. Berta was quieted and taken from the room. Waiters materialized and swept away the wreckage. New tablecloths and place settings were laid. Alexander, having attended his wife, now returned to the room.

"I think," he said, "we will skip the cheese."

{ TENDER MERCIES }

Tender Mercies (1983) won Robert Duvall his only Academy Award in six nominations. It contains one of his most understated performances. It's mostly done with his eyes. The actor who shouted, "I love the smell of napalm in the morning!" here plays a character who wants to be rid of shouting. The film itself never shouts. Its title evokes its mood, although this is not a story about happiness. "I don't trust happiness. I never did, I never will," Mac Sledge tells Rosa Lee, in a scene framed entirely in a medium-long shot that possibly won him the Oscar.

Mac was a country-and-western star maybe 20 years ago. Also an alcoholic, which is how he lost his career, his wife, and his daughter. What he has done in the years since is far from clear, until the morning he wakes up on the floor of a desolate motel six miles outside of Waxahachie, Texas. He was knocked out in a fight over a bottle of whiskey, by a man who has disappeared.

Mac doesn't have a dime on him. The motel and filling station are run by a young widow named Rosa Lee (Tess Harper), who lives there with her son Sonny (Allen Hubbard). Mac asks if he can work off his bill. Since he could have just scrammed, this reveals values that have survived the booze. Rosa Lee puts him to work picking up cans from the roadside, screwing on screen doors, and pumping gas. She tells him he can spend the night.

They hardly speak. Sonny breaks the ice over dinner: "Mister, what's your name?

"Mac."

Mac pumps some gas and is holding the payment. Rosa Lee puts out her hand for it. He hands it over, as if there was any doubt. They speak mostly about business. They regard one another. Days pass very quietly. A school bus picks up and deposits Sonny. One day they're weeding her vegetable garden. He stands up and says, "I guess there ain't no secret how I feel about you. Would you consider marryin' me?"

Rosa Lee looks up from her weeding. "Yes, I think I might."

There has been no courtship. The film shows them twice in church, where she sings in the choir, but there is no wedding scene. Is that strange? Think about these two people, and you realize how much you don't *want* a wedding scene. The characters are too unlike ordinary people for them to fit into a movie cliché. They are married offscreen. The movie has bigger fish to fry.

In most of their work, both the director, Bruce Beresford, and the screenwriter, Horton Foote, tell you about what you need to know, and leave it at that. They never go somewhere just because another story would have gone there. We don't even see Rosa Lee and Mac making love. The film is more about other things in their lives, other baggage they bring to the movie. He doesn't even tell her he was once a country-and-western singer, and she may be too young to have known it herself (the two actors are 20 years apart, and look even more widely separated).

How she finds that out, some young guys from town pull up in a band after one of them recognized Sledge. They tell Rosa Lee they have their own band and are great admirers of Mac's. Word spreads around town. At the grocery store, a woman asks him, "Hey, mister, were you really Mac Sledge?" He's friendly enough: "Yes, ma'am, I guess I was." Was he keeping it a secret from Rosa Lee? I don't think so. It was not important to him any more. That was another lifetime.

They share some details. She was pregnant at 17, married at 18, a widow at 19, when her husband was killed in Vietnam. "He was only a boy," she tells Sonny. "But I think he would have grown up to be a good man."

He was married to another country-and-western singer, Dixie Scott (Betty Buckley). The drinking ended that. There is a court order forbidding him to have contact with his daughter Sue Anne (a young Ellen Barkin), who is about 18 now. One day the kids in the band stop by and tell them Dixie will be appearing in town. Mac goes, not to see her, but in hopes of seeing his daughter. No chance of that.

We meet their old manager and friend, Harry (Wilford Brimley), who has that way about him of patiently explaining the truth, not unkindly. The story introduces some elements and we think we know how they will develop, such as the kids recording a new song Mac has written. It gets a lot of radio play, but the results are not what we'd expect. Life, unlike art, has a way of introducing elements that never do develop into anything.

Horton Foote won his second Academy Award for this screenplay. His first was for *To Kill a Mockingbird* (1962), for which he recommended Duvall for his first screen role, and he also wrote their wonderful *Tomorrow* in 1972. He died at 92 in March 2009. Above all a great playwright, he could hardly write a false note. The down-to-earth quality of his characters drew attention away from his minimalist storytelling; all the frills were stripped away. When interesting people have little to say, we watch the body language, listen to the notes in their voices. Rarely does a movie elaborate less and explain more than *Tender Mercies*.

Bruce Beresford, born in Australia in 1940, had great success with *Breaker Morant* (1980). *Tender Mercies* (1983) was his first American film, and its five nominations included best director, picture, and original song. He took a chance on casting Tess Harper in her first movie, after discovering her at an open audition in Texas. As Janet Maslin pointed out, the movie's "endless and barren prairie" could be in Australia. Even the country singing would fit there. With the cinematographer Russell Boyd, Beresford maintains a certain tactful distance from some scenes, such as the marriage proposal. There are alternating close-ups, but the movie isn't punched up that way and prefers to see these people in the context of where they live.

Tender Mercies isn't simply about country singers. It's about country songs. It's notable that Beresford doesn't cut away after a few establishing lyrics, but stays to listen. Country and western is about the stories it tells, which is why you can always understand the lyrics, and the stories are windows into the heart. Duvall himself performs a couple, and Buckley, as Dixie, sings the nominated "Over You" in a way that makes the Broadway star sound authentically country. You never know all the reasons why an actor will take a pay cut to accept a role. A lot of men have always wanted to play cowboys. Maybe a lot of women have always wanted to play country-and-western singers.

A theme running through the movie is the absence of fathers. Sonny questions Rosa Lee about his father: What was he like? How was he killed? Her answers are always honest: they don't know how he was killed. There were three battles in that area going at the same time. His body was only found after a while. Sue Anne has grown up wondering about the absent Mac. She must have heard some of his records. Where is he? Why doesn't he ever contact her? When she elopes with a young drunk who plays in her mother's band, is something Freudian going on?

During the course of the film Mac begins to fill the gaps in both of those lives; we sense his hunger to be a good father as he throws around a football in a field with Sonny. His greatest yearning is to be reunited with his daughter. That's another element that doesn't quite lead where we expect.

While writing this, I softly played a Hank Williams album. It seemed like part of the review.

{ Veronika Voss }

Rainer Werner Fassbinder premiered *Veronika Voss* in February 1982, at the Berlin Film Festival. It was hailed as one of the best of his 40 films. Late on the night of June 9, 1982, he made a telephone call from Munich to Paris to tell his best friend he had flushed all his drugs down the toilet—everything except for one last line of cocaine. The next morning, Fassbinder was found dead in his room, a cold cigarette between his fingers, a videotape machine still playing. The most famous, notorious, and prolific modern German film-maker was 36.

Does this film represent a premonition of his own death? It tells the story of a German actress who worked tirelessly and achieved great fame, but began depending on drugs and alcohol and eventually became so addicted that she sold her body and soul for drugs. Her fortune spent, her marriage destroyed, she began to live as an inpatient in the clinic of a sinister Berlin woman who billed herself as a psychiatrist but was also a Dr. Feelgood who strung along her patients on morphine and controlled them by withholding their supply. Their arrangement was that after Veronika Voss's death, her suburban villa and its art treasures would be inherited by the doctor.

The film opens in 1955 with Voss (Rosel Zech) looking at one of her own prewar classics (that's Fassbinder himself in the audience, leaning on the seat-back behind her). There was a time when she was welcomed in the offices of producers, greeted by headwaiters, recognized on the street. That time has passed, and it is painful to hear her remind people who she is—or was. One night, drinking without funds in a cabaret, she falls into conversation with a soft-faced sportswriter named Robert Krohn (Hilmar Thate), who is old enough to remain under her spell. She grandly says she will pick up the check, then "allows" him to do it, and invites him to come home with her. All the furniture in her villa is covered in white sheets, the electricity is disconnected, and she has them light candles "because they are so much more flattering to a woman." The starstruck journalist has without realizing it walked into the last act of Veronika Voss's life.

Ending their evening suddenly, Veronika demands to be taken to the clinic of Dr. Katz (Annemarie Duringer), one of the stylish lesbians often found in Fassbinder films (*The Bitter Tears of Petra Van Kant*). This clinic could be imagined as the setting for a bizarre Fred Astaire dance number. It's all blindingly white—walls, floors, furniture, grand staircases, everyone's clothing. In an eerie touch, a wall of windows looks upon a waiting room, where other patients peer in needfully. Katz lives with a woman apparently her lover, and another constant companion is an African-American GI and drug dealer (Günther Kaufmann). This man is in the background of countless shots, never says anything, lurks when needed like a security guard, and was Fassbinder's sometime lover and an actor in many of his films (including the one he made just before his one, *The Marriage of Maria Braun*).

We observe Veronika's frantic relationship with Katz, who berates her sadistically and extracts details of the hours with Robert Krohn. Finally Veronika is shown to her narrow, cell-like room, and given the drugs she craves. In this room, and throughout the clinic, we hear incongruous American country-and-western songs ("The Battle of New Orleans," "16 Tons"). In *Maria Braun*, where Günther Kaufmann plays Maria's GI lover, similar music is heard, probably via Armed Forces Radio, a reminder of the presence of American occupying forces in postwar Germany. At Veronika's own "farewell" party, she performs "Memories Are Made of This," in a low, throaty torch-song voice perhaps intended to remind us of Marlene Dietrich. Indeed, Fassbinder's focus on Rosel Zech reminds me of von Sternberg's Dietrich in *The Blue Angel*.

When Robert Krohn returns that day to his own apartment and girl-friend Henriette (Cornelia Froboess), he is almost proud to tell her where he spent the night, and she, also a writer for the newspaper, accepts this as an expression of his nature; she wants to know what Voss was like. Krohn, whose beat is hockey, convinces his editor he has lucked upon a major scoop about the decline and fall of a star.

Throughout Fassbinder's work we find such figures, great stars, man-nered, decadent, in various stages of their decay. This film was inspired by the real life of Sybille Schmitz, a German star of the 1930s who also fell athwart of a clinic supplying drugs. Many critics look at Veronika Voss and are reminded of Gloria Swanson in Billy Wilder's *Sunset Boulevard*. Perhaps the association is intentional. When Veronika finally, with great difficulty, wheedles a bit part from her former agent, the director of the scene (Volker Spengler) wears glasses and has his hat pushed back on his head, Wilder-style. She only has two lines in her scene, but blows them again and again. She's rattled and craves a fix. She is watched by Robert Krohn and by her ex-husband Max Rehbein (Armin Mueller-Stahl), who wearily explains to the sports writer that his former wife is a hopeless addict.

Two other patients of Dr. Katz figure importantly: a sweet elderly couple named the Treibels. Their story figures tragically in the history of Germany, as you will find. The psychiatrist, indeed, seems poised at the cen-ter of a cynical web of postwar corruption, including drug authorities and the police; when they twitch the web, she senses it immediately.

Fassbinder (1945–82) was an immensely productive filmmaker. In his 37 years he directed 40 features, 24 stage plays, and two long TV minise-ries (notably *Berlin Alexanderplatz*). His death seems to have interrupted this flow in midstream. Powerfully influenced by the heavily stylized works of the German-Danish-American director Douglas Sirk (*Written on the Wind*), he may have worked at a feverish pace but his films always look carefully planned. In this film, for example, he evokes period black and white with a diversity of wipe shots, iris shots, pans, tracking, and the careful positioning of foregrounds. In other films he often uses zooms-in to under-line dramatic points. His films are visually mannered, formal, and far from seeming improvised; the visual strategy of *Veronika Voss* suggests he was moving even closer toward the classic Hollywood style.

What an impression he made when he was alive! At Cannes every year he seemed to have at least one film, and you would see him at Le Petit Carlton, the famous bistro behind the Palais du Festival, on rue Felix-Faure, behind the Hotel Carlton. Fassbinder and his posse would be gathered inside, close inside the doorway, looking as discontented as usual. In August of 1983 at the Montreal Film Festival, as his close friend the director Daniel Schmid and I both served on the jury of the World Film Festival, the ghost of Fassbinder seemed almost like another presence in the city. Fassbinder had attended the 1981 Cannes Film Festival, nine months before his death, and I remember him at dinner, unshaven, defensive, always smoking, ignoring the food, and ordering a bottle of Cognac to be placed before him.

During the last weeks of his life, Schmid said, during those sad telephone calls at three in the morning, Fassbinder often repeated the same thing. "He would shout at me: How are you able to just sit there and look outside the window? How can you? How can you just sit on a rock and look at the sea? How can everybody else be so lucky?"

{ VIRIDIANA }

I can't think of a more mischievous filmmaker than Luis Buñuel. After you get to know him, you can catch him winking in the first few shots. Under the opening title shot of *Viridiana* (1961), we hear Handel's "Messiah," but knowing Buñuel we doubt this will be a religious picture. In the second and third shots, we see a Mother Superior advising a novice at a cloistered convent to visit her old uncle before he dies. No good can come of this in a Buñuel film. The fourth shot shows a girl skipping rope. Well, not the whole girl, just her feet, observed for a little too long. "That was a wonderful afternoon little Luis spent on the floor of his mother's closet," Pauline Kael once observed, "and he has never allowed us to forget it."

So: Buñuel the satirist, Buñuel the anticlerical, Buñuel the fetishist. That's the usual litany, but we should not exclude Buñuel the grandmaster of black comedy. None of his films is lacking a cheerfully sardonic view of human nature. His object is always dry humor. Even when he was working for Hollywood studios, recycling the sets and costumes of English-language pictures into Spanish versions of the same screenplays, or later simply dubbing them into Spanish, he slyly slipped in a few touches that were lacking in the sources. He is one of the great originals, creator of satirical delight, sometimes hilariously funny, and if you love great movies you sooner or later get to him.

Buñuel began as a surrealist, and in Paris collaborated with Salvador Dali on *Un Chien Andalou* (1929), which is only 16 minutes long but remains one of the most famous films of the century. His *L'Age d'Or* (1930), a surrealist attack on organized religion, was unseeable for 50 years after his wealthy patron, Le Vicomte de Noailles, decided to suppress it. Buñuel returned to his native Spain but left after the rise of Franco's fascists, and found work in America. After the war, Buñuel became a Mexican citizen and lived there until his death, although he made many films in France and *Viridiana* in Spain.

Why, his admirers wondered, would he return to Spain, where the dictator Franco was still in power? He told various stories. One was that he was offered four times his salary by a producer. Another was that he felt nostalgia for his homeland. A third that he didn't mention was, I suspect, to make this particular film.

Buñuel was anything but a sentimentalist, and Spain was wrong if it expected a joyous homecoming. His film was not anti-Catholic nor against the ruling class, but it established his virtuous nun, her rich landowning uncle, and his son, her cousin, in a dark and scandalous story. It ended with the nun, having left the convent, quietly entering the bedroom of her handsome young cousin. The government censors flatly rejected the screenplay. Buñuel rewrote it so that she found the cousin and his mistress playing cards in the bedroom. As she joins the game, the cousin says he was sure that sooner or later they would be playing together. Fade out on the unmistakable implication of a ménage a trios. "Even more immoral," Buñuel observed year after.

The film left Spain for France, shared the Palme d'Or at Cannes in 1961, and wasn't allowed back into Spain until after Franco's death in 1975. In the 1960s and 1970s Buñuel (born 1900, died 1983) became established in the first rank of directors, with Fellini, Bergman, and Antonioni, and scored one international success after another, most famously with *Belle de Jour* (1967).

There was always the sly subtext: the virtuous but disgraced blonde of *Belle de Jour* mirroring Viridiana, or the kidding anticlericism in *The Discreet Charm of the Bourgeoisie* by the bishop whose fetish is pretending to be the gardener. And everywhere the shoes. Who but Buñuel would film a scene of Catherine Deneuve being dragged through a forest and focus on her feet? I am giving the wrong impression if you think Buñuel was by then a dirty old man. I think of him more as amused. There's never anything blatant about his eroticism; he finds fetishes funny, as indeed they are except for the hapless fetishist.

The most famous sequence in *Viridiana* (apart from its scandalous reenactment of *The Last Supper*) involves the cousin, Jorge (Francisco Rabal), observing a dog tied to the rear axle of a cart and being pulled along the road on a rope. He stops the peasant and buys the dog to free it. He doesn't notice another dog tied to another cart, going in the other direction. This summarizes Buñuel's world view.

In the larger world of the film, Viridiana (Silvia Pinal) visits her old uncle, Don Jaime (the Buñuel favorite Fernando Rey). For her it is an act of charity. Don Jaime is thunderstruck: having not seen her for years, he realizes she is the double of his late wife on their wedding night. As a favor, he begs her to put on the dead wife's wedding dress. As a favor, she does: form-fitting, with a white corset, and of course much attention to the shoes. He is transfixed. He is in love. He asks her to marry him. She is shocked and tries to leave. He apologizes, gives her drugged coffee, and then . . .

Later, he hangs himself. Viridiana has by now given up the idea of a cloistered life and is determined to perform works of mercy in the world. She gathers up 13 of the most wretched beggars in the town (a drunk, a leper, a crippled man, a blind man, an angry dwarf, a prostitute, and so on) and brings them back to live on the estate. This does not redeem them, and they quarrel, fight, prove shiftless at the tasks she sets for them, and ostracize the leper (who says his sores are only ulcers). Meanwhile, Jorge arrives with his mistress and moves into the big house, while Viridiana abnegates herself by living in an outbuilding. Her experiment comes to a climax when the beggars, left on their own, throw a drunken feast and demolish the dining room. Then, alone or in small groups, they slink away from the place that gave them shelter. Cut to the card game mentioned earlier.

The film is deliberate and controlled. It is funny in that way where you rarely laugh aloud but expand in mental amusement. It is elegantly photographed; each shot conveys something concrete and specific, which is to be expected from a fetishist. It makes no clear and precise statement, but instead conveys Buñuel's notion that our base natures are always waiting to pounce. Despite my plot description, he makes Don Jaime into a not altogether evil man—more of a lonely and sad one, who desires to sin but lacks the necessary indecency. Nor is cousin Jorge a lecher, nor is Viridiana a fallen woman, and the beggars, after all, only behave as they have been taught by the world.

A film like this is bracing. It is made by a strong, individual mind. It is not another marked-down version of comforting feel-good lies. It is possible to imagine Buñuel watching a dreadfully cheery romantic comedy like, say, *The Back-Up Plan*, and laughing tears of derision. He knows the world has its own back-up plan. There is always another cart and another dog tied to it.

$\Big\{$ YELLOW SUBMARINE $\Big\}$

*O*nce upon a time, or maybe twice, there was a land called Pepperland. Eighty *thousand leagues beneath the sea it lay, or lie (I'm not too sure).*

Yellow Submarine was released in 1968, after the Summer of Love but before Woodstock, when the Beatles stood astride the world of pop music, and "psychedelic art" had such an influence that people actually read underground newspapers printed in orange on yellow paper. That was the year *2001: A Space Odyssey* was released in reserved-ticket engagements with an intermission, and hippies would mingle with the ticket holders on the sidewalk outside the theater, and sneak back into the theater for the film's second half, to lay, or lie, flat on their backs on the floor in front of the screen, observing Kubrick's time-space journey from a skewed perspective—while, as the saying went, they were stoned out of their gourds.

Yellow Submarine was also embraced as a "head movie," leading to an observation attributed to Ken Kesey: "They say it looks better when you're stoned. But that's true of all movies." All of that was many, many years ago, and now here is a restored version of *Yellow Submarine*, arriving like a time capsule from the flower power era, with a graphic look that fuses Peter Max, Rene Magritte, and M. C. Escher. To borrow another useful cliché from the 1960s, it blossoms like eye candy on the screen, and with 11 songs by the Beatles, it certainly has the best music track of any animated film.

The story begins at a moment of crisis in Pepperland, which is invaded by the music-hating Blue Meanies. They hate the power of Sgt. Pepper's Lonely Hearts Club Band, which has inspired a big YES to sprout near the bandstand, not to mention a towering LOVE and all sorts of bright and cheerful decorations. So the Meanies freeze everything with blue bombs that bleach out the colors and leave Pepperland in a state of blue-gray suspended animation. Old Fred, conductor of the band, escapes the Meanie treatment and flees in the Yellow Submarine to enlist the help of the Beatles.

This is a story that appeals even to young children, but it also has a knowing, funny style that adds an undertow of sophistication. The narration and dialogue are credited to four writers (including *Love Story*'s Erich Segal), and yet the overall tone is the one struck by John Lennon in his books *In His Own Write* and *A Spaniard in the Works*. Puns, drolleries, whimsies, and asides meander through the sentences:

There's a cyclops! He's got two eyes. Must be a bicyclops. It's a whole bicloplopedia!

The animation, directed by Tom Halley from Heinz Edelmann's designs, isn't full motion and usually remains within one plane, but there's nothing stiff or limited about it; it has a freedom of color and invention that never tires, and it takes a delight in visual paradoxes. Consider for example the Beatles's visit to the Sea of Holes, a complex Escherian landscape of oval black holes that seem to open up, or down, or sideways, so that the Beatles can enter and emerge in various dimensions.

(Ringo keeps one of the holes, and later gets them out of a tricky situation by remembering, "I've got a hole in my pocket!")

Such dimensional illusions run all through the film. My favorite is a vacuum-nosed creature that snarfs up everything it can find to inhale. Finally it starts on the very frame itself, snuffling it all up into its nose, so that it stands forlorn on a black screen. A pause, and then the creature's attention focuses on its own tail. It attacks that with the vacuum nose and succeeds in inhaling itself, after which nothing at all is left.

The film's visuals borrow from the mind bank of the twentieth century. Consider a visit to a sort of image repository where we find Buffalo

Bill, Marilyn Monroe, the Phantom, Mandrake the Magician, and Frankenstein (who, awakened, turns out to be John Lennon). Dozens of images cascade out of the doors in a long corridor, including Magritte's big green apple and his pipe. And real-life photography is built into other sequences, including the one for "Eleanor Rigby."

The songs of course are the backbone of the movie, and they include "Yellow Submarine," "Eleanor Rigby," "All Together Now," "Nowhere Man," "Lucy in the Sky with Diamonds," "Sgt. Pepper's Lonely Hearts Club Band," "All You Need Is Love," and (in a live-action coda) the Beatles in person wisecracking and singing "All Together Now." The movie's original soundtrack was monaural, and it sounds a little muddy on my rare laserdisc of the film. The restored version, in six-track digital stereo, remastered at the legendary Abbey Road Studios, blossoms with life and clarity. I was able to compare the two versions as a friendly projectionist switched back and forth between the original and restored tracks, and the digital stereo is like somebody turning the lights on.

The story of the restoration, like the story of the film itself, is a saga of triumph over Blue Meanies in the distribution business. It is widely known that the *Yellow Submarine* project was only approved by the Beatles in the first place because it offered a way for them to get out of a three-picture deal (after *A Hard Day's Night* and *Help!*) without actually having to appear in a third picture. Their input was reportedly marginal (they didn't even dub their own voices), but when they saw the rough cut they liked it so much they agreed to appear in the live-action final scene.

The movie was a success in 1968, but has never had much of a life since then. Gary Meyer, a programming executive for the Sundance Channel, tells me the film was pulled off the theatrical revival circuit in 1982 and hasn't been available in any form of video for 12 years (the laserdisc is going for $50 on eBay). The movie has only had one TV showing, Meyer says, and has never been on cable.

Why such obscurity for a Beatles movie? It was so much a child of the 1960s, apparently, that the copyright holders considered it a dated period piece. Well, every movie is a period piece; that's what's wonderful about them. The movie was revived in 1997 at the San Francisco Film Festival, where the reception encouraged this restoration project. As Meyer told me: "The head of post-production at MGM, Bruce Markoe, got involved and took *Yellow Submarine* to Abbey Road Studios, where they remixed the soundtrack. The picture quality has been cleaned up too, and as a bonus, the 'Hey Bulldog' number, which only showed in England, has been reinserted with the narrative parts that make it part of the story."

The result, like *Fantasia*, is a music-based animated film for the ages. The songs sound dramatically better, and the story avoids the usual gee-whiz urgency of so much animation and reflects the same deadpan understatement that the Beatles used in *A Hard Day's Night*. Perhaps because the Beatles were considered such a draw, perhaps because the songs were counted on to sell the film, there was no agenda to dumb down the material or hard-sell the story. Instead of contrived urgency, there's unpressured whimsy, and the movie exists as pure charm, expressed in fantastical imagery. And then there are the songs.

ESSAYS APPEARING IN
THE GREAT MOVIES (2002)

Essays Appearing in *The Great Movies*

ESSAYS APPEARING IN
THE GREAT MOVIES II (2005)

12 Angry Men

The Adventures of Robin Hood

Alien

Amadeus

Amarcord

Annie Hall

Au Hasard, Balthazar

The Bank Dick

Beat the Devil

Being There

The Big Heat

The Birth of a Nation

The Blue Kite

Bob le Flambeur

Breathless

The Bridge on the River Kwai

Bring Me the Head of Alfredo Garcia

Buster Keaton

Children of Paradise

A Christmas Story

The Color Purple

The Conversation

Cries and Whispers

The Discreet Charm of the Bourgeoisie

Don't Look Now

The Earrings of Madame de . . .

The Fall of the House of Usher

The Fireman's Ball

Five Easy Pieces

Goldfinger

The Good, the Bad and the Ugly

Goodfellas

The Gospel According to Matthew

The Grapes of Wrath

Grave of the Fireflies

Great Expectations

House of Games

The Hustler

In Cold Blood

Jaws

Essays Appearing in
The Great Movies III (2010)